"This book can help people understand the artistry involved in bringing sitcom material to life."

—ROBIN BARTLETT, Actor, *Mad about You*

"I have the best job in America. I make hundreds of thousands of dollars a year to dress like a slob, sit in a room with a bunch of witty people, crack lots of dirty jokes, and laugh until my sides hurt. Oh, and people bring me free food from the best restaurants, and their only job is to make sure that I'm happy. And did I mention the three months of the year off for vacation? Well, if you want to have a job like mine…READ THIS BOOK!"

—JAMIE WOOTEN, Writer, *Golden Girls*, *Half and Half*

"No matter how a producer, director, studio or network executive couches the note they are giving you—'Can we up the emotional stakes? Can we start the story sooner? Can we make the character more likeable or redeemable?' They all just really want to say, Louder! Faster! Funnier!"

—NANCYLEE MYATT, Writer, *Night Court*, *Living Single*

"The ultimate let loose and laugh guide in a very fast-paced, stressful industry."

—KEITH JOSEF ADKINS, Writer, *Girlfriends*

"This book's value will be as a road map because there isn't a book in the marketplace for an aspiring writer!"

—MICHAEL LANGWORTHY, Writer, *8 Simple Rules*

"Every week has a new show. Every week has a completed assignment…and then you move on to a different one the following week. It is rarely boring."

—MADELINE CRIPE, Director, *Fresh Prince of Bel-Air*, *Malcolm & Eddie*

"Almost everyone in show business has had someone to give them a break, lend a hand, or teach them the ropes. If not they were just lucky enough to be in the right place at the right time. This book can't replace luck or nepotism but it comes damn close."

—RICK HAWKINS, Writer *Sister, Sister*

"The process from the initial audition to the martini shot on Friday night is grueling, boring, exciting, frantic, stress inducing and well worth every second of it. Granted, as long as you didn't get written out in one of the 25 rewrites since the script was first delivered to your door."

—REGAN BURNS, Host, Spike TV's *Oblivious*

"Since the stakes are so high in a sitcom, one has to come on set already knowing the job. There's little room today for on-the-job training."

—MARTIN GOLDSTEIN, Camera Operator

"The biggest misconception about writing for television is that it's just like *The Dick Van Dyke Show*. Writers are almost never home by 5:30 (or leave work by 5 to catch the train to New Rochelle). Only the actors have those hours."

—CARMEN FINESTRA,
Co-creator and Executive Producer, *Home Improvement*

"Laughter is the remedy for our souls and television has created the situation comedy to provide that remedy. From the beginnings of television and into the 21st century the sitcom has been an everlasting and ever evolving means of entertainment.

"Mary Lou Belli and Phil Ramuno have written what no one else would ever attempt...the secrets behind a successful situation comedy. They take the sitcom and move it into a respectful art form that has its own unique methods and processes which only experience and a keen eye can relate. This can only be done by seasoned professionals and not academics who look at it from the outside.

"Only insiders like Belli and Ramuno can give the details of what makes not a good sitcom but a great sitcom. A must for actors, writers, directors, and students and those just interested to know what goes on behind the camera—this book should be on everyone's shelf!"

—MYRL A. SCHREIBMAN,
Producer, Director, Author, Professor,
UCLA School of Theater, Film and Television

"Auditioning for a sitcom is like having a ball thrown at you. You've got to catch it and throw it back—otherwise it hits you on the head, bounces on the floor a few times and the game's over. You've got to be smart enough to know where the jokes are and skilled enough to make them land. Read this book and find out how!

—MARILYN MCINTRYRE,
Actress, Instructor, USC School of Theatre
and The Howard Fine Acting Studio

"At last! Many of us have been looking for this book for years, and now it's arrived. This is a 'must read' for anyone interested in learning about sitcoms. This is the best kind of craft book: clear, concise, and full of insight. Belli and Ramuno have done an excellent job of explaining the rules, principles, traditions, vocabulary, and common practices that make up the world of situation comedy and of breaking down the 'how' and 'what' of funny. They take the reader on a detailed ride through the process of shooting an episode of a sitcom, delivering a wealth of information with a light touch as they revel in the joys of the form."

—DAN CARTER,
Director of the School of Theatre, Producing Artistic Director,
Pennsylvania Centre Stage, The Pennsylvania State University

The Sitcom Career Book

The Sitcom Career Book

A GUIDE TO THE LOUDER FASTER FUNNIER WORLD OF TV COMEDY

MARY LOU BELLI

PHIL RAMUNO

Back Stage Books/New York

Senior Editor: Mark Glubke
Cover Design: Pink Design
Interior Design: Michelle Thompson
Production Manager: Hector Campbell

First published in 2004 by Back Stage Books,
an imprint of Watson-Guptill Publications,
a division of VNU Business Media, Inc.
770 Broadway, New York, NY 10003
www.wgpub.com.com

Library of Congress Control Number: 2004103244

ISBN: 0-8230-2874-7

Manufactured in the United States of America

First printing 2004

1 2 3 4 5 6 7 8 9 / 11 10 09 08 07 06 05 04

To the casts and crews of the early sitcoms that I watched as a child. To Nat Hiken, who published scripts of *Sergeant Bilko*, which was the first book I ever bought. And mostly to my Dad, who unknowingly uses perfect sitcom joke construction when he makes me laugh.

—Phil Ramuno

For Richard Marion and Linda Mancuso, both gone too soon, richly valued and never forgotten.

—Mary Lou Belli

Table of Contents

Chapter 1

1 Getting the Job!

In this chapter:

How to prepare for an audition
Accessing information on a show
Analyzing a sitcom script
How to learn by watching
Dos and Don'ts for auditioning
Why Ks and Ps are funny
How to make strong memorable choices
What to wear to an audition
How to get your script read
Advice for getting the job
Audition tips
How a director prepares
Career profile of a sitcom casting director

Chapter 2

29 Monday (except when it's not)…The Table Read

In this chapter:

How to survive the table reading
How to best utilize the rehearsal
Dos and don'ts when working with a star
Set and stage etiquette
How to identify jokes in a script
The role of the script supervisor
Advice to the aspiring comedy writer
Career profile of a sitcom costume designer

Chapter 7

ACKNOWLEDGMENTS

We would like to thank the people whose assistance helped make this book possible, especially: Mark Glubke, Garry Hart, Steve McPherson, Marcy Ross, Kate Zentall, Steve Rosenthal, James Dunn, Howard Devine, Meredith Hightower, Ellen Waggoner, Steve Stark, Dinah Lenney, Dan Maltese, Karen Kondazian, Barry Van Dyke, Jana Sue Memel, and Jeff Black.

We also wish to thank the people who were instrumental in guiding the acquisition of our sitcom knowledge including: Jay Sandrich, Will Mackenzie, Aaron Rubin, Jim Drake, Bob Broder, Michael Kagen, Sy Rosen, Jeff Harris, George Quenzel, Michael Lembeck, Scott Arnovitz, Nancylee Myatt, Linda Mancuso, Peter Engel, Kerry Holmwood, Robin Schwartz, D. L. Hughley, Lee Shallat Chemel, Michael Lessac, Andy Cadiff, Andrew D. Weyman, Rick Hawkins, Al Burton, Alan Rafkin, Bob Claver, James Burrows, Robert Greenblatt, David Janollari, and, of course, Charlie Dougherty and Jackie Zebal.

FOREWORD

If you want to make a good living, spend weekends at home, and create something with a second family that has a possibility of being very funny, situation comedy is for you!

I went to work for 11 years on Stage 19 at Paramount Studios and had the most extraordinary time. This truly was my second family. My *Happy Days* family. Garry Marshall (the creator and executive producer) along with Eddie Milkus and Tom Miller were the Dads. The cast and Jerry Paris (the director) were the kids. We played softball all over the country. We toured Germany and Japan playing baseball with the American troops. We played charades at Jerry's house. We ate together. We bought our first homes around the same time. We all went to each other's weddings…and kept on asking Tom Bosley what the hell a debenture was.

I loved the camera people, the boom people, and the craft service person, Louie. I loved that crew. Without a crew, no one will record your voice or the picture. No one will write it or direct it. The show couldn't exist. The cast and crew are two halves of a circle. You cannot bring your stardom or celebrity to the center of the stage. You have to leave that in your car. You are a team and you are going to create a story. You will make it as funny as you possibly can in four and one half days and shoot it on the other half of the fifth day. Then you start a new one on Monday.

It's all about timing and trusting your instinct. When I'm in the middle of the process, it is as if the joke is desperately trying to breathe…is screaming its way out of my mouth. I have no control. It needs to come and it needs to come NOW. If I go against that instinct, I'm boring. And if I listen to that instinct, hopefully I'm funny.

Comedy is instinctual, but the craft of comedy, for the most part, can be honed. I believe the discipline of sitcoms can be learned: the lines, the blocking, the not-eating-donuts during the day. I had to learn how *not* to put handles on the beginning of jokes—not to say "oh, by the way," or "hey, did you know." I also had to learn not to embellish a joke by adding a word or two after the punchline.

I used every morsel of my training from the Yale School of Drama in every area during my career and certainly during *Happy Days*. I always saw sitcoms as a one-act play with opening night every Friday. If the show is scheduled for 7:00, you don't start at 7:10. You don't amble in saying, "I'm ready now. I just got off the phone." You must do it with discipline. In structure comes freedom.

If you are going to an audition, you can't be right, you can't be wrong. The producers might know exactly what they want, but most of the time they don't. If you go with your instinct…just go with your muse…you *can* change their minds. I say that because I did. The Fonz was based on someone that Garry Marshall grew up with in the Bronx. As written on the page, the Fonz was much larger, much more imposing, much more Italian than I was. I never researched this character but I lived in New York City and knew these people…actually, I was scared of these people. I just improvised. The person that read with me was standing. I made a decision that I was going to use the six lines that I had to make him sit down. That was my objective. He did. Now I was the only one standing in the room. Then I stayed in character, turned around, threw the script in the air and walked out of the room with my muse.

The bond formed on the soundstage of a situational comedy should be, can be, and must be as emotional, thoughtful, empathetic, and tension filled as your family at home. It does not work if any person on the set thinks he is more important than the group. You are an undulating, pulsating organism that *together* figures out one of the most difficult questions on the face of the earth: What is funny?

If you've ever thought about a career in situational comedy, this book is an unbeatable resource. This book gives you a detailed look at what goes on in front of, as well as behind, the camera.

HENRY WINKLER
Actor, Author, Director, Producer

PREFACE

The sitcom. We all know what that is. It's *Lucy*, or *Happy Days*, or *Mary Tyler Moore* or *Cosby* or *Friends*. But even though we were weaned on these familiar icons—they come into our living rooms night after night—they're not as simple as they seem. And don't get me wrong—they're meant to look simple. Not in a derogatory way, but in an elegant way. It's the closest thing to a perfect one-act play, a comedy form that started with the Greeks and has endured for over 2,000 years.

These 22-minute confections are part of our lives. We either watch them religiously or we have them on in the background while we're reading the paper, eating dinner, feeding the dog, changing diapers. They're literally part of the cultural soundtrack of our lives. You'd think something so familiar and so ubiquitous would be easy, right? Wrong!

When all the elements come together the sitcom is magic. (Think of the candy factory episode of *I Love Lucy*.) But that kind of magic doesn't happen without inspired writing, brilliant performances, and pitch-perfect direction. And the goal isn't to get it right once in a while; we're supposed to do it week after week and year after year. Anyone who's ever worked on a sitcom, anyone who's ever watched, knows instantly when it's happening and when it's not. And it usually doesn't. For every success there are literally dozens that fail and are quickly forgotten.

In short, the sitcom is truly an art form. Oh sure, scholars and critics will argue that television is disposable pop culture, but no one can deny the power and artistry of the sitcom when it all comes together. Everything is carefully crafted. Writers spend hours—even days or weeks—crafting the story and the script, creating rich, textured characters. It's not simply the "jokes" that are pored over and refined, but it's from the depth of the characters that the right jokes will come.

Making comedy is not simple and it doesn't "just happen." Five days isn't much time to block, rehearse, hone, and ultimately shoot an entire episode. Everyone, from the Executive Producer to the caterer, has to know exactly what he or she is doing for an episode to come together. This obviously takes careful planning and preproduction, but once we all assemble on the stage for the actual shooting phase, a great deal of money is at stake and there's very little margin for error.

So how does it all work? Well, this clever book is the first of its kind to dissect and analyze the sitcom with wit, style, and, of course, humor. An enormous amount of skill goes into each aspect of a show and *The Sitcom Career Book* is a rare glimpse into the creative process. When it all comes together, everyone is in sync with everyone else. The entire organism—which can amount to as many as 150 people—all sees the same thing. And though many people try to reinvent the system or breathe new life into it, sometimes the tried-and-true is the best path.

There are so many facets to sitcom production: writing, casting, directing, acting, wardrobe and set design, camera and technical operations, editing, sound effects, music and scoring. When it all comes together the end result looks easy and effortless. Think of Fred Astaire dancing; every step and breath are meticulously choreographed, but it looks absolutely spontaneous.

There's nothing like the rush of production night, when you have the audience for the first time and everything clicks. Despite the ups and downs of the production week, on show night when you have the perfect audience and everything is "working," you will hear that honest-to-God, rolling, real laughter. It's the greatest sound in the world and proof that all the hard work of the week—the rewriting and careful blocking, the arguments about just the right prop or costume, the meticulous guest casting, even the perfect jokes—pays off.

And the greatest thing is that the audience won't think twice. They just laugh. It looks simple. It looks easy. And that's exactly what we want them to think.

This book, written lovingly with a first-hand perspective, chronicles all aspects of production. Devour it, savor it because, short of actually being there in person, this is the next best thing.

Read on. See how we do it....

Robert Greenblatt
Executive Producer/The Greenblatt Janollari Studio

The Sitcom Career Book

THE LOUDER FASTER FUNNIER WORLD OF TV COMEDY

INTRODUCTION

This book is for anyone who wants to know about sitcoms. Louder! Faster! Funnier! These three words may be the oldest rules for comedy. And they still work! However, as comedy has evolved, so too have the rules! This is a career handbook for the most popular form of comedy: SITCOM.

Situation comedies are an enduring form of television entertainment. From *I Love Lucy* through *Everybody Loves Raymond*, they have not changed substantially. They have a half-hour format, are written in two acts, and are filmed or taped simultaneously by multiple cameras in front of a live audience. The basic goal of sitcoms has been to make people laugh!

If you want to work on a situation comedy, this book has all you need to get started. A lot of the material is addressed specifically to actors. Since almost everyone interacts with the actor at some point or does a job that helps the actor on a sitcom, we hope this information will give insight into their process.

We have provided a broad spectrum of information for many other positions on a sitcom. We have ended each chapter with a SITCOM CAREER PROFILE to give specifics about various sitcom jobs including what training is needed, what unions to join, and advice from people currently working in the job you hope to have.

Knowing what makes a sitcom work will help every person involved in a sitcom make the right choices.

Each chapter contains a SITCOM INSIDER article. These sitcom professionals have generously spoken about their specialty subject in their own words such as actor/writer/comedian and author of *The Other Great Depression*—Richard Lewis:

> Getting a laugh as a comedian versus one as an actor is like being raised by a good mother or by a wolf. Two different worlds. I've spent nearly four decades as a standup comedian and I needed to find my "authentic voice" and then learn to trust it and connect with the audience—assuming they are willing to. I don't believe in the adage, "It's never the audience's fault." Trust me, I could get a standing ovation at Carnegie Hall, and I don't mean to be grandiose, but I got two and did nearly two and a half hours on stage and if I did that same set the next night to an audience of Klansmen, believe me, it wouldn't have been my fault had I bombed.

Richard's passion and expertise and those of other generous contributors will provide you with inside information.

We think that sitcom-acting techniques can be taught. We believe that the first step to "being funny" is "knowing funny." We are shocked by how many people who want to work on sitcoms never watch sitcoms. In every chapter, we include tools for watching a show that will allow you to learn the form, not just enjoy the form. These SITCOM RULES, SITCOM VOCABULARY, SITCOM EXERCISES, and SITCOM VOCABULARY QUICK REVIEW are designed as interactive tools to systematically help you understand the fundamental and more complex aspects of sitcoms.

We have worked on hundreds of episodes of sitcoms. We learned this form at the feet of the masters. We have read countless scripts and watched thousands of rehearsals. We sat through fascinating note meetings with writers/producers, network executives, and studio heads. We've waited into the wee hours of the morning for rewrites. We have been lucky enough to work on sitcoms that survived long enough to go into syndication. Conversely, we've also worked on pilots, both good and bad, that never saw the light of day.

Starting as assistants and eventually becoming directors, we want to pass on what we've learned from our on-the-job training. We want to share our additional knowledge from coaching and teaching. Actors talk to us after taking our sitcom technique class or working on an episode with us. We wish we could have a nickel[1] for every time we heard those actors say, "I wish I had known...."

We inherited our first class from the late Richard Marion who taught the first sitcom scene study class we ever knew existed. Richard was a wonderful actor, a perceptive director, and a great guy. Taken just as his directing career was blossoming, Richard was valued as a comedy coach and friend. Richard Lewis writes of Marion:

> I have studied acting and used coaches. Everyone is on their own journey and have different methods. I enjoy the method acting approach a lot and have studied it. I have also studied improvisation. For many shows and some movies, in particular, *Anything but Love* with Jamie Lee Curtis and the film *Drunks*. I relied a lot in a wonderful man, actor, director and coach, Richard Marion. Richard died suddenly and shockingly too young. I credit him a great deal with learning to allow me to be able to focus and not just break down the role but each speech, each line and each nuance. I trusted him unconditionally. Sure it's good to know your lines so you can put down the script and start to really feel the role but way before that someone like Richard was able to help me see when what I was rehearsing was truthful or rang false. Talents like his come along very rarely and if you find one, like finding a good shrink, pray they have time to help you along the way.

---

[1]   Make that a dollar...some things have changed!

The last show Marion directed was *Everybody Loves Raymond*. National TV audiences may know Marion's name from Ray Romano's Emmy acceptance speech when he acknowledged Marion's contribution.

A sitcom is a tight little world with its own rules, its own language, and its own traditions. We find some recent college graduates, successful stand-up comics, and even Academy Award–winning actors, ill prepared for their foray into this field. We believe that with a little background material, these individuals would feel more at home on a sitcom stage.

College students may have studied comedy from Goldoni and Moliere to Noel Coward and Neil Simon, but may never have seen a sitcom script. Broadway musical comedy actors often can't identify the specific rhythm of a sitcom joke. Dramatic film actors can be overwhelmed by the constantly changing dialogue and fiery pace. Stand-up comedians may be experts at making an audience laugh, but not know how to use the rehearsal process to their best advantage. Improv actors, though highly creative, may not see the necessity of "locking in" to a written script. This book will fill in the gaps you may not know about sitcoms.

Director Steve Zuckerman sees the need to learn this unique style:

> The form is very rigid. It's hard to do 22 minutes and have a beginning, middle, and end. Some actors can't do it. They need all that setup to do their character. In a sitcom, you need to have the ability to lay pipe[2] and be funny at the same time.
>
> There is an ancient theatrical form "Commedia dell' Arte" that did this. Both use scenarios. The scenario might be "Lucy makes a bet with Ricky." There's no real plot. It's just that scenario. The Commedia did little scenarios. Lots of little bits. The Commedia had stock characters. There was always the father figure. In every episode there was always the braggart captain, the "Ted Knight" who is always shooting his mouth off. There also was the ingenue. The familiarity with these characters is what sitcom is all about. You don't need a lot of setup because you know who they are. As the Commedia went to different towns, people would decide if this troupe did the characters better than the others did.

The Sitcom Career Book will teach you how to get a jump on others competing in this field and what to expect on a sitcom set.

This book is laid out in chapters that follow the traditional five-day sitcom schedule. We will take you through each typical day. Other chapters cover auditions/preproduction and postproduction/how to get the next job. Knowing this information will be your password to the sitcom club. *It will serve as a guide toward getting a job in this field.*

You'll learn what casting directors look for at an audition. We'll show you

---

[2] Hey, it's only the intro! We'll get into this and many other unique terms later.

what qualities a producer looks for in hiring a writing staff. We'll tell you what qualities or qualifications industry professionals in management positions value in an employee. For example, Steve McPherson, visionary[3] president of Touchstone Television, described to us the qualities he is looking for in a television executive. "I look for really smart, really energetic, really dependable people who have some sort of background in literature or English so that they can look at material, understand material, and know how to develop material." McPherson looks for someone who has both creative and salesmanship skills. As well as a broad education, Steve also values the experience that comes from moving up from the lowest possible job.[4]

We'll tell you how people got their very first TV job such as technical coordinator Dan Fendel who spent one summer "moving walls and hanging scaffolding as a grip" or cameraman Randy Baer who began as a "crewperson at a local TV station in Tucson, Arizona" or director Madeline Cripe who "wrote letters to producers telling them how lucky they would be to have me work for them…somebody took me up on it."[5]

You will be surprised at the myriad routes that people take to get that first sitcom job. Actress Katherine Helmond will share with you some first-timer tips because this form was new even for someone with her experience. "Since I spent 20 years working in the theatre (still do regularly) going into sitcom was a new adventure for me. I had to learn how to deal with an entirely new medium. Although I had many years' experience in acting I had never had to deal with anything electronic. The greatest asset I brought with me was 10 years in a row working in summer stock doing 10 shows a summer."

Our routes to sitcom were different: one of us from musical theater and one from local television. Both of us had college training that prepared us to succeed in this field, but unlike many professions, no one ever asked us about our education. They only were interested in what we could bring to the show.

In our experience, most sitcom cast and crew have college educations, usually with their emphasis or degree in theatre, television, or film. Other complementary routes are speech and communications or creative writing. However, we both know people who established sitcom careers after being lawyers, psychologists, or social workers. A few have no higher education.

Linda Day who was not the first female sitcom director but was the first to direct an entire series says, "The most asked question I get is, 'Is it hard being a woman director?' First off, it's hard simply being a director, man or woman.

---

[3] McPherson has spearheaded one of the most aggressive campaigns to increase the hiring of minorities and women in Hollywood.

[4] McPherson himself has both experiences, starting out as a production assistant in Hollywood and an education from Cornell University with a pit stop between the two working on Wall Street.

[5] Cripe was the Assistant to the Associate Producer on the hugely funny Norman Lear sitcom *One Day at a Time*. She started in the fifth season. It ran 9 years altogether. "Who knew my first show would last five years." She directed episodes of *Charles in Charge*, *My Two Dads*, *It's Garry Shandling's Show*, *Fresh Prince of Bel-Air*, *In the House*, and *Malcolm and Eddie*.

But yes, the pressure was really on in the beginning, because if I failed, I failed for all women. Once when I interviewed for a job, I was actually told, 'We tried a woman and it didn't work out.'…lord help us if one of their male directors didn't work out…which was why I was being interviewed in the FIRST place."

Today there are still barriers but efforts are being made by unions and network diversity programs. Some are more aggressive and successful than others. Certainly some of the job categories are underrepresented by some races or by women. There are certainly more men directing sitcoms yet there are fewer men being script supervisors. Throughout this book, we will use the generic "he" rather than bore you with "he or she." Instead of using politically correct terms such as "camera operator," if we are talking about a guy, we call him a "cameraman." We happen to work with many topnotch "camerawomen" as well. Many writers, directors, and actors also have fewer employment opportunities once they pass that thirtysomething gateway. Having the luck to do your good work on a show that becomes a hit always gives you a free ride into more employment no matter what your color, religion, age, or shoe size.

Robert Wilonsky of the *Miami New Times* quotes sitcom writer Howard Gewirtz about his job prospects between *Just Shoot Me* and creating *Oliver Beene:*

> "Ageism is definitely prevalent in this business," Gewirtz says, his matter-of-fact voice hinting at little bitterness. "In Hollywood it's all about heat—is there heat on you or not heat on you?—and at that time there was very little heat on me, which I found to be an unacceptable situation. But there it was. So, you can moan and bitch and say it's not fair, and it wasn't, but the only way to fight it is to just draw upon your reserves and challenge yourself and see if you're relevant or not, because no one's gonna turn around and go, 'Oh, gee, he's such a nice guy and worked on *Taxi*, so let's give him a job.' It doesn't happen that way. You'll only work if they think, 'Hiring him's gonna make us money.' But at the moment, things could not be better."

Each chapter will begin with one of the SITCOM RULES. We will show you when each rule applies. We will tell you the back-story on many traditions. You will learn how sitcom rhythms developed from the Jewish Catskill comedians.[6] Each chapter will also introduce you to commonly used SITCOM VOCABULARY words. We will give examples of how these words are the unique shorthand in the sitcom world. We will then give you a SITCOM VOCABULARY QUICK REVIEW to let you see how these words are used in context every day. We will provide SITCOM EXERCISES to familiarize you with sitcom story, structure, and camera technique. Some of these exercises will ask you to view a sitcom; some will ask you to analyze a scene from a sitcom script. Finally

---

6 Writer/Producer Jamie Wooten advises writers to "Learn Yiddish. If you don't know why, oy."

(because we know you're curious), we will pass on apocryphal and legendary stories that we have gathered over our years in the business.

For example, we will show you the difference between:

➤ A celebrity/comedian-driven show versus an actor/ensemble-driven show

➤ A multi-camera sitcom versus a single-camera half-hour comedy

➤ An 8:00 show versus a 9:30 show

➤ A tape show versus a film show

We are still in awe of the shows that were created in the hallowed soundstages where we work. We delight in stories about Desi Arnaz, *George Jefferson*, Jackie Gleason, *Sgt. Bilko*, Mary Tyler Moore, *The Fonz*, Carroll O'Connor, or the *Golden Girls*. We can tell you stories about actors who were replaced and then went on to star in movies or another sitcom series that made them multi-millionaires.

We want to acknowledge the generous contribution made by the people who are quoted in this book. Some appear in the text, on the cover, in sidebars, and some in our SITCOM PROFILES and SITCOM INSIDER. We especially want to acknowledge Henry Winkler and Robert Greenblatt for their insightful comments and support.

THE SITCOM CAREER BOOK will show you why working on a sitcom is one of the best jobs in Hollywood. The hours are great. The work is creative. And someone is actually paying you to go to work all day to laugh.

Chapter 1 GETTING THE JOB!

In this chapter:

How to prepare for an audition

Accessing information on a show

Analyzing a sitcom script

How to learn by watching

Dos and Don'ts for auditioning

Why Ks and Ps are funny

How to make strong memorable choices

What to wear to an audition

How to get your script read

Advice for getting the job

Audition tips

How a director prepares

Career profile of a sitcom casting director

The audition is an actor's job interview. He or she shows up, résumé in hand, at an appointed time to meet someone who has a job to offer. Similarities with job interviews in the real world end there. Getting a normal job is based on experience, job aptitude, education, salary requirements, and personality. NOT IN SITUATION COMEDIES!

GETTING THE JOB—ACTOR

In sitcoms, an actor has to audition, which determines two things: Are you right for the part? And are you FUNNY?[1]

Being right for the part encompasses a lot of things. The most important begins and ends with how you look. Most people might think that means how beautiful. It is not that

> **SITCOM RULE**
>
> **Comedy comes in three.** *A pattern is created with the first two items. The audience is fooled when the third item is not the expected completion of the pattern.*

---

[1] You might wonder where your acting skill comes into play. We're going to assume you wouldn't even get to the audition if you can't act.

simple. A dynamite actress may audition for the "best friend" part. If she's prettier than the lead actress (whose name just might be the title of that new show), she can kiss that part good bye!

Being funny is next. Rick Kushman of the *Sacramento Bee* describes *Friends* as "One of TV's most consistent comedies throughout the years, partly on the strength of funny and just-goofy-enough writing, but mostly because the cast is so special. They each have that precious gift of comic timing..."

It is no coincidence that many sitcoms have been developed for stand-up comedians. Hollywood descends on Montreal's and Aspen's annual comedy festivals in search of new talent. This may not be tapping the most experienced acting pool in Hollywood, but it usually guarantees the laughs. Bruce Hills, COO of Montreal's Just For Laughs Comedy Festival tells us:

> In the late 80s, network talent executives realized that the Just For Laughs Festival was one-stop shopping for them. Within a couple of days, they could see the best stand-ups from around the world, including the best unsigned talent from North America. Basically, we scout all year round and take the pulse of comedy around the world and present them with the best of the best. Over 70 deals have been cut here at the Festival, involving every major studio and network in the U.S.

British actor Adrian Lester (*Primary Colors*, The Royal National Theatre *Henry V*) told us about his first American sitcom:

> I think you can tell a lot about a culture by what makes its people laugh. I spent a while doing nothing but watching all the sitcoms I could get my hands on. I had to learn very quickly to put away the classical theatre muscle and work on my funny bone.

We do not mean to EVER minimize the art of acting. We have great respect for those who are gifted artists and practice their craft with intelligence, creativity, and integrity. But good acting is not enough on situation comedies. "Dying," as the saying goes, "is easy. Comedy is hard." Okay, you are a talented actor. Can you act and BE FUNNY?

Al Martin of the New York Comedy Club talks about his club's connection to the comedy scene.

> We get great, diverse audiences here from all over the country. It's the same people who watch TV so it's the perfect place for people to try out material. We get new acts, top acts who are rehearsing material for HBO or *The Tonight Show* or comedians who want to test material before they go to a major venue. It's a great place to be seen.

BEFORE THE AUDITION

So how does that interviewer (casting director) know if you are "right for the part" *and* FUNNY?...by your audition. Casting director Patricia Noland (*Married...with Children*) explains what she likes about being a casting director: "My favorite part of my job is working with the actors. It is a real joy to nurture talent, and help to launch a new career or participate in moving an existing career to the next step." Noland also cautions,

> I think one of the most common mistakes an actor makes (especially a novice one) is to confuse the audition in a casting director's office with that of an acting class. Although it is perfectly okay to ask a question or two if the material isn't clear to them, they need to come prepared to do the scene, and not expect us to coax it out of them, or even coach them for any length of time. Often, we see many, many people for each role, and time just doesn't permit us to do that pre-liminary work. I've had actors flat-out tell me, "Well, I read it over once, and I didn't really get it, so since I knew I was coming in to see you, I thought I'd just wait and let you walk me through it." NO! After I see what an actor has prepared, I often do have comments or suggestions, but only in a tinkering kind of way—not in a let's-build-it-from-scratch way. Actors need to realize that our job is to see many people (cast a large net) and then narrow down the choices we think our producers will respond to the strongest. Of course, this is why many agents and managers would prefer to bypass this step alto-gether, and have their clients go "straight to producers." I've found overall, however, that the best producers' auditions are the actors who have come in for me once, taken some small direction (be it a wardrobe suggestion or a small adjustment—"Let's try it again, and take about half the anger out"), and then have the confidence to really nail it in front of the director and producers.

An actor auditioning for a sitcom will often get only a few pages of the script. Known as **sides,** these pages are an actor's guide to the story and character. An actor will go in and read the sides (consisting of a part of a scene, an entire scene, or multiple scenes) with the casting director, reader, or an actor who has already been cast.

Sides come from one of the versions of the script...and there have been many. A sitcom script starts with a story premise that is developed into an out-line. This process starts about six weeks before the show goes into full production.

Many scripts are completed before actors show up for the first episode of the season.[2] One writer or writing duo turns the outline into a first draft, often

---

[2] A full season is usually 22 episodes. First-time show creators have lots of butt to kiss just to get an order of six.

known as the pretable draft. As writer Keith Josef Adkins (*Girlfriends*) remarks, "The first draft is written by one entity. It comes to the writer's room, and it's read aloud by everyone. Then we begin pitching on jokes, arcs, etc., in order to shape it for the table. The point of this is to make sure the script feels and sounds like the TONE of the show. With so many writers, each one is bringing their very specific flavor and personality to the show. Although this is encouraged and gives the show its juice, ultimately each script must feel as if it is birthed from one mother."

This birthing process delivers a **table draft.** This is the version of the script that actually gets read the first time the cast is assembled. It takes place around a table: hence the name. At any time from premise to table draft, revision notes and comments may be given on the content and structure by network, studio, and production company executives to the head writer. This writing position has evolved into a position of great power. The head writer is usually just referred to as **show runner.**

A clever and informative article entitled "15 Steps to No Fat" authored by Marsha Scarbrough appears in *Written by*. It describes the evolution of an *Everybody Loves Raymond* script entitled "No Fat" written by Ellen Sandler and Susan Van Allen. Phil Rosenthal is the show runner and Ray Romano is the star of that show. The first few steps involve the initial pitch and outline. Then Scarbrough writes:

> The two-pager defines the spine of the story in a condensed narrative. It's re-written once with Rosenthal's input before being distributed to all the writers and discussed in The Room.... After this "two-pager" is refined, it is sent to the network, the studio, and Romano. At this point Rosenthal suggests that Sandler work with Susan Van Allen on the first draft of the script... Sandler and Van Allen collaborate by writing some scenes together line by line at the computer and some scenes individually, then trading and revising each other. After a first pass, they solicit input privately from some of the other staff writers and do a rewrite. That version goes to Rosenthal who writes notes and jokes in the margins and returns it to Sandler and Van Allen... Sandler and Van Allen rewrite incorporating Rosenthal's notes to create the "writer's first draft"... "The writer's first draft goes to the table in The Room. After an hour or more of general discussion on the overall script, the staff starts with the teaser and goes through the script line by line. A writer's assistant types this version into a communal computer as it is being revised. This process may take the better part of two or three days in The Room but the result is a funnier, fast, more focused script... The script is sent to Romano, who can only be in The Room when he's not involved in rehearsals on stage. After reading this "table draft," Romano spends lunch hour in The Room giving his notes on the script page by page.

The casting director has received either some version of the script, a scene, or sometimes as little as a description of the character and basic idea of the scene. He or she sends this to Breakdown Services,[3] which synthesizes the information about each character in a script. The casting director edits the character descriptions and adds details they want the actor or agent to know. What results is a **breakdown.** Gary Marsh of Breakdown Services describes these sheets as the "Cliffs Notes on the characters." Ideally, a breakdown is a description of the character and what makes that character tick. Often, it's merely a summation of how a character serves the plot. A breakdown is the tool by which agents submit their clients for a possible audition.

Most actors receive the Breakdown Services info sheet from their agent along with their sides. This gold mine reveals what the project is, when it's set to go, and where it's being done. More importantly, it is "the who" of the character. It is the tool that can give an actor insight into what the writers had in mind.

Sometimes the sides and info sheet are limited or sketchy. In this time of advanced information technology, it is assumed that the actor can access additional information. For example, nearly every current series on the air has a Web site. Go to it! An actor can figure out the style of the sitcom based on the writer's previous work,[4] the network's demographic, and the time slot. Do an Internet search. For example, if you wanted more information on Fox's *Oliver Beene*, you'd find that Robert Wilonsky, of the *Miami New Times*, wrote:

> If quality alone guaranteed success in the TV biz, then *Oliver Beene* will live long eough to enter puberty, if not college. It's the sort of

---

CASTING CAREER TRACK

I was head of casting for Turner Television, an in-house production company for the WB Network. Before that, I was the Casting Director for various pilots and series, which included the Saturday morning teen lineup for NBC.

I began my training in Casting with John Levey at Warner Bros. Television. I started as his Assistant, and was later promoted to an Associate Casting position under his supervision. Together we worked on such shows as China Beach, Head of the Class, Growing Pains, Life Goes On, *and* The Adventures of Briscoe County, *among others. Later I also worked under such terrific Casting Directors as Marion Dougherty, Joel Thurm, and April Webster before starting on my own projects.*

I got my first job when the producers of Married…with Children *were looking to cast a spinoff from their show during the final season. Their casting director, Vicki Rosenberg, was too busy to take on another project at that time, so I was hired to cast the spinoff (called* Radio Free Trumaine*) with her as a supervisor. Later, when one of the producers, Stacy Lipp, was hired to Executive Produce another pilot for Columbia TriStar, she asked me to be her Casting Director on that project. And so it began.*

Patricia Noland,
Casting Director, *USA High, One World*

---

[3] If you can tear yourself from this chapter, see Breakdown Services in the Appendix.

[4] A writer's credits can often be found at Internet Movie Database (www.imdb.com).

show that defines FOX, home to the dysfunctional-family comedy ever since the Bundys moved into the neighborhood and started lowering property values. The show makes sense on the network that airs *The Bernie Mac Show* and *That '70s Show* (*Oliver Beene* is, in a sense Fox's *That '60s Show*), and it's the perfect Sunday-night closer, a curveballer from the bullpen after a lineup of *King of the Hill*, *The Simpsons*, and *Malcolm in the Middle*.

Knowing this should help you understand the style of the show.

If a writer was known for an edgy show like *Married...with Children*, this can clue you into the tone of the new material. If the network is targeting viewers 18 to 45 years, like the WB Network, an actor can tailor his delivery for a younger crowd. For example, if an actress is playing seductress, the acting choices she makes for an audience of 8-year-olds would be very different from those she would choose for an audience of 30-year-olds. If a show is currently playing in an 8 o'clock time slot, it has closer scrutiny from a network's Standards and Practices[5] department because the average viewer may be younger than those watching a 9:30 show. If you are interviewing or auditioning for an established show, your own viewing habits and familiarity with the style of the show are invaluable. Watch sitcoms!

PREPARING FOR THE AUDITION-ANALYSIS

So how does an actor best prepare for that all-important chance of actually getting a job? ANALYZE THE MATERIAL, then REHEARSE THE SCENE. First, read a script for content. Understand every line of dialogue and stage direction. Then identify the jokes. This is sometimes harder than it seems. When we teach, we begin each class with the same exercise: We call it FIND THE JOKES. All the students are given the same sitcom scene and are asked to circle the jokes. We ask for a total. We poll for who finds the most. You'd be surprised at how widely the totals vary! An old rule of thumb holds that sitcoms contain three jokes per page.[6] When you study a page carefully looking at odd character traits and reactions, you will often find many opportunities for a laugh.

What exactly is a joke? A joke is the funny part of the scene. It may not be a classic type of joke that a comic might say in a stand-up act, but it is something that makes you smile or laugh[7]. Sometimes jokes are not easy to spot. As you read the later chapters in this book, you'll find out more about the structure and types of jokes common in sitcoms.

---

[5] This department regulates the material that can or cannot be aired on that network, i.e., nudity, profanity, violence, commercial references, etc. With the increase in basic cable viewership, the standards are quickly changing.

[6] Sitcom dialogue is double-spaced and therefore covers about 30 seconds per page unlike dramatic scripts' approximate one-minute pages.

[7] Not everyone would actually laugh out loud at most sitcom jokes, which is why sitcoms are performed in front of an audience of 200 people. Let's hear it for group dynamics!

Just to give you a head start, here are two clues to easily spot jokes: Responses that end with words with *K* sounds and speeches that have a pattern of three. The *K* sound jokes are more than words with the letter *K*. Any hard consonant that sounds "foreign" to the audience's ear will make them laugh.[8] This creates "funny-sounding" words. The letters *C*, *T*, and *P* in a word will often make it funny. Sounds weird, but it's true.

Here's an example from the episode "The Ring Cycle" written by Jon Sherman, from the series *Frasier*, created by David Angell, Peter Casey, and David Lee. Frasier (Kelsey Grammer) spars with his father Martin (John Mahoney) after a celebration dinner.

> MARTIN
> (as he sits) I already said thank you for dinner.
> What am I supposed to do, get down on my knees and
> kowtow to your fancy-ass American Express card?

> FRASIER
> No, I was referring to the gift we have for them.

> MARTIN
> (clambering to his feet) Oh! Right, I forgot about
> that. Yeah, and thanks for dinner, Fraizh, it really
> was excellent. I didn't think I'd like beef cheeks.[9]

Here's another example from the episode "Pop Art," written by Susan Nirah Jaffe, from the series *One on One*, created by Eunetta T. Boone, another Paramount sitcom. This is the episode where Flex (Flex Alexander) meets Natalie (Melissa De Sousa) for the first time. Flex is unaware that Natalie is his daughter Breanna's (Kyla Pratt) art teacher. Flex is making fun of the art teacher he thinks he hasn't met yet. He begins saying she sounds like one of those…

> NATALIE
> Feminists?

> FLEX
> Worse. She calls herself a "womanist." That's French
> for ugly.

> NATALIE
> (GASPING) No! They're the worst. She's probably

---

[8] It is no coincidence that the German Colonel Wilhelm Klink (played by two-time Emmy winner for Best Actor in a Comedy Series Werner Klemperer) on *Hogan's Heroes* received so many laughs. The same goes for Apu on *The Simpsons*.

[9] Paramount Pictures Corporation. All Rights Reserved.

```
                    NATALIE (cont'd)
      filling your daughter's head with outrageous ideas
      like equal rights and self-respect. I bet she
      doesn't even shave under her arms.


FLEX GASPS.


                         FLEX
      She probably wears Birkenstocks.¹⁰
```

Jokes that have a pattern of three follow the sitcom rule that begins this chapter: **COMEDY COMES IN THREE.** These jokes are easy to spot because the two alike items in the list are separated by commas with an odd choice for that list coming after the word *and/or* it may be three separate lines that follow a pattern. We all subconsciously identify patterns when two similar items are mentioned. We are already thinking of the next item in this identified list. When the odd choice comes up, it surprises us. Surprise is the key to making someone laugh.

Here's an example from the same *Frasier* episode. This occurs at the moment when Niles (David Hyde Pierce) and Daphne (Jane Leeves) put rings on each other's fingers. Sam Johnson played the Officiant.

```
                      OFFICIANT
      By the power vested in me by the state of Nevada,
      county of Washoe, and the all-new Lucky 7 Resort and
      Casino, I now pronounce you Husband and Wife. Good
      luck!¹¹
```

Notice the word *casino* also has a K sound. When the third item in the list ends with a hard consonant, it provides a natural emphasis.

Here's another example of a run of three from the episode "Take This Job and Love It," written by Susan Nirah Jaffe, from the series *One on One*, created by Eunetta T. Boone. Duane (Kelly Perine) is scolding Candy (Shondrella) for trying to find a date through the personal advertisements.

```
                        DUANE
      ...the personals. The last bastion of the lonely.
      I, too, was like you, Candy Cane. Looking for love
      in all the wrong places. Bars. The car wash. Idaho.¹²
```

---

¹⁰ Paramount Pictures Corporation. All Rights Reserved.

¹¹ From the episode "The Ring Cycle" written by Jon Sherman, from the series *Frasier*, created by David Angell, Peter Casey, David Lee. Paramount Pictures Corporation, All Rights Reserved.

¹² Paramount Pictures Corporation. All Rights Reserved.

Did you notice the *K* sounds in Candy Cane and car wash?

Sitcom Exercise

This exercise is to help you watch sitcoms with a keener eye and understanding of the genre. Record one entire episode of a sitcom. Play it back the first time. Simply watch as a normal TV viewer. Turn off the VCR. See if you can write a one-sentence blurb describing the plot of the episode. Next, make a note of the three funniest moments you remember in the episode. Turn the TV back on. Fast-forward to one of these funny moments. Watch it three times in a row. See if you can figure out what made you laugh. Do this with the other two memorable funny moments. Do any of these jokes end with K sounds or lines that have a pattern of three?

PREPARING FOR THE AUDITION—REHEARSAL

After studying your sides or the script, the next step is to rehearse. This means saying the words ALOUD for one character, with a partner saying the lines for all the other characters. This partner is **cueing** the actor. Practice the scene in this manner repeatedly until you are entirely familiar with the scene. There is a great debate as to whether material should be memorized for an audition. That is up to the individual. The better an actor knows the scene, the freer and funnier he is in the audition. The point is to be comfortable and free of tension. An actor's tension is not funny.[13]

Whether or not you have memorized the material, we still recommend that you hold the script, for two reasons: Under pressure, you just may forget the lines. With the script in your hands, you can find the line. Then there's the subliminal message. An audition is not a final performance...or at least that is what an actor wants the producer to think. By holding the script, you let the producer know you are directable and there is even more to your performance to come.

However, here's the catch: Even though you're holding a script, an audition REALLY IS a performance! And a strange performance it is! Great acting is reacting. It's playing a scene moment to moment with another character who needs something or wants something. The problem with auditioning is that other character may or may not be present. If the casting director you are reading with is not emotionally present, reacting is difficult...but not impossible.

Some casting directors are good actors; they give a lot to the partner with whom they are reading. Casting director Robi Reed (*Girlfriends, Sister, Sister*) believes that a casting director's training should include acting and directing classes to prepare for the job. Even with the best training, though, some may fall short. When this happens, an actor can't react because *nothing is going on.*

---

[13] Well, actually it can be! Comedian Richard Lewis has had a very successful career with his self-effacing humor about his personal neuroses. Richard's tension is funny. Richard co-starred with Jamie Lee Curtis in a short-lived, yet wonderful show *Anything but Love* created by Peter Noah.

What to do in this case? PRETEND. For example, suppose a parent (played by the actor) is being begged by a child (played by the casting director) to go to a party. Suppose no begging is really going on. The auditioning actor must then go through the same thought process AS IF he were being begged.

In our experience, the actors who get seriously considered for each role are the ones who come into an audition with strong choices of how to play that character. Marc Hirschfeld, who was the casting director of dozens of series from *Married...with Children* to *3rd Rock from the Sun* and now heads casting for NBC says, "I look for an actor who commits to the audition material. I want to hire an actor who makes strong, intelligent choices. I want to hire an actor who is prepared and has obviously put some thought and energy into the role."

Actress Diane Delano (*Northern Exposure, The Lady Killers*) lives and works by the philosophy, "I am what I am, and that's all that I am." She advises actors, "Don't apologize and never compromise what you are to fulfill another person's view of what you should do." Delano's strong choices allow her to be creative and approach her craft with a deep personal integrity.

As directors, we have been asked our opinion about a specific actor after an audition and responded that he or she was "okay." Okay doesn't get the part. One producer once described to us why he had not cast an actor whom he had used many times before. This producer assured us that he was a big fan of that actor's work. He also said that actor was perfect for the part. So why didn't he cast him? "You know, at the audition, he didn't nail it!" he explained. If you intrigue the decision makers with a strong choice, you will be seriously considered for the part. If the strong choice does not intrigue, it might be considered odd or inappropriate. At least you tried.

Peter Engel (executive producer of *Saved by the Bell, USA High, City Guys,* and many other Saturday morning hits) has a theory about young actors. "When you hire young actors, how much experience can they have?" he asks. Engel, who launched the careers of such actors as Mark-Paul Gosselaar (*NYPD Blue*), expounds on his litmus test for actors. "The key is that some young people fill space, others take up space." He gives an example. "I was looking for kids who would captivate me with their personality. I was looking for that before they ever read."

Engel says making an impression is key. "First thing is make me interested in you—then try and do something with the part that makes it you. Don't change the character but do something that is memorable, something that makes it better." He also cautions, "Don't make it worse, and don't re-write it. Take what's there and make it you. We only need one of each character."

PREPARING FOR THE AUDITION—COACHING

Some actors get coached. That translates into paying money to someone who knows sitcoms better than you do. There are three reasons to get coached. First, a coach allows you to rehearse exactly what you will be doing at the audition. Second, a coach may know more about the material than you do. Third, the coach can help you make better choices about the material.

Academy Award–winning actress Louise Fletcher (*One Flew over the Cuckoo's Nest*) shares that her coach "can take the fear and panic and replace those with confidence and ease. I can concentrate!" She explains that her coach "knows how to focus on the material and relate it to my own strengths which I have forgotten I had (because the fear and panic are in full command when we meet). Meeting with her coach for an hour before an audition has been one of the "great finds" in her career.

Why rehearse an audition? An actor who prepares by himself is only studying the material; he isn't actually practicing the scene. Sitcoms are predicated on timing and rhythm. Stage, film, and television actress Robin Bartlett (*Mad about You, The Powers That Be*) says about sitcoms, "Making it natural and musical at the same time is the challenge and the fun." Musicians just don't study their music. They play it. A coach, reading the lines of the other characters in the scene, helps an actor simulate an audition. So many obstacles can interfere with an actor's concentration when he walks into an audition. The only thing an actor has control over is his mastery of the material. Being well rehearsed allows an actor to perform with confidence.

Why are a coach's choices better than yours? They aren't always. But a coach can be a second pair of eyes. A coach may spy a joke you missed or an impulse you had (but didn't follow). A coach allows you to simply act and not analyze. An actor who is analyzing or watching himself during the scene is not fully

AUDITION HINTS

What separates the good actors from the bad actors and the good writer from the hack, is that good actors can take a hack script and make it blossom into more than that writer deserves. The good writer can watch a bad actor make him or her seem like a hack. The point is, it's a synergy. A good actor will read a difficult piece of writing, like Brecht, Albee or Neil Simon, and even if they don't understand the writer's point (and if they don't understand Simon, there are other lines of work), their own uniqueness will embellish it because the words are there. Do not fuck up or add to the words. Writers hate that. They might not tell you to your face, but they do. That can come after you get the job (unless it's Simon and he'll fire you in a New York minute). And a good writer will create characters that are vivid, even in their dullness, for an actor to wrap his or her mind around. If an actor says of a script, "But there's nothing for me to grab onto" he or she is saying, "Please fire me." Find something. If the actor makes a writer see something they hadn't thought of before, he'll take credit for it and hire you, even if you're thinking inside, "This is shit."

Ian Praiser, Writer, *Alf, Suddenly Susan, Caroline in the City*)

present in the material. So, what makes an excellent audition? Bartlett says, "Spontaneity above all. Bringing yourself to the material, which is often written formulaically."

Choosing a coach for a sitcom should depend on whether that coach is an EXPERT in the field of sitcoms. Just making good acting choices is not enough. Sitcoms are different from other material because their aim is to make people laugh! Sitcom writer, producer, creator Nancylee Myatt (*Night Court, Social Studies, The Powers That Be, Living Single*) was asked to describe the difference between sitcoms and other material. She replied, "It's funny. If your script doesn't make people laugh, and I mean out loud, not just smile, perhaps you should write a drama." So, make sure your coach has a sense of humor. Your immediate reward will be making him or her laugh!

THE AUDITION

How does an actor get an audition appointment? After an agent receives notices from Breakdown Services, he submits his clients for the roles. The casting director sets up appointment times. The actor auditions for the casting director. Then the actor sometimes auditions again (a **callback**). Then the actor sometimes auditions again (final producer session). Then, in the case of a pilot, the actor auditions again ("going to network"), maybe on tape. Before this final pilot audition, an actor signs his contract called a "test deal."

Actors should foster relationships with casting directors. The secret is how to do this without being a pest. The best sales tool an actor has for this purpose is the reputation of doing consistently good work. There are workshops where actors pay a fee to meet casting directors.[14] They usually involve doing a prepared scene or pairing up with another actor in the workshop to read a set of sides. These workshops DO NOT come with any job offers or guarantees. They are merely a way of getting a casting director to see your face and view a sample of your work. After one of these workshops, a casting director may agree to look at a sample reel of your work. Sample reels should never exceed five to seven minutes. You're lucky if a casting director will watch more than two minutes. Sending postcards or flyers alerting casting directors that you are in a play, performing stand-up, or appearing on an episode of an upcoming show is a great way to keep your face or name in front of them. Quoting good reviews or mentions in newspapers or magazines gives them an unbiased assessment of your work. Invite them, but don't ever expect casting directors to actually come to an event. They couldn't possibly see everything. You just want it on their radar that you're out there working.

Casting directors are asked to vouch for an actor's reputation. They should know that you're cooperative, professional, and PUNCTUAL! It's also helpful when they know you have a life. An articulate or funny comment made about current events, a recent movie, or a book you just read may leave a more

---

[14]   To prevent scams, the Casting Society of America supports the regulations that the State of California sets up on how these types of workshops should be run.

lasting impression than bragging about your latest gig. An actor who talks only about himself and his career is boring, boring, boring.[15] One sitcom writer interviewed for this book commented on actors giving bad writing notes. He followed this insult with "I can say this safely because actors don't read books that aren't about themselves." The perception that actors are self-absorbed is hard to live down.

At the same time, it is important to note that the audition is NOT the time or place for long chitchat. An actor should come in, ascertain with whom he is reading, do the material, thank the casting director, and leave. Casting director Beth Goldstein (*The Naked Truth, The Hughleys*) also offers some other advice: "If you don't connect with the character and know you'll give a poor audition, pass on the audition. If you are sick, don't come in: Chances are you'll give a bad audition and can get everyone else sick, plus you might have the good fortune of being able to reschedule when you are well. In both cases, remember: better not to be seen than to be seen poorly."

> **AUDITION HINTS**
>
> *Always bring a picture and résumé...even if your agent tells you that the casting director already has it on file. Be on time or early for your audition! Don't make a mountain out of a mole hill. Some actors are under the mistaken impression that the longer you're in the audition room, the better shot you have at booking the role. Wrong. Go in, do your scene, and get the hell out so we can talk about you while the audition is fresh in our minds. Don't feel the need to shake everyone's hand when you both enter and leave the room. Don't second-guess your audition: If you have a bad start on the first line, ask to start again. Otherwise, shake it off and keep going. And don't ever finish the audition and then ask to do the scene again because you were unhappy with your performance. It just shows that you were insecure with your choices the first time around. If the Producer or Casting Director asks you to read again, make sure you take their direction. Don't ignore it.*
>
> Marc Hirschfeld,
> Ex. VP Casting, NBC Entertainment

PROPS AND COSTUMES

Actors often ask about wearing a costume or bringing a prop to an audition. Wearing something that gives the flavor of a character is often helpful. Wearing a costume is trying too hard. For example, a loose-fitting garment would be better for a pregnant character than a pillow or pregnancy suit. Similarly, a black shirt and dress pants would give the flavor of a minister rather than an actual clerical collar. NBC's Marc Hirschfeld thinks this is the most common audition mistake: "An actor should dress to *indicate* the role, but don't come in wearing a uniform. If you're auditioning for a steel worker, don't come in wearing a hard hat. Wear casual clothes, blue jeans, work shirt."

Then there are always exceptions to the rule, and it all comes down to being comfortable. Actor William Forward (*The Gilmore Girls, Babylon 5*) found he got more work in his own comfortable, nice, casual wardrobe than when he tried

---

[15] There are many jokes told about actor narcissism. One story tells of an actor going on and on about his last role and then realizing that he's been talking only about himself. The story ends with the actor saying, "Enough about me...what do you think about me?"

for a look. His jeans and cashmere sweater booked him a job as funeral director: He was the only actor not wearing black. His khakis and sweater did not prevent him from being cast as an Ivy League admissions director: It helped him stand out from the sea of tweed. Forward said, "Dressing in what suits you can show them you are a confident actor, not trying desperately to please."

With props, think substitution. Our rule of thumb is, if it's something you normally carry, you can use it. We have seen portable phones, pagers, water bottles, and pens substitute for anything from a gun to a cattle prod. If an actor commits to that prop, his audience at a casting session will believe it too.

Casting director Beth Goldstein also advises, "Do not bring unnecessary props. Small props are fine such as a cell phone, candy bar, etc. Guns are tricky. The two times I've seen them brought in, the actors actually booked the job! If you do choose to bring it in, show everyone in the room, BEFORE THE AUDITION, that it is not real or loaded. At no time during the audition do you point the gun at anyone in the room. My director on a film actually responded to the actor who brought in the gun because many other actors had a hard time pantomiming having the gun."

Auditioning is hard. The pressure can be excruciating; the stakes are high. Landing a pilot can lead to six years[16] of continued employment plus syndication. As if auditioning isn't hard enough, respect for actors can be sometimes less than it should be. We have heard two great pieces of advice about auditioning: (1) enjoy yourself, and (2) don't replay it! Marietta Diprima (*The Hughleys, Dear John*) loves to act. She says, "Auditioning is an opportunity. I'm a character actor. Auditioning is my chance at creating my own little repertory theatre company!" Moreover, she "gets to play all the parts…one audition at a time." An audition is the first, last, and only time an actor gets to create a character without other people's input. Diprima says, "It belongs to you! You go in, you do it, you do it right, and whether they cast you or not, you KNOW that you did it." Marietta believes in living or dying by her choices because they're hers.

Sitcom audiences know Betty Garrett as Irene Lorenzo on *All in the Family* and *The Jeffersons* and as Edna Babish-DeFazio on *Laverne and Shirley*. Garrett, a lovely actress, a very funny lady, and a wise sage, says, "I treat an audition as a performance. I just get out there and enjoy myself. And if I get the job, that's just gravy!"

Try to remember: They have a problem (casting this role) and you have the solution. You are the doctor. Don't go in to be funny; go in to be the character. Don't hit the jokes too hard; let the material do the work for you.

---

[16] Actors sign contracts before they audition for a pilot that contracts them for the first six years on a sitcom series. The goal of most series is to produce enough shows so that all episodes produced can be sold into syndication. Syndication means lots of residuals. The target number for a syndication package is 100 episodes. That's five seasons of 22 episodes a year. The sixth season is the last season to make more shows without renegotiating with the actors. In the case of a megahit like *Friends,* renegotiations are done earlier than six years in good faith because the show has been such a financial success.

Always give your auditioners the benefit of the doubt. They're fallible. Remember they're people, too. Scott Bakula (*Enterprise*, *Quantum Leap*, *Murphy Brown*) shares a perfect example:

> I'm a theatre guy. When I came to L.A., after 10 years in New York doing mostly musical comedy, the sitcom world was a natural fit for me. I loved and understood the live audience, and I loved the sense of performance, of getting ready for "Show" night! I was lucky enough to land the guest-starring role on the *Designing Women* pilot, which was an exciting, complicated, but very visible introduction to the L.A. scene. People had started to know who I was when I went into an audition later that year, an audition that I've never forgotten.
>
> It was to replace the lead in a pilot that had been picked up already. (I won't name names because this is about the audition process). I went into a room to read for the Executive Producers and Writers, one of whom was sitting down in a big, soft chair, and never got up. I plowed into the scenes but couldn't help but notice that as I went on, the man (who had never gotten up), sank lower and lower into his chair and that by the time I was done, he was basically fully reclining. He said "thank you" from the reclining position and I left; immediately called my agent telling them I almost put the guy to sleep, the whole thing was a disaster, what a rude S.O.B., etc., etc., etc. Oddly enough, to my surprise, I got the job.
>
> Turned out he was the Executive Producer and his back was out, and he was in terrible pain at my audition. Hence his posture and attitude. The moral of course being that you never know what will happen at any given audition. Every one is different. You need to stay positive, as positive as anyone can, during that mind-bending, necessary evil of "the audition."

Replaying an audition can be destructive. Do not waste time rerunning your last one in your head, worrying if you made the right choices or amount of chitchat. Actress Kate Zentall warns about such obsessing. "Auditioning should be like going to the bathroom," she begins in her own irreverent way. "Just do your business, flush, and then forget about it!"

Nevertheless, actors have a lot of valid questions after they leave the room. One is "Who were all those people?" Another is "Did they like my choices?" And "Would they have validated my parking?" The answer to the last question is definitely no.[17] The people in the room might include the casting director, a casting assistant who reads the scene with you, the producer/writer who wrote

---

[17] Not-yet-cast actors are at the bottom of the food chain. Directors and writers often get their parking validated.

[18] For some unknown reason, a lot more male producers show up when a girl in a bathing suit is being cast.

that episode, the show runner, the line producer, and the director.[18] If you're auditioning for a series regular, network and studio people may be there as well. On rare occasions when the audition is for a particularly important series regular, the series' star might be there to read. As an actor, don't try to get everyone's name. Just focus on the work!

Richard Lewis, actor/writer/comedian and author of *The Other Great Depression*, suggests:

> Find yourself in every role. The best screenplays are generally written—at least the personal ones—by writers who know their subject matter first hand. To me, I need to find the part of me that is very much a part of whomever I am playing to make it real or I'm through. This holds true in the auditioning process. What's the point when you usually have one shot not to do it your way? Even if you don't get the role and that can be for a zillion reasons that have nothing to do with you or your talent, if you drive home after an audition knowing you didn't do it the way you truly believed was the way to go, to me, it's a waste of time. And on screen, obviously directors can do take after take but all I can say is I hope that you never find yourself in a position where you cave in to a direction that you feel, in your gut, is so wrong. Trust me, months later when it airs or in a year in the darkened movie house you will cringe and all you had to do is not do it. It's your career and your "being" up there, regardless of the role so be compassionate to your instincts and yourself because sadly, it's a world of a lot of ego-trippers and power hungry people who need to justify their creative existence. Well, guess what, so do all of us, so fight for what you believe in!

The best feedback on your choices is the laughs that you can earn from the people in the room. Stick by your choices. Trust us, if there is interest in casting an actor, someone will offer an adjustment if it's necessary. The choice is yours whether to take the offer. The changes may be asked for immediately in the casting room. Be open. If you want extra time to rethink the scene, you can ask to go into the waiting room and return shortly. More often, feedback gets filtered through an agent. You may be asked to change something for a callback. If no requests are made, *do the scene the way you did it the first time.*

Casting director Beth Goldstein suggests, "Don't invade the reader's space. It makes the reader feel uncomfortable and it's difficult for us to see you so

---

[19] Of course, one you're as famous as Ashton, you'll get offers without auditions and will never have to slate again.

[20] Fourth wall is a theatre term referring to the imaginary wall through which the audience is watching. Breaking the fourth wall in theatre is when a character speaks directly to the audience. Breaking the fourth wall in television is when the actor looks directly into the camera lens and appears to be talking directly to the viewers. *Malcolm in the Middle* and *Bernie Mac* regularly use the device for effect.

close up. If you can't play the character from across the room, you can't play it. Do not have actual physical contact with the reader during the audition. If the character you are playing is supposed to kiss the other character, SKIP IT and any other inappropriate contact. The only time this is acceptable is if you are told to do it, perhaps for a screen test."

Increasingly, auditions are being videotaped. If someone making a casting choice was not able to attend the audition, or would like to review an audition, this can be a very valuable tool. Actors are asked to **slate** their name. This means announcing your name as the first thing on the videotape to identify yourself. Such as "Ashton Kutcher, Endeavor Agency."[19] The casting director or assistant who is reading will usually stand right next to the camera. Play the scene to the person, not the camera. Playing to the lens will give the appearance of breaking the **fourth wall.**[20] If an actor knows that an audition is going to be taped, we recommend rehearsing as if there were a camera in the room.

Casting is the most important single task of a sitcom. Producer Peter Engel says, "Casting is the key to television." Engel continues, "In the perfect casting situation, when you see the right actor come in, there is no one else in the world. You know 'that is the person I wrote it for,' there's no one else!" If a show is not cast well, it doesn't matter how well the script was written, how masterfully it was directed, how beautifully it was lit and shot, or how stunning the designs. What matters is can these characters come into TV viewers' homes every week and consistently entertain them. That's why the actors on hit shows make megabucks. Actors are treated like royalty on sitcoms. A show is identified with the faces that make them laugh every week!

Some stars define a series. Mark-Paul Gosselaar who stars on *NYPD Blue* starred on the original *Saved by the Bell.* Engel describes the talent of Gosselaar as "awesome. He understood it, he got it. He *was* 'Saved by the Bell.' He was the most popular kid in the school and the biggest geek was his sidekick." Engel talks about casting him, "I said to casting director Robbin Lippin, if we don't find a Zack, we don't have a show. When Gosselaar walked in the room, I said, 'If he can speak English, he's got the job' because he had a sparkle." Even though in real life, Mark-Paul was nothing like the character he played, he had the ability to become Zack. "And nobody else did! Mark-Paul could look you in the eye, lie to you, and you knew he was lying to you and you still loved him. Brandon Tartikoff likened the Zack character to the early sitcom character Bilko."

Actress Kate Zentall offers a realistic picture:

> Chances are you will be auditioning for a smaller guest-star role, a probable one-episode gig. Chances are your character will be there to further the plot, create situations to be overcome by the series regulars. Chances are your ability to be unique and interesting and sincere, and charming will get you the part. Chances are also that once you do get the part you will notice that it gets progressively smaller and less funny with each day of rehearsal. Chances are you

will take this personally. Do not do this. The very charming and funny thing that got you the part may very possibly be excised from the script by taping day. You often become a straight man to one of the regulars. It hurts, but so does childbirth, strep, or other unfortunate conditions of life. The more you anguish and worry, the worse it is all around. You are a hired hand, a professional. Watch, listen, be a good guest, a helpful participant. Know your place. Be a grown up.

GETTING THE JOB—WRITER
The Pilot

A writer gets a job on sitcoms in an entirely different way: He gets read and then he pitches…or in the case of a **pilot,** he just pitches. A pilot is the very first episode of any television show. It is the model on which a series is based. The cast, the scenery, the "look" and style of a show are set during a pilot. Pitching is telling your idea: your idea for the pilot or your ideas for future episodes.[21]

Nearly always, a writer pitches his pilot to a network in the hopes that that network (or another) will like the idea enough to order a script. The game in Hollywood is to be one of the individuals who gets to pitch. That game is often set up by only the most powerful of agents, or by a producer or studio with a track record, or a manager with a hot client. Comedian D. L. Hughley sold his pilot *The Hughleys* based on his pitch. His already successful stand-up career got him the pitch meeting! If a writer has a hit show on the air, his chances are far better to get the opportunity to pitch.

Before the network pitch, a studio will often get involved. Touchstone's Stephen McPerson explains that, "We find a writer we like, or have an idea that he likes and wants to develop, and pitch that to the networks."

It can also happen the other way. The network can ask a producer to develop something they have in mind. Peter Engel gives an example about his series *Saved by the Bell.* "NBC's Brandon Tartikoff wanted me to do a Saturday morning show.[22] The premise really was six kids 'who were starting high school: the wondrous wonder years.' The pitch was telling these kids' stories from the opening bell at eight o'clock on Monday to four o'clock on Friday." Peter and his writers laid out the show for Tartikoff, who asked, "What shall we call this?" Writer Tom Tenowich suggested *Saved by the Bell.* The title cleared[23] and the next day a sign was up.

The last and most unusual way to get a show on the air is to write a spec pilot. This does not involve pitching. Howard Gewirtz did this with *Oliver*

---

[21] Writers also pitch individual jokes as part of an ongoing rewriting process.

[22] NBC wanted to capture the ten- to 13-year-old market. Research said it would never work.

[23] Shows use an outside contractor to check for legal clearances or conflicts.

Beene. Even though a network might buy a pilot idea and commission a script to be written, it does not guarantee that the pilot will get produced. Once a pilot script is bought, the next step is getting a commitment from a network to make it. Many pilots are made each year. Few actually make it to the air. The way a pilot makes it to the air is with star power or audience testing. Over the years, we have seen some very funny pilots not make the schedule while another, not-so-sharp pilot with a major star in the lead, gets the pickup. A recent trend in sitcoms is for networks to buy shows that they have produced by a studio "in house." For example, CBS network owns CBS Productions. When it comes time to sell that product into syndication,[24] CBS reaps more profits because it is both the buyer and the seller.

A pilot script is different from other episodes in that it must entertain while containing more expository information than a normal script. A pilot has to introduce all the regular characters and the basic premise of the show. When viewers watch a sitcom from week to week, there's a familiarity with these characters. The pilot lays the foundation for this. When test audiences view a pilot,[25] they give specific feedback on how much they like each character. Characters are often recast if the audience test group is favorable toward the show but unfavorable toward the actor.

Getting staffed on a pilot (AND DOING A GOOD JOB on that pilot) often will ensure a job for future episodes of that show if it gets on the schedule.

GETTING THE JOB—WRITER
Staffing

Getting the writing job on an existing series is another matter. First a writer gets read, then he pitches. **Getting read** means an agent submits writing samples of his writer client. This may be scripts that have been produced or speculative scripts from popular shows on the air. Every year, there are different shows in vogue to write as spec scripts. The writer has copied the format of the show and supplied his own story using the regular characters and some guest stars. It shows what the writer can create for an already existing show. Not any show will do. There is a practice that only certain shows are worthy of copying. For years it was great to have a *Frasier*, but now everyone has a *Frasier*, so it might be better to do a *Scrubs*. Writers need multiple writing samples if they want to go to a new show. Writer/producer/creator Nancylee Myatt advises the aspiring sitcom writer. "Writers write. Write something. Then write something else. Then another thing. Until you have so many samples from different

---

[24] This is where sitcoms make huge profits! It's like selling something twice but the second time you have no production costs, other than residuals.

[25] Pilots are viewed by test audience private screenings in different cities. Each audience member has a dial, which they turn up if they like something and down when they don't. Some of them are interviewed in depth right after the viewing. The results are crucial to determining whether a show continues. A show can live or die by the turn of a dial.

genres that you'll be covered for any opportunity. By genre I mean: a family show, a workplace comedy, a twentysomething ensemble, or whatever is popular. Because invariably the spec script you have will be from the one show that the producer who can give a job hates."

For writers, a job interview is the next step. "I'm looking for people with passion for what they are doing," says Peter Engel. "People came in like Leslie Eberhard (*USA High*). Who is this guy? Why does he want to work for us? I had read his 'Frasier'[26] which was totally wrong for us, but when he came in, there was so much enthusiasm…and he had done his homework. Knowing what we're doing, that's what it's about!" During the interview, the writer may have to pitch stories for the series. These are multiple ideas for episodes. When a writer successfully pitches his ideas for an already existing series and gets hired, it is called **staffing.**

When Engel looks for a writing staff, he "casts the room." "I try to cast a room with diversity, and I don't mean diversity female/male, black/white. I mean diversity in ages[27]. I wanted to get a diversity of ideas so that the older guys could teach the young guys and the younger guys could teach the older guys. I cast the room like I'd cast the show. It's great because you don't have just one point of view!"

Engel has read many spec scripts. "What I'm looking for in reading a writer is finding something that pops off the page. Yes, I've read this kind of scene a hundred times, but this is a different attack on it. For instance, I read Jeffrey Sachs's (*9 to 5, City Guys, Hang Time*) script of *The Wonder Years*. Obviously, my doing all these young adult shows, *The Wonder Years* was a good sample. I didn't want to read *Homicide*. Jeffrey Sachs's script talked about a bully who Kevin (Fred Savage) could not avoid. He had to fight him after school at 3 o'clock. Jeffrey dealt with leading up to the fight and then the confrontation, and how Kevin got out. Jeffrey treated it differently, and that's why I hired him. I was looking for something that was very real emotionally but treated differently or uniquely."

GETTING THE JOB—DIRECTOR

Directors being considered for sitcom jobs also interview. Instead of a spec script, an agent sends over an already produced episode on tape or a sample reel of a director's work. For the newcomer this may be a student film, commercial, etc. Director Steve Zuckerman (*Everybody Loves Raymond, Friends, Murphy Brown*) says,

> If you put together a reel or show someone an episode, it doesn't show too much about you. It looks the same as the other episodes

---

[26] In this case a produced episode, not a spec script.

[27] Tomes have been written about ageism in the TV business. Mr. Engel seems to have walked to the beat of his own drum for which we applaud him.

of that show. What it doesn't show is how the week went. Did you do it on time? Did you do the shots or did the TD or AD do them? By the time it is edited, all sitcoms look the same. But my agent said I had to give them a reel so you try to give them something that they are looking for. They might be looking for a lot of physical comedy. That will help. If you are up for a single camera show, you might have an episode with some single camera elements.

Picking the right style of show is as important as the right quality of show. In addition to the ability to actually produce a good finished product, a director is judged on whether he can handle the cast and crew. Being at the helm is great responsibility and there are many big personalities involved.[28] A producer takes a big leap to hire an unknown or unproven quantity. For this reason many journeyman directors "observe" on a sitcom in order to gain familiarity with a show and, more importantly, gain the confidence of the regular director and producer. A verbal vote of confidence or recommendation can make all the difference as to whether a young director gets a break. Director Michael Lembeck (*Friends, Mad about You, According to Jim*) has very generously helped many careers this way. Producer/director/actor Jonathan Prince (*American Dreams, Dream On, Throb*) agrees. He told a theater full of Director Guild members that the key to employment in this industry is "who you know." "Mentors," he said, "get you in the door."

There are also training programs sponsored by the studios or networks. ABC and Disney, in association with Touchstone Television, have fellowship programs for both writers and directors. Warner Brothers has a long history of developing writers. Writer Nancylee Myatt (*Night Court, Social Studies*) talks about that program:

> **WRITING CAREER TRACK**
>
> *My advice to anyone who wants to become a writer of sitcoms (or any other form of writer) can be summed up in three words: write, write, write. The difference between people who talk about being writers and those of us who are writers is the difference between a blank page and one that is filled with words. I carve out a space every day to write, if not on a project or script, then in my journal. Learning to create with words, like making music from piano keys requires practice. It's a use it or lose it proposition. Writers write.*
>
> *As a kid I was a television addict—still am. Back in the days before VCRs, I used to write out the story in dialogue of a favorite series I'd seen the night before. By the time I was in high school, I would amuse myself by making up my own "episodes" of my favorite shows. When I had my first interview with an agent and he asked to see my material, one of the things I gave him was an original sketch I'd written for* The Carol Burnett Show. *That sketch landed my first job, a summer replacement series produced by the writers from the Burnett show. To my good fortune, we all learned I could write more than just "pretend" sketches and was ultimately brought on staff of* The Carol Burnett Show.
>
> Rick Hawkins,
> Writer, *Major Dad* and *Sister, Sister*

---

[28] Madeline Cripe when talking about a director's responsibilities includes "walking on egg shells and talking to the actors…who will occasionally listen."

I believe the Warner Bros. Writer's Workshop originally started as a minority program for the studio. The studio would choose writers who met the minority criteria with an eye to putting them on the shows that were being produced by Warner Bros. Writers and producers who were working on Warner Bros. shows at that time taught the class. I ended up teaching there a couple of years when I was working on the lot. The studio would help place the graduates on their shows, pay the writing salaries—that way everyone got a break. When I went through the WBWW in the late 80s it was still geared toward minorities somewhat, but was starting to open the doors to all writers who turned in a good sample which rose to the top of the very tall stack of submissions. I hit the minority status on two levels—I'm a woman and a Native American (and yes I can prove it, I'm a card-carrying member of the Cherokee Tribe. Being a woman has been much easier to prove over the years). And I had the good fortune of having producers who were running shows for Warner Bros. recommend me to the workshop. I had been their writer's assistant and they told the studio that if I got into the class and showed promise they would hire me. It all came down that way and they gave me my first job on *Night Court*. Of course, everyone who got hired out of the workshop had to then prove they were worth keeping around—because the studio was only paying our salaries for the first 13 weeks as a term writer. After that, the producers had to keep us on as staff writers and pay the salary from the writer's budget on the show. It's my understanding that the program is still going on—but is no longer focusing on minority hires and making no promises about staffing. And once you get accepted, you have to pay a fee to the workshop. I understand Disney has a similar program. So it took a while, but the studios have finally figured out a way to get writers to pay them for writing.

GETTING THE JOB—DESIGNERS AND CREW

Department heads and designers are hired at the very beginning of the pre-production period. That period is usually about 6 to 10 weeks for a series and may be just a few weeks for a pilot. To save time, the heads and crew from a show that is just finishing its season might be hired to continue as the staff for a pilot that is being done by the same production company. For example, many crew members from the already running *The Hughleys* worked on the new pilot *One on One*, both for the Greenblatt Janollari Studios. When *One on One* got on the air, the crew members who only worked two days a week were able to do both shows simultaneously for the years that both shows were in production.

After the show runner, director, writers, and department heads are set, the line producer fills all of the approximately one hundred positions it takes to make a sitcom. Line producer Coral Hawthorne (*The Hughleys*) clarifies, "I let the department heads choose their own staff. I just have veto power." She goes on to explain that she rarely exercises that veto and that it is rare for a department head to not have recommendations.

So how does one get to know that department head who uses people they know? Any way you can! A common route is starting as production assistant, or PA. Madeline Cripe who wrote the blind letters to producers started out this way.

Work breeds work! It is easier to move laterally from a position in the company. Script supervisor Kit Wilkinson "took the only job available" and explained her other interests to her employers once she was already in the job. Oscar-winning producer Jana Sue Memel believes it's all about relationships. "There are a lot of qualified people in this business; it's assumed you can do the job well, or you wouldn't be considered. The deciding factor is whether the person hiring feels comfortable with you." Costume designer Emily Draper (*Oliver Beene, Grace under Fire*) explains about breaking into her field: "I do think you have to be willing to work on almost anything to get experience and connections. You also need to try to get into the union by working in a costume house or on a movie that goes union. Usually, if you keep working hard and are easy to get along with, you will keep working." Director of photography Bruce Finn (*8 Simple Rules*) gives this advice, "Befriend and call huge volumes of business potential clients." Writer/producer Rick Hawkins (*Sister, Sister*, and *Major Dad*) credits luck and nepotism: "Almost everyone in show business had had someone to give them a break, lend a hand, or teach them the ropes. If not, they were just lucky enough to be in the right place at the right time."

There is a popular cameraman in Hollywood named Vito Giambalvo. Actors love him. Producers love him. Crews love him. Why? Vito has a great laugh. When Vito sees a scene, he is the best audience anyone could ask for. Line producers hiring **below-the-line**[29] staff have kept Vito employed continuously for 30 years because they want him and his great sense of humor around…and he's a great camera operator. **Above-the-line**[30] are the actors, director, and producers or as Second Assistant Director Marcia Lapin wryly defines it as "the people who get big **residuals**.[31]" Residuals are payments negotiated by a union for reuse of a TV show. When a line producer is staffing, it is a crucial time for resumes of all personnel to be already at his or her disposal. Keeping in touch year-round is the smartest thing to do so you don't appear at the last minute, too hungry for the job. People can smell panic in Hollywood.

---

[29] Below the line refers to the crew and production staff. Some are paid only for the weeks they work. Others are "carried" and receive payment for the weeks that a show is not in production and on hiatus.

[30] Above- and below-the-line staff are either under contract to the studio, sign a production company deal-memo, or get paid by the day.

[31] Screen Actors Guild, Writers Guild, and Directors Guild negotiate payments for reuse on behalf of their membership. Second Assistant Directors get a *much* smaller residual payment than Directors. According to Teri Benton of the DGA, only the sitcom director earns a residual for Free TV, syndication, and foreign reusage. Below-the-line Guild members share a percentage of video sales and Pay TV rights only.

Designers and below-the-line crew interview for jobs. Even for well-established people it is sometimes difficult to get a foot in the door. We recommend always asking someone to make a call on your behalf for that entrée or recommendation. If that person knows you well, and likes your work, it will make a difference in whether you get the interview. Remember, ONLY YOU CAN GET THE JOB!

PREPRODUCTION

If you land the job, all departments have a certain amount of preproduction work that begins with reading the script. The production designer is drawing up blueprints for scenery and getting it built within the production's budget. A copy of the production designer's set plans[32] are sent to the director and lighting designer. The designer must understand the physical requirements of shooting four cameras simultaneously (see Chapter 5) and creating a space that fulfills the requirement of the script. Finally the designer must understand what aspects of the scenery will enhance the comedy. More confined spaces, for example, make a scene funnier than a wide-open area. The production designer supervises the set decoration department in selecting all furniture, rugs, drapery, etc. Ann Donahue in a *Daily Variety* article entitled "Sitcoms set in their ways" writes:

> The look of the family sitcom was established in the late 60s and early 70s with *The Brady Bunch* and *All in the Family*. Little has changed since: There's a couch in the middle, a staircase to nowhere and a swinging door that provides fodder for comic entrances and exits.

In that same article Donahue quotes Multi-Emmy winner John Shaffner for *Friends* who acknowledges the challenge.

> The sitcom set is a vernacular that everybody recognizes...Doing sets for multicam is like that line from Ginger Rogers...you have to do everything on three walls that movies get to do with four walls. Ginger Rogers had to do everything Fred Astaire did, but backwards and in high heels.

Donahue also quotes art director Roy Christopher (*Frasier, Murphy Brown*) who explains that the usual set design is the fallback that makes it easiest for thesps to time their lines.

> You want it so they can go down the stairs, say their line, and head out the front door. On *Frasier* we have Niles' beautiful Montana

---

[32] See the sample plan in the Appendix.

apartment, and to walk through the front door and go to the kitchen it's about 40 feet. The writers are always telling me, "Roy, it's really hard to fill all that."

The wardrobe department can begin shopping or pulling wardrobe once the actors are cast. The lighting designer can hang a general lighting plot before the set is loaded in. The properties (props) department will shop for specific props for the show and have an array of general props available for weekly use. The script supervisor does an initial timing of the script. The line producer usually rents the camera and sound equipment. The editor can use either rented equipment or rent space and time at a postproduction house. The camera, sound, and editing department have limited preproduction work.

Preproduction generally has an ease to it because less is going on. Hours tend to be more regular and for some departments nonexistent if there is nothing that can be done ahead of time. A master list is generated from the office with the name and contact information of each crew member. When you get it, make sure your information is correct. Our last piece of advice is to take it easy during preproduction because production will be more hectic and pressured.

Sitcom Vocabulary Quick Review

Read these sentences. If the director gave you these notes, would you instantly know what he meant? If not, go back and review the explanation in this chapter.

*We don't have to worry about overtime because he's **above-the-line.***

*This is a **below-the-line** problem.*

*There was no information on it in the **breakdown.***

*Let's see what she does at the **callback.***

*The only one who should be **cueing** is the script supervisor.*

*Don't break the **fourth wall.***

***Getting read** on that show is harder than childbirth.*

*Did they refer to a sister in the **pilot**?*

*This is not what was **pitched!***

*Syndication would mean more **residuals.***

*Let's leave it up to the **show runner.***

*We aren't going to use the **sides**, turn to page 15 in the script.*

*I started feeling confident right at the **slate.***

*They're done **staffing.***

*Is everyone looking at the **table draft**?*

Sitcom Insider

One of the aspects of directing that has always been very important to me is preparation. When I first receive a script, I read it through from beginning to end. In doing so, I get an overall sense of the story to be told. How does it move from point 'A' to point 'B'? Is the story told through a specific point of view? How do the events in the story impact each of the characters? What makes it funny?

I read the script again. Then I read it a third time. I make note of all the production requirements; props, set dressing, set design, wardrobe, lighting, camera, special effects, etc. If there is anything about the script that is confusing to me, I make a note of it so that I can talk with the writer to clarify his or her intent. I also note script changes I will suggest to the writer. At the same time, I block the action of each scene. I decide on where actors will be at the beginning of each scene, when and where they will move and why. I create 'business' for them to do. I stage scenes in each set and vary the playing areas as much as possible to allow for visual variety.

I love to walk onto the set and have my game plan. If a prop master asks me where to put a hand prop, I have an answer. If a special effects team asks me which kitchen sink drain needs to be practical, I know immediately. If the director of photography asks me where I plan a lighting change, I can give him the details.

I'm right there with an answer when an actor looks at me and says, "Where do you want me?" "What am I doing in this scene?" "Why am I moving here?" I never consider my plan written in stone. I use it as a jumping off point. If an actor has a good suggestion about some other approach he or she would like to try, I try it. If rehearsal should reveal better choices, I go with them. If an actor tells me something's not working for him or her, I always have some alternate plans ready to go.

A director must have the wisdom and confidence to recognize a good idea, no matter where it comes from. I once listened to what a stand-in had to say about a particular piece of business and I incorporated it into the scene. It got a huge laugh and I gave him credit for coming up with it. It improved the show in more ways than one. The audience thoroughly enjoyed it and as a member of the crew, he felt appreciated.

For me, preparation is very important. Having a plan, along with a back-up plan or two, has proven invaluable to me. I've found that by working this way, I can maintain my vision for how I want to tell the story and at the same time, create a secure collaborative atmosphere on the stage.

Andrew D. Weyman, Director *Roseanne, Ellen, Two and a Half Men*

Sitcom Career Profile

ROBI REED
CASTING DIRECTOR

Robi has an amazing ability to find great acting talent. Her sessions are an embarrassment of riches! She is creative yet discerning, and is well-liked by actors because she treats them with respect.

What shows have you worked on?

Girlfriends; In the House; Sister, Sister; Roc; In Living Color; A Different World; Out All Night; The PJs; The Robert Guillaume Show; Sparks; Good News; The Kirk Franklin Show.

What are your responsibilities?

I'm responsible for casting all principal roles (speaking parts) in each show.

Did you have specific training in this field?

My training primarily was on-the-job training. I interned in a casting office for a short stint before receiving my first paying gig as a casting coordinator on a movie. I did, however, study acting and directing in school and received my BA in Speech Communications and Theatre. I believe both areas are invaluable to the casting director.

How did you get your first job?

I knew the production coordinator on a feature film. She hired me to work as her assistant—so I was assistant Production Office Coordinator. I did well; however, it wasn't my desired area. On her next film—the Casting Director didn't have an assistant—I met her and she hired me. That was 19 years ago, and I've been working ever since. Interestingly enough, that same Casting Director and I are still good friends and when she's in LA (She lives in NY) we often visit comedy clubs together.

What advice would you give someone who wants to do what you do?

Preparation. You can never be too prepared. Take an acting and directing class—it will help you in your casting sessions. Intern in a casting office to gather experience. Most casting offices want actual experience. See lots of movies and television. Go to plays, showcases, and comedy clubs. Don't ever limit yourself—and keep an open mind. I've discovered many people who are "stars" today. Everyone needs a break. What is five minutes in the room when it can change someone's life. If you become bored—get out of it. You'll stop being good at it.

What do you like best about your job?

Helping people achieve their dreams.

CASTING DIRECTORS
Union: None
Typical Weekly Salary: $2000–6000
Hours Per Week: 60–84

Chapter 2 MONDAY (EXCEPT WHEN IT'S NOT)...THE TABLE READ

In this chapter:

How to survive the table reading

How to best utilize the rehearsal

Dos and don'ts when working with a star

Set and stage etiquette

How to identify jokes in a script

The role of the script supervisor

Advice to the aspiring comedy writer

Career profile of a costume designer

Arriving for the Monday table read of a new show is always exhilarating. It's a new script and a new story! It's often a different director and writer from the week before! A new guest cast is arriving. There are new **swing sets**[1] being erected and **dressed** (decorated) on stage. Each Monday is a new beginning.

A Monday table read doesn't always take place on Monday. Most sitcoms run on a five-day schedule: table read on Monday, rehearse on Tuesday and Wednesday, camera block on Thursday, and film or tape on Friday night. There are any numbers of reasons to alter this schedule. The stand-up comedian, who is the star of the show, may have a gig on Friday night or be flying to the city where he or she is performing. Executive producer Michael Jacobs (*Charles in Charge, Boy Meets World*) doesn't work on his Sabbath, which begins on Friday night at sundown so his shows always shoot on Thursdays. A very common reason for altering the schedule though is to accommodate the studio who may have more than one show on the air. For example, Robert Greenblatt and David Janollari are hands-on executive producers. Until Greenblatt started running *Showtime,* they attended the taping or filming of every episode. When they have two shows in production, they can't be in two places at once on Friday night. Finally, since certain members of the crew such as camera operators only work on two days of the sitcom week, they try to work two shows each week

> **SITCOM RULE**
>
> *Hold for laughs. Laughs are an important part of sitcom rhythm. Actors must wait to deliver their dialogue or business when the audience is laughing.*

---

[1] These sets are new to this particular episode. On some very busy shows, the crew actually "swings" them into a space between two regular sets. See the set plan in the Appendix.

of the season. They also can't be doing two shows on the same days. A good camera crew is worth the change in schedule. Therefore, the most typical schedules are Monday through Friday or Wednesday through Tuesday.

THE PRODUCTION MEETING

An hour before the cast arrives to read the new script, there is always a 30- to 60-minute production meeting. The production manager (**UPM**[2] or Producer may be his official title) sits at the same table with the **show runner,**[3] director, and all department heads to discuss the upcoming episode. Usually, the assistant director (AD)[4] runs this meeting. The AD will go through the script page by page discussing anything that is relevant. Each department head has previously read the script and marked it for their individual needs, highlighting the places where the dialogue or stage directions call for anything pertaining to their department. They pose questions during the production meeting.

For example, on one episode of *Fresh Prince of Bel Air*, there was a gag where Will Smith burns down the kitchen. All the department heads had lots of questions for director Madeline Cripe. "Will we be doing this in front of the audience or preshooting?" "Will we need props and costumes for the next scene that look as if they have burned?" "Will we be burning the actual set or building a duplicate?" "Will a representative of the fire department have to be on set?" "Will the special effects person need to have a safety meeting with the cast and crew?" "How will we keep characters in the next room from knowing the kitchen has burned?" Cripe explains further:

> One of the biggest issues was one of reality. (Although reality is usually stretched to the limits in half-hour sitcoms.) The *Fresh Prince* set was designed so that the kitchen opened directly into the living room. After the kitchen burned there were scenes to be played out in the living room. These characters would look directly into the burned out kitchen and supposedly not see it. (Let's not even discuss what they would smell.) In discussing this issue with the producers and set designer the solution was a shutter panel and sliding shutter doors. This piece was installed for this one episode, never to be seen again in the Bank's house. We should all be so lucky to have a set department at our disposal.

---

[2]   Unit Production Manager, Directors Guild members since 1964.

[3]   This is the executive producer who actually runs the show. He is usually the head writer.

[4]   The director's assistants evolved differently in film and live television (which became videotaped television). Film shows have an assistant director, second assistant, and sometimes a second second AD. Taped shows have an associate director, stage manager, and second stage manager. The new 24P digital camera systems (which is really tape) use both hierarchies, depending on the studio. The new DGA contract will change the title of technical coordinators to associate directors.

ARRIVING AND SEATING ASSIGNMENTS

As the production meeting is winding down, the cast arrives for the table read. For a guest cast member, locating the table read is not always easy. The table read is in a different location from where that actor auditioned. It is often in a different location from where that actor will be doing the show. Security differs from studio lot to studio lot. At some studios, the parking lot is a good ten-minute walk from the sound stage. *Allowing enough time to get on to a studio lot is mandatory.* It is much harder to get laughs at the table read if you've kept everyone waiting.

If the production meeting is taking place on stage, anyone arriving for the table read should keep their conversations to a minimum. If the reading will take place in a conference room, don't enter until the meeting is over. This may seem obvious, but many an actor has opened a conference room door, only to have 30 people turn around and glare at them for the interruption. This is usually avoided by posting a note on the entrance saying, "Production Meeting In Progress." If you are early and there is no sign, but the door is closed, wait.

There is usually assigned seating for the cast at a table read. As a guest actor, you will want to ask the AD, "Where do I sit?" There are probably 60 to 75 chairs in the room. You will not be welcome in most of them. A network executive doesn't necessarily want you overhearing a conversation he is having about the strategy for sweeps week.[5] The writers may be discussing a future script. It's a great idea to greet and thank the casting director who was instrumental in getting you the job.

Actress Kate Zentall describes her feelings as a guest actor and gives some valuable advice:

Sitcoms are great for any actor because it's a job. You can only pray the writing is good and the all-important show runner is hard working and writes true to the character you have developed—which is a combination of what the writer had in mind and hopefully was flexible enough to take your input. I have had joyous times and miserable times on sitcoms. Recently, four years into Curb Your Enthusiasm, *albeit no script but a tight outline, although I am able to ad-lib—the star is a brilliant writer and producer and allows the best to come from you as an actor. Many other shows I have done there are oftentimes the writers versus the actors mentality and if there isn't a strong show runner with a vision and a lot of clout an actor gets notes from what seems like an army of people and that's before the director. It's more fun doing drama on TV as you usually deal more with your director and not a ton of writer-producers who for better or for worse have their two cents and it can at times get very frustrating and hard to focus on what you, the actor, and the talent behind the role really wants to do. There is so much luck involved in getting a good role and having producers and directors more into the scene than the power. If you get the former scenario, consider yourself blessed and enjoy every moment as one day you'll get directions that only visitors from outer space "might" understand.*

Richard Lewis,
Actor/Writer/Comedian and
Author of *The Other Great Depression*

---

[5] This week is defined by the key ratings periods. Networks battle for their share of the television viewers. The shows airing during sweeps week may be stunt cast (casting big-name stars) in order to attract an even larger audience.

Few things are more exciting than anticipating your first day on the set, that initial "table read." Chances are you have had yet another script delivered (*delivered!* At like 11 PM by a friendly human who has found your abode without needing directions!)—and what a feeling to walk onto the same lot you trod only a few days before for the audition, when you were not quite so sure you belonged. But belong you now do. You even get to park with the big boys. If you have any theater experience, the thrill notches up a few points, because sitcoms are the closest thing to theater television has, and what a luxury to have a *whole week* of rehearsal time. So you find the soundstage, step into the darkness, and...huh? Where are you exactly, what are all these flats and clusters of furniture, and where is everyone? Are you even in the right place?

You probably are. First thing is to find an AD (assistant director). Ask anyone, and you'll be pointed right. The 2nd AD is usually in charge of keeping track of you, and it is your responsibility to find him or her and check in, and not vice versa. Chances are you will be on time (you'd better be), but ahead of the rest of the cast (that's their prerogative, but not yours). You'll be pointed to the coffee and donuts. Make yourself comfortable, and wait. Cheerfully.

As the cast drifts in (and they may all be there already; it depends on the kind of set and show and how long it's been running; usually the more well established a show is, the looser the atmosphere), you will probably be introduced, or they will do it themselves. And then there's the star. It's usually someone you feel you have known onscreen for years, but remember this: That star has not known you, and despite how much like a play this seems, it is not like theater, where you all instantly become one family. The hierarchy is very much there.

Stars carry the show, and despite all the red carpets and entourage and assistants, the pressure is on. Some of them are remote and "difficult"; others create a more relaxed ambiance and joke around. But make no mistake—either way, they are on the line, and they are working hard. Even when it doesn't look that way. Years ago when I did a *Cheers* episode, Ted Danson was easy and funny and relaxed and instinctively seemed to understand how his mood set the tone for the rest of the set. It took me a few days to see how he used his charm and grace and humor to serve the needs of the show; it greased the wheels and created a wonderful counterpoint to the slightly nerve-wracking end-of-day rehearsals in front of the producers and writers. Years later, when I guested on *Becker,* his MO hadn't changed much. But he was working harder than ever— though he still made it seem effortless. And the unwritten rule had also not changed: Respect the delicate web of privacy around him, and take your cue from him. I have watched some sitcom guests breezily, cluelessly violate this, sometimes never realizing their gaffe, and sooner or later it catches up to them. Do not interpret an easygoing facade as an invitation to conversation or engagement. Keep your distance; respect the star's space.

Series regulars usually take the same seats; the director and executive producers are seated nearby at the head of the table configuration. The AD will try to place you close to the other actors in your scenes. You'll get a strong sense of the show from the amount of banter that goes on before starting. On a successful show, people may be discussing the houses they're buying. On a friendly show, people may be discussing their weekend. On a show with declining ratings, there is little chatter except for cell phone calls to agents. The AD will signal when everyone[6] has arrived, and the table read will begin.

The table read is the first time the writers will hear their whole script read aloud by the cast. Now they get to hear it from the mouths of the people playing the characters that they created. They want to hear what they wrote, *exactly how they wrote it!* This may be the only chance to hear their vision before everyone starts "improving it." (Read Chapter 3, SITCOM INSIDER Michael Kaplan.)

READING THE SCRIPT

Everyone is settled for the reading. The show runner or director will congratulate everyone for their hard work on the previous episode (unless it's the pilot), then introduce the guest actors, and finally the director starts the table read with the title and author of the episode. Then the performance begins!

Broadway and daytime drama veteran Marilyn McIntyre (*Gemini, Search for Tomorrow, One Life to Live*) describes the enormous pressure she felt at this moment on her first sitcom, *Who's the Boss?*: "You look up and see the amount of people in the room and you have this realization: They're looking right now to see if what they've written is funny, and if you're funny doing it. The pressure is intense."

While the actors read their parts aloud, and the director reads the stage directions, the studio and network executives are making notes on content and structure. The writers are noting when a joke has **landed** or scored (gotten a laugh). This may be simply a check mark in their script. These laughs are important! The sitcom rule, which begins this chapter, states **HOLD FOR LAUGHS.** If an actor tries to speak his next line while the people at the table read are laughing, no one will hear the information in that next line. Holding for laughs may seem unnatural but it is essential to sitcom rhythm. This rule applies not only at the table read, but the entire week.

---

[6] Network executives, studio executives, the entire writing staff, nonwriting executive producers, the cast and guest cast, the casting director, the parents of child cast members, the teacher, the department heads, the script supervisor, and the director's team all attend the table read. There might also be people that you won't see again until shooting such as publicists, executive assistants, and the postproduction teams.

Laughs are noted because everyone wants to know what works and what doesn't. In addition, the script supervisor is timing the actual reading and then adding a reasonable amount of time for staging and full audience laughter. This timing will guide the extent and length of the rewrite. Script Supervisor Ellen Deutsch (*The Golden Girls, Malcolm & Eddie, Regular Joe*) says she reads the script at least twice before the table read and times it for the anticipated action and business.

The crowd attending the table read might be the toughest audience the cast has all week. They must do their best to sell this story to everyone. Nothing will infuriate a writing staff more than a half-hearted performance at a table read. A guest cast member is expected to duplicate what he did "in the room" at the audition. This performance got him the job! This is sometimes a challenge, especially if the part has been substantially rewritten.

This is only the first of many challenges for the guest star. Regan Burns (star of Spike TV's *Oblivious*) whose sitcom guest appearances include *Curb Your Enthusiasm, Mind of the Married Man, The Ellen Show, 3rd Rock from the Sun, Titus, Suddenly Susan,* and *The Drew Carey Show* shares: "Guest starring in a sitcom can best be described as asking for a girl's phone number, calling her up, asking her on a date, going out for a romantic dinner, finding out you have a lot in common, continuing to see her, falling in love, deciding to move in together, emptying out a drawer for her, introduce her to the folks, planning the wedding and then finding out she left you for your best friend. Oh, and this all happens in five days!"

It's also important that the guest actor look the same as when he or she auditioned. Changing a hairstyle or dressing weirdly doesn't make the best first impression…and this is the first time many people on the show have seen you. While we're on the subject of changing your appearance…*DON'T!* Even if you're a series regular. On one sitcom, a very hip, youthful cast arrived at the table read, after a week off, with three new tattoos, two body piercings, and one change in hairstyle and color. The cast was read the riot act after the reading. On another sitcom, a hairstyle change (and unwillingness to change it back) caused a permanent rift between a star/executive producer and his studio head…also an executive producer. Remember that actors are hired not only for their talent but also on their appearance. You are under contract to play a character. Don't screw up and do anything that changes that without first consulting the show runner. That includes extreme sports on weekends. The writers don't want to accommodate a full leg cast unless they have to.[7]

Not radically changing appearance has to do with how the shows air. They are not necessarily programmed in the same order they are made. If the show is lucky enough to re-air for years to come, it is disconcerting to the audience if the characters look different every time they turn on the TV.

---

[7] Stage and TV actor Jon Cypher broke his leg in a theater accident during *Major Dad*. Producer Rick Hawkins wrote it into the script. Cypher made his performance in a wheelchair and with a cane even funnier.

NETWORK AND STUDIO NOTES

Body casts, hair-dos, and tattoos aside, the cast is usually dismissed from the room after the reading. The show runner, his second in charge, and director (with the script supervisor to write his notes) stay for notes with the network and studio executives. This can be very tense. The writing staff has created what they think is a worthy product. The **"suits"**[8] may disagree. Now the tearing apart begins. When asked for comments about notes after a table read, one writer told us, "I'm not going to say much about network and studio executives, because a few of them can read, and I hope to continue working."

The tone of this comment is common in sitcoms. Sitcom writers are some of the smartest, wittiest, most creative individuals you'll ever meet. They are well read, well educated, and socially and politically astute. They are proprietary about their responsibility for the literary content of a show. They consider themselves artists. Network and studio executives often possess these same qualities but ultimately they are the money-people, and report to a corporate entity. Many writers feel the "suits," who are asking for changes to "their" script, don't know dick[9] about writing!

Another writer warns, "Never make an enemy of a network or studio executive. Network and studio executives never die or lose their jobs. They just keep trading places. So that enemy you make at NBC today will be your enemy at FOX tomorrow. They also never forget or forgive...."

It's not all bad. *Home Improvement*'s Carmen Finestra explains it from his point of view, "Notes are given by the network and studio, often in collaboration with the producers and writers, i.e., if the network and studio have a problem, generally a compromise or solution gets worked out."

A show sometimes works well with complete cooperation and artistic vision from its network and studio. After the table read for *All about the Andersons,* a pilot developed by Warner Brothers Television Network, there were no notes. Comedian Anthony Anderson, along with his co-creators Marco Pennette and Adam Glass, walked away from the table read with complete confidence that they had written a pilot that WB would support.[10] Stories are rarely told about great situations like this because it's easier to be funny relating a story that has a good guy and bad guy. In most of the stories you hear on stage, the suits are the bad guys. When the writers are considered the bad guys, they just stop getting hired and start telling funny stories![11]

While notes are being given, the rest of the writing staff goes to the writers' room and begins the rewrites. Some changes are obvious from the reading

---

[8]   Suits are so named because of the odd uniform they wear.

[9]   Dick is a technical term with a "K" sound.

[10]   The WB nurtured and developed this script from the beginning.

[11]   Although we are not sure he has ever been out of work, Leonard Stern of *Get Smart* and *The Honeymooners* fame has assembled a book of notes from studio and network executives, called *A Martian Wouldn't Say That!,* and is working on a sequel.

so they waste no time getting started even though the show runner will have more changes from the network and studio meeting. Writer Nancylee Myatt describes the process in the writers' room: "A bunch of adults with arrested development will sit around a table and pitch jokes. Whichever joke gets the biggest laugh in the room will land in the script. Unfortunately, the best joke is usually the filthiest joke and cannot be said on network television. Thank God for cable."

Guest actors are usually shown to their dressing rooms during notes. Wardrobe fittings may begin during this break. The **load-in** of this week's set continues on stage.

After the meeting, Carmen Finestra tells us, "Producers and writers go upstairs and begin the rewrite. Some producers and writers may pair off and divide scenes, while others concentrate on coming up with new stories for future episodes. Work on existing drafts for future episodes may also occur at this time."

REHEARSAL

On stage, rehearsal begins…or sometimes the actors are sent home. Finestra says that this is rare unless the entire script is being changed.

Whether to rehearse or not is the choice of the director but it is dictated by many factors. Reasons for going home include: giving the stage to the crew to complete the new set's load-in; everyone is exhausted because they shot an episode until late last night; this show (usually it's the third or fourth season) normally and efficiently rehearses only four days a week; or the star of the show has a 2 o'clock tee time.

The more years that a show is on the air, the more comfortable the regular actors are with playing their characters. The writers have been writing their dialogue to fit closer to the actors' own personalities. These shortened weeks make it harder for a guest actor to discover the finer aspects of his character.

THE SETS

If rehearsal begins on this day, actors may be working on a half-built or impro- vised swing set. If you spot anything that appears unsafe on the set, report it to the AD *immediately!* The sets that are used every week are called the **standing sets** and remain in place for the whole season. Although inviting,[12] sets are never to be used as a lounging or eating area. Often, a "Hot Set" sign will remind you.

UTILIZING THE REHEARSAL

Every show rehearses differently. Monday may be the time that the director allows the actors to explore the material more on their own. If this is the case, it is the perfect opportunity for the guest actor to try anything different from his

---

[12] The sets are supposed to appear inviting to the TV audience. If they do, the set decorator has done his job well.

audition choices. Actor Regan Burns suggests that being a "guest star can be one of two things. Either your chance to feed stale straight lines to the star of the show who gets all the zingers; or, an opportunity to seize the moment and make the role memorable as your own." He continues, "The process from the initial audition to the martini[13] shot on Friday night is grueling, boring, exciting, frantic, stress-inducing and well worth every second of it. Granted, as long as you didn't get written out in one of the 25 rewrites since the script was first delivered to your door."

Stage actors are always surprised at how quickly scenes are rehearsed on sitcoms. This week, the director has about twenty or so hours to rehearse what is essentially a short two-act play. He then has about the same amount of time to film it.

Guest actors, explore your relationship with the cast and director. Try to fit in! If this show is easygoing, flow with it. If the cast seems very private, don't invade their space.

> *Be proud of even the smallest role on a sitcom. Many would kill to be in your shoes saying, "I have a package for Chandler."*
>
> Regan Burns, Host of *Oblivious*

Michael Lembeck, Emmy award–winning *Friends* director, calls this "taking the temperature of the room." Remember that these people are a family (or at the very least, a working unit), and you are a guest. Remember your manners. On most shows, the series regulars will come up, introduce themselves, and welcome you to their show. Sometimes it is less pleasant. Just remember you don't always have the inside scoop, and the cast may seem aloof because they don't want to air "family" laundry. Or maybe, as Kate Zentall says,

> They are simply preoccupied, with (a) the size of their part that week, (b) the size of their paycheck after recent contract renegotiations, (c) the size of the audience share that week, (d) the size of their new house, (e) the size of their butt. The point is, you never, ever know, so do not take it personally, or let it affect your performance in any way. And speaking of performances, remember the scene you nailed and the great laughs you got at the audition? Be prepared for those lovely lines to morph and even be whittled away by shooting day. The script changes daily. You might have been hired because you were funny, but you may notice that you are increasingly becoming a straight man for the regulars. That's normal. You may even start to feel like an exchangeable Lego part. That's also normal. And if you can accept that and still have fun and take pride in your work, you just may have a career in sitcoms.

WAYS OF WORKING

Actors have many different ways of working. As perennial movie butler Arthur Treacher said about his acting theory: "Say the words, take the money, go

---

[13] Completing the last shot on any production signals that IT'S TIME TO PARTY!!!

home." Actors who do this earn instant respect because they know what they're doing, don't demand a lot of attention for doing it, and have a life to go to when they've done it. Katherine Helmond (*Who's the Boss?*, *Coach*, *Soap*, *Everybody Loves Raymond*) is also from the simplicity school. She told us, "I don't have high-flown ideas about acting. I just work by doing."

Other actors have complex ways of working. Some need to do a scene repeatedly, trying to find the core. Others are looking for every opportunity to add a new joke or modify an existing one. Some actors need repetition to help them learn their words or to work the words and movement together. Others don't want to move much at all. Gerald McRaney (*Simon & Simon*, *Major Dad*) minimized the number of props he had to handle. At home on stage, screen, and TV, he always considered rehearsal time a private time for actors and their director to rehearse. Very much an artist, he would seek the truth of a character's core and the integrity of a script's story within a safe environment where actors were free to try things (that means often failing) in an effort to make the show the best it could be. When the words "Closed Set" appear on a sound stage door, he expected them to be respected.

Matt LeBlanc of *Friends* is quoted in *Daily Variety* saying, "I'm more confident, which is one of your biggest assets as an actor especially in comedy. In comedy, you have to be unafraid to hang from the tree branch naked in the high wind and you have to be absolutely unafraid to look ridiculous and silly."

Some actors have to work beat-by-beat so their character logically and organically progresses from moment to moment. Some are selfish. Some are generous. Some are easy. Some are difficult.

The late motion picture and TV actor Richard Mulligan (*Little Big Man*, *Soap*, *Empty Nest*) was questioning every direction and note that the director was giving him during one rehearsal. He stopped in the middle of second-guessing the director and said to him, "I love what you are doing, but I need to do this." Challenges and struggle helped Mulligan feel that the scene was fully explored for its potential.

We asked Robin Bartlett (*Mad about You*, *Powers That Be*) about the challenges of working on a sitcom. She remarked, "Don't ask! Well, okay. I was in a sitcom with an unnamed movie star. It was a terribly pressured situation; the difficulties were myriad. Staying focused on my own work was the only solution. Otherwise I would have been pulled into the drama and very unfunny world of the woman I was working with."

CELEBRITY/COMEDIAN-DRIVEN VERSUS ACTOR/ENSEMBLE-DRIVEN

Shows are divided into two genres: a celebrity/comedian-driven show or an actor/ensemble-driven show. The first builds on the established talents of that person. For example, comedians such as Jerry Seinfeld, Tim Allen, and Roseanne Barr had established audiences and uniquely identifiable material from their stand-up careers. Their hit sitcoms were designed to appeal to these target audiences and expand from there. Hip-Hop artist Eve and Chef Emeril Lagasse were given opportunities to move into a sitcom after their success in their individual fields. The expectation is always that they will bring a built-in audience.

An actor/ensemble-driven show starts with a premise before a star. Although a well-known comedian, actor, or celebrity may very well be cast in the leading role, this genre always begins with a writer's premise. *All in the Family* is a perfect example of this type of show. Plotlines came out of the characters that the writers created and the themes that the show wanted to explore. Howard Gewirtz talked in the *Miami New Times* about finding his characters for *Oliver Beene*. "I really wrote a lot of it based on people in my world—my mother and father provided inspiration, as did my brother. Our actual family dynamic was significantly different, but it was a starting-off point, and the material breathed for me." Tim Goodman of the *San Francisco Chronicle* speaks of another successful comedy. "The vision that made *Sex in the City* so attractive to viewers is back. The great majority of these stories are believable, the characters [are] fleshed out in a way rarely seen (especially in a comedy) and the writing [is] crisp and fun as ever." We wholeheartedly agree with Goodman but we don't actually consider *Sex in the City* a sitcom format.

In our opinion, the best sitcom writing combines the best aspects of both joke-based and character-based genres. Here is one of our favorite character-driven scenes from the pilot *Style and Substance* by Emmy award–winning writer Peter Tolan. Jean Smart played Chelsea, Nancy McKeon played Jane, and Heath Hyche played Terry.

> *Originally, the position of the script supervisor was that of a secretary, taking director's notes to give the editor. It soon became a position with a lot more responsibility. I can't tell you the amount of times that I have had fellow crew members come to me and say, "You have the toughest job on the show." I believe because the position is held primarily by women, the industry still does not value it. I have always said my job is like that of the anesthesiologist; there are times that it looks like you are not doing anything but when all hell breaks loose, you better know how to fix it.*
>
> Marcia Gould, Script Supervisor, *Wings* and countless others

Sitcom Exercise

Read this scene and find the jokes! Identify things that make you laugh. You already know how to identify words with "K" sounds and patterns of three. In addition, look for character-driven jokes. Understand that Terry is a somewhat inefficient male secretary, Jane an insecure but ambitious office manager, and Chelsea an empire-building superwoman, founder of a Martha Stewart–like company. We have identified the first two jokes for you with a ✓✓✓ where we think the audience is expected to laugh. You can find all the jokes identified in the Appendix. Don't cheat!

<u>STYLE AND SUBSTANCE</u> - Pilot

(B)

<u>INT. CHELSEAS'S OFFICE - LATER THAT MORNING (D-1)</u>

(Chelsea, Jane, Terry)

CHELSEA IS LISTENING TO TERRY, HER YOUNG MALE SECRETARY, RUN DOWN A LIST OF PHONE MESSAGES. CHELSEA MAKES HIM NERVOUS.

> TERRY
>
> Francine Messinger called and said thanks for the padlocks.

> CHELSEA
>
> That's Nancy Kissinger, and she's thanking me for the gravlax. ✓✓✓

> TERRY
>
> Right. Franklin Carter called...

> CHELSEA
>
> Frank Langella. ✓✓✓

> TERRY
>
> Okay. Needs advice on planting an urban garden.

> CHELSEA
>
> An herb garden. Breathe, Terry.

> TERRY
>
> Okay. Ken Klein called...

> CHELSEA
>
> Kevin Kline?

> TERRY
>
> No.

> CHELSEA
>
> Calvin Klein?

TERRY SHAKES HIS HEAD NO.

> CHELSEA (cont'd)
>
> Kelly Klein. Carol Kane. Carole King. (A BEAT) Beverly Sills?

> TERRY
>
> Yes. You're good at this.

                    CHELSEA
Thank you. Terry. Much better today.

                    TERRY
I thought so too.

TERRY EXITS AS JANE ENTERS.

                    JANE
Hi, Chelsea. Listen I don't want to be a bugaboo,
but have you had a chance to sign that budget
agreement yet?

CHELSEA STARES AT HER FOR A SECOND.

                    JANE (cont'd)
Jane Sokol. From Ferber Communications?

                    CHELSEA
Jane, please. I know who you are. What a darling
suit.

                    JANE
Thanks. I really need you to sign that agreement.
Being put in charge of your office is the first major
assignment the company's given me, so I want to keep
Mr. Ferber happy happy. So sign sign.

                    CHELSEA
I'll look at it right away.

JANE NOTICES A PURSE ON THE DESK.

                    JANE
We have the same purse.

                    CHELSEA
Really?

                    JANE
Yes. It's exactly the same purse.

                    CHELSEA
How about that?

                    JANE
I mean...it's the same purse. (A BEAT) That's my
purse, isn't it?

                    CHELSEA
Why don't we talk about something else? (PICKING
SOMETHING UP FROM THE DESK) Oh, look. A recipe for
flan.

                    JANE
Chelsea. You have my purse.

                    CHELSEA
Don't get upset, Jane. You're new here, I want to
get to know you. You know the old saying. The
fastest way to get to know another woman is to look
in her purse.

                    JANE
Here's another old saying. I want my purse back.

                    CHELSEA
You have something to hide?

                    JANE
No.

                    CHELSEA
I'd let you look in my purse.

                    JANE
I doubt that.

                    CHELSEA
I would.

                    JANE
Right.

                    CHELSEA
Go ahead.

                    JANE
Where is it?

                    CHELSEA
At home. But if it were here, I'd let you look at it.

                    JANE
Chelsea, this is a major invasion of my privacy.

CHELSEA HOLDS OUT A SMALL JAR OF JAM TO JANE.

                    CHELSEA
Jane, I'd like you to have this. It's a jar of my
lovely homemade preserves. I hope you like rhubarb.

                    JANE
Do you honestly believe that giving me a little jar
of jam will make this okay?

                    CHELSEA
I have a bigger jar.

                    JANE
That is so not my point.

                    CHELSEA
Oh, I get it. There's a jam hater in our midst, is
there?

                    JANE
Oh, please. I love jam.

                    CHELSEA
I wish I could believe that.

                    JANE
I am crazy about jam.

                    CHELSEA
You do not seem jam friendly to me.

                    JANE
(AFTER A BEAT) Okay. Okay. You want to look in my
purse? You go right ahead. This is unbelievable.

                    CHELSEA
Oh, pooh. You really know how to take the fun out of
things.

CHELSEA STARTS DIGGING AROUND IN THE PURSE.

                CHELSEA (cont'd)
  Somebody clips coupons.

CHELSEA TAKES A COUPON OUT AND GRIMACES.

                CHELSEA (cont'd)
  Macaroni and cheese? From a box?

                JANE
  It's filling and inexpensive.

                CHELSEA
  I can't argue, Jane, but if those were the only
  criteria for nourishment, there'd be a lot more
  recipes for dirt. (DIGGING) Lip gloss, rouge...I see
  tweezers. Eyebrows on the march, Jane?

                JANE
  Are we done yet?

                CHELSEA
  Oh, Jane. Jane, Jane, Jane...

CHELSEA REMOVES A PACKAGE OF HOSTESS SNOBALLS FROM THE PURSE.

                CHELSEA (cont'd)
  Hostess Snoballs? Why, Jane?

                JANE
  I like them. They're fun.

                CHELSEA
  Have you heard the expression, "You are what you
  eat?" Add bangs and a business suit, this is you,
  Jane.

                JANE
  I'll be going now...

JANE GATHERS UP HER PURSE AND STARTS TO EXIT. CHELSEA HOLDS UP A
SMALL PHOTOGRAPH.

                        CHELSEA

Who's this?

                        JANE

Give me that, please.

                        CHELSEA

Brother?

                        JANE

None of your business.

                        CHELSEA

Friends?

                        JANE

I'm not telling you.

                        CHELSEA

Fiance?

                        JANE

(A BEAT) No.

                        CHELSEA

You paused.

                        JANE

Darn!

                        CHELSEA

What's his name?

                        JANE

Why would I tell you?

                        CHELSEA

Because I really think you want to talk about it. Mint?

CHELSEA HOLDS OUT A SMALL CONTAINER OF MINTS.

                        JANE

(GRABBING THEM) Those are mine. Chelsea, I
appreciate your trying to be friendly, but I'm not
going to discuss my personal life with you.

                    CHELSEA
He looks like a Paul.

                    JANE
I'm here to do a job. It's a job I take seriously.

                    CHELSEA
Doug? Dennis?

                    JANE
There's a line between business and personal...

                    CHELSEA
Tony? Mike?

                    JANE
I'm a professional, and I'm going to maintain a
professional...

                    CHELSEA
Chuck?

                    JANE
(END OF ROPE) Steve! Steve! The man's name is Steve!
Are you happy now?

                    CHELSEA
I knew you wanted to talk about it.

                    JANE
I don't! This is the office. The office is where we
talk about office things. My ex-fiancé is not an office
thing.

                    CHELSEA
Your ex-fiancé?

                    JANE
Darn!

                    CHELSEA
What happened? He hit you, didn't he? (TO THE PHOTO)
You bastard.

JANE

This is really inappropriate. How would you like it if I just waltzed in here and started asking you about your divorce? Which by the way, I would never do. I know it must've been difficult and I hope you're okay.

CHELSEA

(THROWN) I'm sorry?

JANE

I said I hope you're okay.

CHELSEA

(COVERING) Well, yes...of course I am. My husband wasn't giving me what I needed, he was a lox, I kicked him out. Let's get back to you.

JANE

Look, I need that agreement signed and on my desk by the end of the day.

CHELSEA

I'll look it over right now. Jane, if I upset you, I'm sorry. It was wrong to take your purse.

JANE

Okay. I'll be in my office if you need me.

JANE EXITS AND CLOSES THE DOOR BEHIND HER. CHELSEA TAKES OUT THE SNOBALLS AND TAKES A BITE OF ONE. JANE ENTERS.

JANE (cont'd)

Where are they?

A BEAT, THEN CHELSEA MAKES A MUFFLED RESPONSE.

CHELSEA

Where's what?

CHELSEA HANDS THE REMAINING SNOBALL BACK TO JANE.

FADE OUT.[14]

THE ACTOR/DIRECTOR RELATIONSHIP

Mondays are the first chance for the actor to work with the director. Some directors are more effusive than others. An actor should assume that the director is pleased with what an actor is doing unless the director asks the actor to change it. A needy actor who constantly needs an "Atta boy" is a pain in the neck. The director has too many things to think about without being the personal cheering section to one individual. Conversely, directors can be the best audience in the world. They are an actor's best ally on the set. Directors have heard all of the notes from the "suits" and the show runner and can help the actor satisfy everyone's needs. No one appreciates talent, craft, and dedication from an actor more than a director. It only makes him look good!

Director Steve Zuckerman (*Everybody Loves Raymond,* series director of *Empty Nest*) gained his first notoriety on and off-Broadway. He has been described as an "actors' director." He explains this in his own words:

> Being called an "Actors' Director" means that I came from the theater and I can read. I can read a script and know about the structure and about the writing. I'm good at knowing what the moments are and knowing what the writer's intent was. No matter how good an actor is, they really approach it from: "Bullshit...bullshit...bullshit...my line!" They also really don't read the stage directions. They might not be getting the meaning of something and I can point out what the intent of a line is. They really appreciate that."

Joe Regalbuto (actor-director of *Murphy Brown,* director of *The George Lopez Show*) regularly works on both sides of the relationship. That has brought him a unique perspective:

> During the very first episode of *Murphy Brown* that I directed, I was so concerned with technical considerations that I forgot that I was also in it as an actor. I finally realized that in the scene we were staging, I was the weakest link.
>
> As an actor in the scene, I was thinking only about what my character wants. As a director, I had to also look at the second, third and fourth characters' needs. I had to know the perspective of everything in the scene. The experience of directing has enhanced my acting. I now see how my part fits into the whole. It has opened me up as an actor. It has settled me into my place.
>
> Actors come in arms out and eyes wide open hoping that the director will see what they are trying to do and will help. Actors can usually find out in thirty seconds if that help is coming.

THE REHEARSAL TEAM

The group attending the actual scene rehearsal is small. It is a close team and generally feels like a family. This group includes the actors, director, AD or stage manager, script supervisor, on-set prop person and on-set decorator. That's it. Others come in and out all day, but this is the core team. And they trust each other. On a show where a director is doing the whole season (directing all the episodes), that director will often request his team. These are the individuals whom that director trusts with seeing the rehearsal process unfold. Script supervisor Kit Wilkinson describes this from her point of view:

> As a script supervisor you need to have the ability to focus on multiple details, understand the actors and their processes so as to help not hinder, and have a sixth sense about when to contribute and when to keep quiet. The rehearsal week early on is a small group— actors, director, AD, and you. It's intimate. But there is no training that really aids with this sensitivity.

STAGE ETIQUETTE AND WRAP

If the rehearsal day is long enough, there may be a lunch break on Monday. All the cast and crew should report to the set (not dressing rooms) to see what's up first after lunch because the anticipated scenes may or may not be rehearsed in order. Never assume that you know what is being scheduled next, because it will change! Reporting to the set every morning and after every meal break is general courtesy. After telling the AD that you have arrived, actors that are not needed will be dismissed to their dressing rooms. That is where the AD expects to find you unless you tell him otherwise. Rounding up actors for the next scene is an easy task *if* the AD knows where to find everyone. In some cases it is simply an announcement over the PA system into the dressing rooms. Others choose to call actors individually on their phones or knock at their dressing room doors. However summoned, an actor should drop what he is doing and come immediately to the set.

After rehearsal, actors may have wardrobe fittings. Work will continue on sets. The prop master is arranging the rental or purchase of key props. The ADs continue their paperwork and planning for the week. Writing is still going on in the writers' room. Carmen Finestra tells us, "Rewrite usually lasts until 9 or 10 P.M. (or into the wee hours if there are real problems, and occasionally that happens. Be sure to sleep well over the weekend)."

At the end of each workday, actors sign out and the crew fills in their time cards. Be sure to know the **call time** for the next day. That's when you are expected to be on stage ready to work. Don't assume that because your day is done, everyone else's is as well. It takes many hands to make a sitcom. All departments are integral to the final product. A simple acknowledgment from an actor leaving for the day to a crew member who is still working is always appreciated. It says that the actor knows that although he is in front of the camera, there is a huge supportive network behind him. His crew always loved actor/comedian D. L. Hughley because when he arrived he would always greet everyone, often with a kiss on the cheek or handshake. When he left the stage for the day, he'd thank everybody for their efforts.

Sitcom Insider

ADVICE TO THE ASPIRING COMEDY WRITER

Three things are important:

1. **Read.** *And not just* Variety. *Read good books—classics with expressive language and nuanced characters, as well as modern fiction that features humorous description and dialogue. Richard Russo is a good choice. If you want to be a good writer, you have to know what good writing is. Don't sit at home only watching television. Much of it is not good. If George Santayana were alive today, I'm sure he'd say, "Those who watch bad television are condemned to repeat it."*

2. **Live.** *Before you can write, you have to live. The best writing comes from life experience. Plato said, "The unexamined life is not worth living." A psychiatrist amended that saying, "The unlived life is not worth examining." I agree. Go to concerts, theater, lectures, play with your children, hug your mate, listen to them, and engage them fully. If you don't presently have someone in your life, try meeting someone. Not just at singles bars or clubs. Do volunteer work, with causes you care about. Invite friends to your place, not to watch videos, but to talk and exchange views. Don't get bogged down in discussing "the business." It just cuts you off from the real world—the world where people work, struggle, cry, laugh, love and hate. If you just want to be a hip cynic, who disdains life, your writing will reflect it. It'll be clever, but not memorable. People who know how to write character and emotion are the ones who keep collecting the residual checks.*

3. **Write.** *Then write some more. Writers become better writers by writing. It's no secret. You have to sit down at a desk and pound it out. Gene Fowler said, "Writing is easy. You just sit in front of a blank page until the blood pours out of your forehead." Keeping a journal might help. It's a good way to start the day. Write everything you saw and heard. Build up your writing muscle any way you can.*

Carmen Finestra, Writer, Co-creator of *Home Improvement*

Sitcom Vocabulary Quick Review

Read these sentences. If the director gave you these notes, would you instantly know what he meant? If not, go back and review the explanation in this chapter.

Take it up with the **AD.**

What's your **call time** tomorrow?

Is the kitchen **dressed?**

The joke didn't **land.**

We won't pretape anything in the **standing sets.**

Have the **suits** arrived?

Is the **swing set** secure?

Did the **UPM** approve that?

Who was the **show runner** on that series?

We'll rehearse as soon as the **load in** is finished.

Script Supervisor's Monday Tasks

✓ Come to table reading having prepped the script.

✓ Time the reading.

✓ Report timing to executive producer and director.

✓ Go to note session, take any notes for director if needed.

✓ Rehearse.

✓ Notate blocking in your script.

✓ Time each scene.

✓ Act as liaison between stage and office.

Sitcom Career Profile

EMILY DRAPER
COSTUME DESIGNER

We met Emily when she was a costume assistant on a delightful sitcom called Domestic Life *created by Howard Gewirtz and Ian Praiser. It was one of those gems that never made it past 10 episodes despite its excellence. Emily reunites with Mr. Gewirtz on* Oliver Beene. *She now heads the costume department and brings the 60s to life in her historically accurate, yet highly creative designs!*

What shows have you worked on?

Oliver Beene, Grace under Fire, Normal Ohio, Oh Baby, many others, many pilots…assistant on *General Hospital.*

COSTUME DESIGNER INFO
Union: IATSE Local 892
Typical Weekly Salary: $2400–$3000
Hours Per Week: 40–50

What are your responsibilities?

I am responsible for reading and breaking down the script, renting, fittings, hiring and overseeing costumers, and the budget. I also have to please the actors, producers, and network!

Did you have specific training in this field?

No. I got my first experience in Equity Waiver theater, AFI Films, and friends' short films—any way possible. There was never any pay on these jobs!

How did you get your first job?

My first job was as a costumer on a pilot called *Mr. Success.* A friend hired me: Howard Gewirtz. He had to foist me onto them—but they ended up liking me.

What do you like best about your job?

Shopping, working with great costumes, working with producers and actors. I love clothes! I love that it all comes together quickly! I love the whole process!

Chapter 3 **TUESDAY...REHEARSAL/PRODUCERS' RUN-THRU DAY**

In this chapter:

How to collate a script

Identifying the setup and punchline

Advice from a sitcom writer

What to do while holding for a laugh

Dos and Don'ts of staging

How to stay focused as a character

Surviving a run-thru

Career profile of a script supervisor

"**W**hy did they change it?" is the most frequently asked (or thought) question on Tuesday. The table read went well. The jokes got laughs. Now, lines are gone when you get the first rewrite. There may be an entirely new script, a new first act, or at least several new jokes.

The reason for the changes can mostly be found from the discussions on Monday's meeting after the table reading.[1] Considerations about character development, plot clarity, and general direction for the series caused the writers to spend many hours working on the pages that you now have. Notes were given by network, studio, and countless other people yesterday. They all have their own needs and desires. Writers must address all these notes. At the same time, they want to rewrite for their own satisfaction of playing with the story and making it all fit together.

So, "Why *did* they change it?" Sometimes your line is gone, simply because the script was too long. Look at the page count; is it shorter? Sitcoms are programmed to the second. The writer is aware of how much of a 30-minute time slot is set aside for the opening credits, the show, ending credits, and commercials. The length of the material that is being rehearsed is probably only 20 minutes or less. Each sitcom has this time adjusted for its specific

> **SITCOM RULE**
> ***Don't move on the joke.*** *The joke is most important. Moving on the joke distracts the audience from listening to the punchline. Moving **after** the joke gives a place for the audience to laugh without missing dialogue.*

---

[1] Nearly everyone involved with the show was asked to leave the room for those notes. The director was there and can explain some of the more perplexing changes.

network, time slot, credit length, and transitions. Most shows try to end up about one and one-half to two minutes "long" at the end of the week. This gives the director and producer the ability to tighten up the pace in editing and remove the occasional lame joke or two. *Seinfeld* was notorious for coming in as much as seven minutes long. This gave creator Larry David the freedom to take out quite a bit of material and keep only the créme de la créme.[2]

The script supervisor timed yesterday's reading. To that timing was added about two minutes for the "laugh spread." This is the anticipated extra time expected from a full audience's laughter. An additional two minutes is added because actual staging and camera transitions usually take longer than just the director reading stage directions.

There are a myriad of other reasons for script changes. After yesterday's rehearsal, the director may have made requests based on difficulties in staging. For example, on *Frasier*, Daphne might have been given the stage direction: "ENTERS AND CROSSES TO KITCHEN." As happens occasionally, an actress might be pregnant and her character is not. In this case, the director could suggest she "ENTERS HOLDING DRY CLEANING AND CROSSES TO KITCHEN." The prop should hide her bulging belly. He may have found something during rehearsal that will tell the story better or in a more visual way than what the writer described on paper. The director may have told the writers that a scene just wasn't working or asked for help in a certain area to better serve an actor.

The script may be shorter because it was too expensive! Revised cost estimates of the sets, props, wardrobe, and special physical effects were discussed in yesterday's production meeting.[3] Line producers who keep track of the physical costs of the production make requests to cut entire scenes! Sometimes there isn't money in the budget to build another set. At times, there isn't enough room to squeeze another set on the soundstage. Marsha Scarbrough, in that *Written by* article, writes about the "No Fat" episode of *Everybody Loves Raymond*: "Because there is not enough room on the stage for both the pharmacy set and the bedroom set, the bedroom scene is eliminated." The line producer's responsibility is to bring the show in on budget. Everyone can love a scene but sometimes it's just gotta go! A *Seinfeld* script described a set once, then explained that the scene took place in the dark. We have to wonder if this was written to alleviate the cost or space concerns over another set.

Finally, the reason for script changes could be that the star didn't want other cast members to be funnier than he is. Although neither of us worked on the series *Cybill*, it was rumored that there was friction over the script almost every

---

[2]   One of our favorite activities is watching that great sitcom and hoping to catch George go into Jerry's bathroom and then see him again on the couch without coming out. Excising jokes could leave a mismatch or two.

[3]   Maybe budgets haven't been turned in yet, but the line producer wishes he had them!

week of the production between the star Cybill Shepherd and the **second banana**[4] Christine Baranski. Once something like this is anticipated, the writers spend much of their rewrite trying to avoid this situation.

A typical Tuesday call time is 10 A.M., with the producer's run-thru scheduled in the mid to late afternoon. That is approximately four or five hours of actual rehearsal, an hour for lunch, and time for the run-thru and notes. Because the majority of in-depth rehearsal takes place today, use that time wisely.

> *During the day, prior to the run-thru, writers are working on future scripts. Producers are also busy editing prior episodes, casting, meeting with potential writers for episode assignments. This happens every day of the week.*
>
> Carmen Finestra, Co-creator and Executive Producer, *Home Improvement*

THE NEW SCRIPT

The writers—there can be as many as 15 of them—work around a conference table with an assistant making each change on a computer. Many writers are looking at the large computer monitor visible to everyone. This scene some-what resembles a hospital's late night emergency room with its motley characters. However, this room feels like *American Idol* with writers competing with each other, performing new jokes that will replace the old. The head writer has the final word.

We know about a couple of exceptions to this collaborative writers' room system. We have been told that Susan Harris almost exclusively wrote the majority of *Soap* episodes. Her scripts had a wonderful emotional base with a wacky style. She had a couple of other writers working along with her during the four-year run of that show. It was evident because of her distinctive flair which scenes she completely wrote and which were written by other fine writers such as Stu Silver who had his own distinct funny voice.

The very talented Aaron Sorkin also worked as a lone gunman...on two shows at the same time! You can't argue with the results: *The West Wing* and the sitcom *Sports Night*. Show runner Tim Doyle had just finished working on the recently **wrapped**[5] *Ellen*. Doyle and most of his writing staff were available to aid sitcom newcomer Sorkin, the feature film writer and playwright. Doyle told us that Sorkin essentially didn't need much help. If you missed Sorkin's comedic voice on *Sports Night*, rent *The American President* for a real treat.

Sometimes the new script or new pages are delivered to the actor's door. It is usually late in the evening when the writers finish this first rewrite. A pro-

---

[4] Second Banana is a term from Burlesque. Today, Burlesque brings to mind strippers. Before television, it was a major form of comedy for the masses. Phil Silvers starred in Broadway's homage to Burlesque *First Banana*. He was a natural to move over to star as Sgt. Bilko in the hugely popular early sitcom *You'll Never Get Rich*. Baranski was the second character of importance, hence the name second banana. Despite Baranski's distinguished Broadway career, it was Shepherd who brought "name value" to the show because she was a more recognizable movie star at that time.

[5] Wrapped means completing the day's work, and episode, or in this case the entire series.

duction assistant stays with the writers to make the deliveries. If it is too late, the delivery might be made by another assistant who comes in at dawn for that purpose. Actors should not leave their houses or apartments until they have checked around their front door or gate for a package with these pages.

If there are fewer changes, the scripts will be left on the stage. Department heads will often get the script delivered to their office or know the designated spot on stage where new scripts are usually left. When in doubt, ask the script supervisor who can always track down the new script. Always assume that there are pages to incorporate. If you need extra time to assimilate new dialogue or prep before rehearsal, consider getting to the set before your actual call time. All departments need to read their new script...all of it!

COLLATING

To begin, check all scenes for changes that affect you. READ THE WHOLE SCRIPT! Sometimes you've been added or deleted from scenes. To help you find changes easily, there are usually asterisks (in the margin) at the place on the page where there is a new line or word. If the entire page is very different, the asterisk will be at the top. If you have not received a completely new script, **collate** the new colored pages into your old script. This means putting the script in order. This can be daunting if you've never done it before.

Here's what you need to know to collate a sitcom script properly. All changes keep to the original page numbers. If page 4 has new dialogue, it replaces the old page 4. If there are now too many lines to fit on page 4, they will continue to an "A" page with the same original number. Page 4 will now be two sheets: 4 followed by 4A. If there are cuts, the original numbers are accounted for with a hyphen. You might see pages 28–31 as the designation of the original page 28 and the missing scene after it. Each show has its own color system for each set of changes. The first rewrite is probably printed on pink paper. The next is blue, then green, goldenrod, etc.

If you have to collate on the set, find a place where you can spread out. Work from the beginning to the end sequentially. Be sure to clean up after yourself. Most stages have a recycling bin for old pages. Then, if you haven't done it yet, READ THE NEW SCRIPT!

> *My job is to train the writer's assistant as to what is needed or not needed in a script for the stage. For me, the writer's assistant is the most overworked and under appreciated job on the show. The hours are terrible and the mistakes are there in black and white. Many have had little sleep and very little leeway given to them. So, I guess part of my job is to tell them I understand and that there is nothing that cannot be fixed.*
>
> Marcia Gould,
> Script Supervisor, *Wings*

GETTING THE MOST OUT OF REHEARSAL

If you are an actor and your script is complete, take the time to study it. Today is your day to do most of the rehearsal for the entire week. Theater veterans are used to a long rehearsal schedule that slowly reveals the subtleties of their character and the plot. Sitcoms have only three days in which to rehearse the script as a stage play. Dramatic television actors are often surprised that sitcoms are much more like theater than they are like episodic series.[6] Stand-up comics often discover how rehearsal can be helpful to creating a rich character and performance. Others don't value that time and want to keep their performances "fresh."

Bill Cosby disdained long rehearsals. He let his stand-in, Samuel L. Jackson,[7] work much of the rehearsal to allow the other actors their time. Audrey Meadows once told us that Jackie Gleason would only rehearse *The Honeymooners* scenes one time. If you watch those reruns closely, you will occasionally see Meadows feeding Gleason his forgotten line. Bret Butler of *Grace under Fire*, would often say, "I don't know why you are taking this long to rehearse. I can *learn* a script in a couple of hours." She knew the intricacies of her character, since the series was based partially on her life.

Guest actors, who are only working on one episode, need to realize that they have to help create their new character in very little time. Robin Bartlett suggests, "Don't overwork the material. It is usually thin enough to be weighted down by too much thought. This does not mean that it isn't worth the time. I think of sitcom as the vaudeville of this era. At its best it is both common and full of wit and wisdom."

SETUP, PUNCHLINE, OR PIPE?

The better you know what the scene is about and the better grasp you have on the words you say, the more profitable your rehearsal will be. Sitcom dialogue can be broken into three categories: the **setup**, the **punchline**, and the **pipe**. A student of comedy can tell the difference.

The setup is the statement or premise that has to be understood for a joke to get a laugh. It immediately precedes the punchline. You will see that this construction is very precise. There are no extra words or thoughts to get in the way of this premise.

The punchline is the other half of the formula. It is the funny part, but will not be funny without the setup. Here is an example of a classic setup and punchline:

```
                    MONICA
(NOTICING HIS TIE) Oh, honey I thought I told you
not to wear that tie.


                    WILLIAM
I thought you meant just that one time.
```

---

[6] Dramatic television actors will often shoot scenes with little or no rehearsal.

[7] Jay Sandrich, the Director of *Cosby*, impressed with Jackson's acting ability as Bill's stand-in, kept trying to get the producers to let "Sam" play a small part in an episode. It never happened. With all of that sitcom experience, we were not surprised at how many laughs Jackson got in the feature film *Pulp Fiction*.

> MONICA
> No, darling, I meant never.[8]

The setup and punchline make up the jokes; everything else is pipe or exposition. The setup is also known as the **feed** because it comes before or feeds into the punchline. Pipe is simply information that helps audiences understand the story. It also can serve as a setup for something that will be coming later. It could be dialogue such as, "So your brother is coming over. I hope you guys can get along for a change." This establishes a premise that won't be paid off right away, but is important to know when he shows up and there is a series of jokes based on the idea of sibling incompatibility. Each of those jokes will have their own immediate setup and punchline.

Pipe is found in abundance in the first scene of a script, or in the first script of a series, called the pilot. Hiding the pipe is the challenge of most pilots. Due to the expository nature of these lines, they are the parts of the script that don't get laughs. Many actors complain that all they are doing is **laying pipe** in such scenes. They feel like a laborer rather than an artist since they are not involved in either the front half or back half of the actual joke. Actor Anthony Anderson (*All about the Andersons*) cleverly disguises the pipe explaining his character's move from New York to Los Angeles in the pilot episode of his show. The secret that Anderson knew was to play the needs of the character. The audience heard a lot of background information disguised as a heated discussion.

Analyze the structure to understand how to deliver it. You should be able to find the **operative word** that is key to each sentence's meaning. That word is not always the funny word but it is usually the premise by which the joke is based. Understanding this script construction is critical so that each line can be framed or presented by the actor in such a way that will make the audience laugh.

As we begin to break down the structure of comedy, we have to admit that over-analysis can be the death of comedy for *some* people. Many naturally funny people will start morphing into a homogenized standard sitcom caricature if they are not careful. Our experience has shown us that *most* newcomers who don't naturally see the structure and hear the rhythm desperately need to understand these sitcom basics. The best way to learn that is to read a lot of sitcom scripts and identify exactly what makes them funny.

Here is a classic scene from the pilot *Luis* by Will Gluck. The very talented actor Luis Guzman plays a gruff but good-hearted owner of a Spanish Harlem donut shop. The character Greg is Luis's daughter Marly's live-in boyfriend.

---

[8] From the episode "Invasion of the Gold Digger," written by Keith Josef Adkins from the series *Girlfriends*, created by Mara Brock Akil. Used by permission of Paramount Pictures Corporation. All Rights Reserved.

Sitcom Exercise

*Read this scene. Identify the **setup** and **punchline** for all the jokes. We've done the first two for you. Complete the rest, remembering that for every **punchline** there is a **setup**. You know where the answers are.*

LUIS

"PILOT"

INT. DONUT SHOP - DAY

(LUIS, GREG, MARLY)

GREG KISSES MARLY. HE NOTICES LUIS WATCHING AND BREAKS IT OFF.

>   GREG
> Oh, I guess <u>I shouldn't kiss your daughter in front
> of you,</u> huh?

>   LUIS
> You can kiss my daughter in front of me. <u>You just
> can't kiss my daughter in front of me without a job.</u>

>   GREG
> <u>What else can I do in front of you if I get a job?
> Grab her ass?</u>

>   LUIS
> <u>A good job, yes.</u>

>   GREG
> What can I do for eighty-five grand and a dental
> plan?

>   LUIS
> You make eighty-five grand a year, you can grab my
> ass.

>   GREG
> (RE: GREG'S SMALL HANDS AND LUIS'S LARGE ASS) I
> don't think that's possible.

LUIS TAKES A BEAT THEN LUNGES AT HIM.

GREG (cont'd)
You know, Luis, most artists don't achieve success
until after they're dead.

LUIS
How 'bout I make you successful right now? (THEN,
RE: GREG'S DONUT) Did you pay for that?

GREG
Of, course.

LUIS
(MENACING) Did you?

GREG
Yes!

LUIS
(MENACING) Did you?

GREG
Marly, can I borrow a dollar? (THEN) I'm kidding. Of
course I paid for it. I mean, come on. (LOUD
WHISPERS) Marly. Dollar bill. Quickly!

LUIS
I don't get it. She's a smart girl. What does she
see in you?

GREG
Maybe a guy who loves her, who's sensitive,
talented, and from time to time (OFF LUIS) not
afraid to show fear. (LOUD WHISPER, TO MARLY)
Dollar...bill. Now. If you love me!

MARLY BRINGS HIM A DOLLAR.

GREG (cont'd)
Here you go.

LUIS
I don't understand you. I mean, how can you let a
woman pay your bills?

> GREG
> It'd be a hell of a lot easier if you didn't bring it up all the time. (THEN, RE: DOLLAR) Do I got some change skating my way, how does that work?[9]

HOLDING FOR LAUGHS

After studying the script, go back and make a note when a punchline is your cue. The cue is the last word spoken by another actor before the next actor's line. It is critical to have an awareness of when the audience is laughing. They can't hear the next line if it is spoken under a laugh. Actors need to get used to this rhythm of the sitcom. Remember the Sitcom Rule: **HOLD FOR LAUGHS!**

Emmy-nominated director Jim Drake (*Golden Girls, Buffalo Bill*) was directing a little-experienced actress in a scene on *Sanford*.[10] During rehearsal he kept warning her about the need to hold for the laugh that she would get in the middle of her own speech. He explained that she needed to give the audience time to appreciate her joke before she continued. Finally, she seemed to understand. On the night of the taping before the live audience, she got to the joke and got the big laugh that Jim predicted. Happily, she held for the laugh. As the laugh was diminishing, before she finished her speech, she turned to the audience and took a bow...Not exactly the activity Jim was hoping for during that laugh.

Holding is waiting...and so much more. Holding requires the actor to remain involved in the scene. The actor must remain in character as well.

If you are an actor, decide if your character knows that the joke is funny. That might call for a different reaction than if the joke was an insult to your character and funny only for the audience. The proper reaction can add much dimension to the comedy of your performance and the scene. It is important for you to discover what your character is thinking during the pause for the laugh. This moment should be a genuine organic moment of the character rather than just an actor waiting for the laugh to end. On *Major Dad*, Beverly Archer (who played Gunnery Sergeant Bricker) could always be counted on for an extra or prolonged laugh when you cut to her **deadpan**[11] face. Ms. Archer had made the character choice that Gunny took her job very seriously. Her stern reaction to anything humorous was always a sure laugh! Regan Burns who has been a guest star on dozens of sitcoms says, "During any comedic argument, I always hunt for the 'deadpan.' That one line that seems to be most powerful when just delivered flat. It's important to find the different levels."

---

[9] Luis ©2003 Twentieth Century Fox Film Corporation. All Rights Reserved.

[10] This was the 1980s series that followed the classic *Sanford and Son* and *Sanford Arms*.

[11] The human face has been referred to as a "pan" since the nineteenth century possibly because the face is broad and shallow like a dishpan.

Similarly, Lisa Kudrow of *Friends* extends laughs by her character's naïveté, bewilderment, or ignorance of something said to her. Observe Kudrow thinking, in character, while she waits for the audience laughter to subside. Matt LeBlanc, also of *Friends*, constantly gets laughs while his character tries to decipher what has been said.

A FEW PRELIMINARIES

Rehearsal on Tuesday will resemble a play rehearsal. Rehearsal will be on a set that may or may not be completely built. For example, the living room walls may be standing, but there may not be a front door. Folding chairs are often substituted for a car set. Actors should use rehearsal props whenever possible even though they are holding a script in their hand. The prop department provides both real and rehearsal props. You should always ask if the prop will be different from the one you are using.

Scenes may be rehearsed out of order on Tuesday. This is common practice in the film and television industry. If there are child actors in the episode, their limited time[12] on the set needs to be optimized. All of their scenes may be rehearsed back-to-back even if they are not sequential in the script. The star might have an interview with the press in the morning and needs to have a later call, if this is the case. Any scene that the star is not a part of would be scheduled early.

It is an actor's job to keep track of what takes place in the scene. The script supervisor is keeping an official record if an actor ever has a script question. Ellen Deutch calls herself and fellow script supervisors the "logic police." However, even the best script supervisor doesn't have the benefit of the organic acting process, which reveals a moment that doesn't ring true because of a gap in emotional logic. This talent comes with an actor's ability to behave in character sequentially from moment to moment.

This is the day to make sure that there is a proper through-line for each character. If you are an actor, ask yourself a few questions: Does everything make sense? What changes are made as each scene progresses and how do they affect me? Did my character have information earlier that would be necessary for my scripted behavior in this scene? Any problems in continuity should be brought to the attention of the director. Since there have been, and will continue to be, changes in the script, some things fall through the cracks. Bringing attention to the problem can remedy these inconsistencies.

There is a difference between being creative and helpful and being thought of as a selfish performer.[13] As a guest actor, you should also be sensitive to monopolizing the rehearsal time. If you have something that you think could help, don't hold it back...but find the right time to share it. If the director

---

[12] Nearby are a classroom and a studio teacher whose responsibility it is to protect the child from abusive working conditions.

[13] The term *selfish performer* is actually never used on the set. These people are always called "pain in the ass."

agrees that it is important, he will bring this to the attention of the writers. They care very much if it causes the story not to work—unless it means losing a really good joke...and then some writers will excuse the logic by telling you that they are taking "comedic license."

By contrast, writers may seem almost uncaring about long-term character continuity. For example, you may come across a line that states your character is meeting his sweetheart at the high school reunion. You may remind the writers that in the pilot, you had a line about not dating in high school. You may be told, "Nobody will ever remember that!" The prevailing attitude is that most of the audience doesn't keep track of these details. Some shows have had a change of careers for some of the characters without any explanation. Next-door neighbors appear and then are replaced in the very next episode. Diana Canova's son in *Throb* went from tall, thin, blond actor Paul Walker[14] to shorter, stockier, dark-haired Sean DeVeritch. Other shows are very strict about the show's continuity and every detail fits together like a giant puzzle.

The actors will put every scene on its feet. It is their time to get familiar with props and the set. It is also a good time to get to know the rehearsal crew. The prop master will give out each handheld prop just before its scene. Props should be returned to the prop department after each scene. Props are the items that are identified in the script to be used by a character. Everything else in the set is part of the set dressing. For any questions about the set or if an actor wishes to use some set dressing as a prop, a set decorator is on hand during all rehearsals.

If you are an actor, become familiar with your props. They are an adjunct to your performance. Let them help rather than hinder you. Ease with props takes repeated rehearsals even for seasoned professionals. On an episode of *Charles in Charge*, guest star John Astin[15] needed to use a medicine case as a part of his scene. He spent his entire lunch hour of Tuesday's rehearsal working at loading and unloading the case (with the permission of the prop master). He worked it repeatedly until the movement was habitual to the character. It became so fluid, that the character and his case were the delight of the show.

STAGE GEOGRAPHY

An actor should be aware of his physical position in relation to his fellow actor and his audience. In order to share the stage with his fellow actor, the physical relationship between them should be **50/50**. This means that each actor is equally visible to the audience. If both actors are facing each other, they mirror each other's position while both attempt to turn their downstage shoulder

---

[14] Paul Walker went on to star in noncomedic action features such as *Varsity Blues, Pleasantville, The Fast and The Furious,* and *Timeline.* He has been called "the next Steve McQueen."

[15] Prior to many guest appearances including *Charles in Charge,* John Astin has had a distinguished career as the star of long-running sitcoms such as *I'm Dickens, He's Fenster, The Addams Family,* and *Operation Petticoat.* His resume goes all the way back to an appearance in a dance sequence from the film *West Side Story.*

outward toward the audience. The audience isn't there on Tuesday, but an easy way to gauge this relationship is by looking at the **set-line,**[16] which lies **downstage**[17] at the edge of the set. This line is called the proscenium line in the theatre. The actors are standing at a slight angle to each other. The upstage shoulders of the actors are closer to one another than the downstage ones. An easy trick is to always lean on your upstage leg. This gives the effect of opening you up to the audience for better viewing, and as we'll learn in Chapter 5, better viewing by the cameras.

During rehearsal, the script supervisor is keeping track of all dialogue changes made with the director's approval. Actors should call out the word "line" to ask the script supervisor to **feed** the words. She is also recording blocking notes and can refresh your memory about movement and continuity during the scene. The AD or stage manager will be keeping everything operating properly on the stage and often give you your entrance cues. Cue lights are sometimes set up backstage in order to cue silently.

The crew is an actor's friend. Everyone needs to treat them respectfully. Everyone on a sitcom is part of a creative team. Each individual is providing his expertise. Often, a crew member is overqualified for his job. He may have surprisingly long and distinguished credits in similar or complementary positions. For example, prior to becoming a prop master, Ron Woods (*8 Simple Rules, Dave's World*) acted at the renowned Oregon Shakespeare Festival. He has been known to fill in for a missing actor during rehearsal and give quite an excellent performance!

Out of respect to your fellow craftsmen, no personal food or drink should ever be brought onto the set. Cell phones and pagers should be set on vibrate. No one should ever lounge in a set when it's not in use. Space allowing, there is always a table and chairs in front of the center set to use for collating, going over your lines, and relaxing.

Each scene will be rehearsed a number of times, until the director is satisfied with it. Notes may be given after each completed scene or the director will stop and start in order to figure out the best way to execute the scene. ACTORS SHOULD USE THIS TIME TO EXPLORE! USE THIS TIME TO ASK QUESTIONS! Remember the rule: **DON'T MOVE ON THE JOKE**. This pertains to your and other character's jokes. Actually, it pertains mostly to the punchline. Nothing should distract the audience from laughing. Any movement or gesture will take their attention away from hearing the funny part. There are always exceptions. D. L. Hughley knew this rule and would purposely defy it to prove his skill at comedy…he always got the laugh!

---

[16] The set flooring, painted or real, is easier to use as a guide than the often-asymmetrical walls.

[17] Downstage is so named because when stages (not audiences) were raked (tilted), the lower part of the stage was closer to the audience for better viewing. As the actors walked away from the audience, they literally were traveling up.

STAGE BUSINESS AND BLOCKING

Actors, write down your blocking! It is also a good idea for the director, his assistants, and is a must for the script supervisor. You can use the shorthand of an up arrow when you rise from a chair, a down arrow when you sit and an X for when you cross the room. Always use pencil because things are always changing. Play with the other actors! Find your moments! Create your own **business!** Business is any physical action: any movement or gesture. It may support dialogue or exist on its own. Business can make a character memorable as in the example of John Astin and the medicine case. Some actors have been hired just for their **shtick.**[18] An extreme piece of shtick is a pratfall. Actors hired for their shtick are expected to enhance their performance with more physicality than most. If Jim Carrey were doing sitcom, he'd be known for his shtick. Michael Richards of *Seinfeld* elevated the humorous physicality of his character, Kramer, to an art form. This was well planned, expertly executed, and inventive work!

Seinfeld director of photography, Wayne Kennan, remembers Richards as a very hard worker who would toil all day long on his physical business, "He would be constantly trying different ways of entering and exiting through Jerry's apartment door. By the end of the series, the bottom of the door was completely beat-up and almost black from Kramer's shoe marks." Kennan watched as Richards developed one piece of physical business when he sat down at a barstool. Kennan said, "Michael didn't smoke and it was pure genius the way he worked with that cigarette and beer. His hilarious antics fit really well in the sitcom arena."

Actors have to find the appropriate business for their character. Most business is naturalistic such as a mother unloading grocery bags and putting the food away in the kitchen cabinets. Actors should make their energy and activities fit their character. It may, however, be more than real life and more than a dramatic character would do. On one episode of *Girlfriends*, actress Tracee Ellis Ross invented a piece of business for her character who was cooking pasta. Her character, Joan, was angry with William (Reggie Hayes) for betraying her. Ross punctuated her line by broadly snapping the dry pasta in half and depositing it into the boiling water at the end of her line.

                        JOAN

You know what? I was wrong. This isn't about Monica.
She doesn't owe me anything. This is about William,
and how he betrayed me as a colleague and a friend.
We are more than friends, we're like family. You
don't turn on family—unless you're Fredo Corleone.
And like Fredo Corleone, his ass is going down.

---

[18] *Shtick* is the old Yiddish term for piece or routine. It described the physical comedy or little dances of vaudeville.

```
ON THE GIRLS' REACTIONS, WE:

                                                        FADE OUT.
```

<u>END OF ACT ONE</u>[19]

This ended the act with a huge laugh!

ADVICE: WORK HARD BUT KEEP IT FUN

Sitcom rehearsals are usually a lot of fun. Everyone needs to stay loose. You may be very good at your job, but if you bring tension to the set, you won't last long in sitcoms. That goes for both actors and others. We knew an individual working in a prop department who was militaristic in efficiency. She made her fellow crew members tense, the actors nervous, and drove us crazy. The laudable attention to detail was overshadowed by the tension created.

Crew members, feel free to laugh! Remember this is a situation comedy. The actors love having an audience during rehearsal. The television audience wants to laugh as well; otherwise, they'd be watching a drama. That being said, rehearsals also have a serious intent. As an actor, this is the time to practice the scenes so that you will perform it, retaining what you rehearsed, at the producers run-thru later this afternoon.

THE PRODUCER RUN-THRU

The producer run-thru is a performance for the writers. Scarbrough defines the *Everybody Loves Raymond* experience. "They watch the cast perform the script 'on its feet' in the sets." Scenes are done in order. Actress Catherine MacNeal (*Cheers, Night Court, Designing Women*) admits:

> When I did my first sitcom, I got very nervous before run-thrus for producers or the network. I worried that if I didn't land the joke, it would be gone the next day. But once the audience arrived, I loosened up and felt like I was back in the theatre, theatre with retakes. With every job, I reminded myself that it was "theatre" and tried to carry that feeling of freedom into every run-thru.

The writers are the audience. They will laugh…a lot. They will also take a lot of notes to aid them in the second rewrite that evening. Actors, you will hear a lot of pencils writing during the run-thru. Don't assume that they are writing criticisms of you. They usually are marking the script for places that need writing help. These markings are their own shorthand. They might spot a place where a joke is needed and write **JTC** meaning joke to come, **LTC** meaning line to come, or some other mark.

---

[19] From the episode "Invasion of the Gold Digger," written by Keith Josef Adkins from the series *Girlfriends*, created by Mara Brock Akil. Used by permission of Paramount Pictures Corporation. All Rights Reserved.

Executive Producer Peter Engel was so noted for his two notes **punch** and **replace**, he received solid gold cufflinks of those words as a warmhearted gesture from one of his writers. *Punch* means to refine the joke to make it better; *replace* means to come up with an entirely new joke. These two instructions may be only marked in the script by a check mark, but the producer or writer knows that this is a place to review during the rewrite. If a joke has been checked in a script, a writer or writer's assistant will say, "I've got it marked."

The more successful a run-thru, the earlier the writers get to go home. For that reason, there is a lot of pressure. Concentrating on the scene and remembering everything practiced in the rehearsals are expected. This is not the time to add anything new. Directors don't like surprises. One of the most important skills for a sitcom actor (this applies to almost everyone in all positions) is to be able to reproduce the exact same performance many times in a row. Once you have arrived at a desired choice, stay with it. If an actor wants to try something different, do it in rehearsal. It is the director's prerogative to keep it or not. If a prop person has a different prop from what was used in rehearsal, he should check to see if the director wants to use it during run-thru. A wardrobe person who wants an actor to wear wardrobe during run-thru should also run it by the director.

HOLDING SCRIPTS, NOTES, AND SIGNING OUT

Today, scripts should be held even if an actor knows his lines perfectly. There will be no expectation that an actor be **off book**,[20] yet there will be little sympathy if lines are muffed or cues are wrong because you should have the words in front of you. If you don't know 'em...then read 'em. The writers want to hear it the way it was written! If they don't have this opportunity, they won't know what to change. Actors should think of this as a performance and dress appropriately for the character. Women should wear makeup. Everyone's hair should be out of his or her eyes. NO GUM! NO HATS! NO SUNGLASSES!

Notes will be given at the end of a run-thru. Actors may or may not be included. Sometimes notes may contradict each other. The director will decipher what is needed. Actors should write down notes if they have less than perfect memories. Carmen Finestra explains what happens to the writers after a run-thru. "Tuesdays are often considered a 'punch up' night, where concentration is given to making the jokes better and funnier. Sometimes certain writers, who are known as great joke writers, are hired for this one night.[21] Obviously, any structural or motivational changes to scenes, if necessary, are also made."

Actors sign out with the 2nd AD or Assistant Stage Manager. Actors may be needed for costume fittings before they leave. They should expect to be in their

---

[20] *Off book* means an actor no longer needs to carry a script in his hands because he has memorized the words. This makes it easier for him to act, handle props, and move about the stage more freely.

[21] Bob Smith, who had worked as a joke writer for Johnny Carson's *Tonight Show* served as a "punch up" genius on several Carsey-Werner shows including *3rd Rock, Grace under Fire,* and *That '70s Show* all at the same time.

cars and stuck in rush-hour traffic by 6 P.M. Now is a good time to find out what the procedure is for having guests at the Friday audience show. Ask the **Second**[22] whom to notify about your guests. Guests are usually given priority seating. The crew doesn't sign out but submits daily time cards. Props, script supervisors, directors, their assistants, and some other crew members may have additional hours to complete their work after the run-thru.

Hope you had a good time! Tomorrow is the last chance to concentrate on just the play before cameras make it into a teleplay. Rest…and come back ready to refine what you've already begun!

Sitcom Vocabulary Quick Review

Read these sentences. If the director gave you these notes, would you instantly know what he meant? If not, go back and review the explanation in this chapter.

*That piece of **business** gets in the way of the punchline.*

*You jumped the **cue**.*

*When you **collate** your script, omit page 24a from the new pages.*

*A **deadpan** reaction will get a bigger laugh.*

*Cross **downstage** on that line.*

*The **punchline** didn't pay off because the **feed** wasn't clear.*

*Stand **50/50** with him.*

***Hold** for the laugh!*

*Don't worry, we'll have a **JTC**.*

*Disguise the fact that you're **laying pipe**.*

*He's the **second banana** on this show.*

*You don't need to be **off book** today.*

*The writers will **punch** it.*

*If it doesn't work, we'll **replace** it.*

*Check with the **Second** before you go to lunch.*

*The **setline** is farther downstage.*

*The **setup** is too far away from the **punchline**.*

*What is the **operative word** in that line?*

*Can you come up with some **shtick** for this scene?*

*What week were you **wrapped**?*

---

[22] DGA position of Second AD or Second Stage Manager.

Script Supervisor's Tuesday and Wednesday Tasks

✓ Make sure all actors, DGA team, department heads, etc., have revised script.

✓ Read Revised Table Draft.

✓ Transfer blocking notes that apply.

✓ Arrange possible informal reading of revised script with actors and director.

✓ Rehearse.

✓ Stay on book (script) in order to prompt actors of their lines if needed.

✓ Advise actors of dialogue if they are having difficulty.

✓ Time producers' run-thru.

✓ Take any notes for the director during run-thru.

✓ Report time to execs.

✓ Go to notes, record any notes for the director.

Sitcom Insider

NOTES ON WRITING SITCOMS

As jobs go, being a writer on a sitcom can be a fantastic way to make a living. You're well-paid, well-fed, and, in most cases, have a lot of fun. A writer on one show I worked on used to say that when he came home from work and his wife asked how his day was, he had to lie. Because, if he told her the truth—that he spent the day laughing and eating and bullshitting with his friends—she would become resentful over being left at home to do the truly hard job of taking care of the kids. In fact, being a sitcom writer is like being a calf raised for veal. And I mean that in a good way. You're kept in a confined space, and fed all day, with the added bonus that when you've been sufficiently fattened up, the slaughter is only metaphorical.

One downside should be obvious: it's hard to get a job on a sitcom these days, as there are fewer and fewer being produced, and budget cuts on those that remain on the air have reduced the number of writers being hired. In any given season, most job openings are on new shows, and most new shows get cancelled before the end of the season. But if you're lucky or talented enough to be working on a show, it can be a lot of fun.

It can be, that is, as long as you don't look to your writing on the show to provide fulfillment to your creative urges. And therein lies the other downside. On most sitcom staffs, the room (meaning the ten or so writers acting as a group) breaks (meaning outlines) a story for an episode (meaning episode). Then one writer goes off to write one or two drafts of the episode. That episode is thereafter referred to as that writer's episode. As in, "We're shooting Michael's episode this week." If you believe this—that it is really your episode—you're going to have your heart broken. You spend two weeks or so pouring your heart and soul into the script, and then bring it back to the room. The room then re-writes the script. There's a certain feeling of being violated, and not a damn thing you can do about it. And the room re-writing one's script is just the beginning of the process. If a writer is able to make it through the room re-write with most of his script intact, then he gets to watch the actors read it and hear the network and studio executives give notes on it.

I've been lucky enough to work on a couple of shows where a well-written first draft can make it all the way to shoot night without being messed up. But this is the exception. All too often, scripts are changed and not always for the better. And even if the changes in your script are all for the better, chances are you don't realize it. Chances are, you think the brilliance that you achieved in your first draft is much better than what ended up getting shot. And sometimes the changes are just lateral, because the process is all about re-writing, whether it's necessary or not. And so, the writer of the script is often left missing his draft, even if he knows, deep down, that the re-write is better.

It helps, if you want to work as a writer on a sitcom, to enjoy the food and the camaraderie, but to look elsewhere for creative fulfillment. Write a novel or a play on the side. Or your own spec pilot or screenplay. Something that's yours, that no one else can touch. (Unless, of course, you actually sell it, and then you'll have to get notes from somebody. But don't worry, that'll never happen.) Enjoy the show as a fun job and not as an outlet for all your creative urges, and you'll have fun.

Michael Kaplan, *Frasier, Girlfriends, Roseanne*

Sitcom Career Profile

KIT WILKINSON
SCRIPT SUPERVISOR

There was one season where Kit was offered 12 different shows! Everyone wants to work with her! Besides being an incredibly gifted script supervisor, she is great fun to be around. She has a goodness and honesty that you can always count on.

What shows have you worked on?

I worked in Accounting and as a Writer's Assistant on *Kate and Allie* (NY). I also worked as a Writer's Assistant the first season of *Golden Girls*. I was Script Supervisor on *Charles in Charge*, *The George Lopez Show*, *The Norm Show*, *Cybil*, and *The Torkelsons*. I was a Technical Coordinator on *The Drew Carey Show* and Associate Director on *The Fresh Prince of Bel Air*.

What are your responsibilities?

As a script supervisor, I am recording and keeping track of information for the actors, director, and writers and finally on show day, for the editor. I make changes in the script—mine is always the most accurate written version of the script at any given moment. I communicate write-ins from the stage to the writers and vice versa. I mark down blocking for actors' and director's reference. I note props and continuity. On show day, I keep a marked script of takes and the material covered, number of cameras filming, word flubs or other mistakes, and record these notations in my script which is then handed over to the editor.

Did you have specific training in this field?

No. All my training was on-the-job...and through observation. I worked first in accounting, then in script processing, and finally was given the opportunity to script supervise.

How did you get your first job?

I talked the coordinating producer into letting me pay bills because it was the only job available. I explained my interest in writing and was eventually moved over to Writer's Assistant.

> SCRIPT SUPERVISORS
> Union: IATSE Local 871
> Typical Weekly Salary: $1500
> Hours Per Week: 40–54

What advice would you give someone who wants to do what you do?

Find a producer willing to give you a shot. Work in some other capacity to start, pay attention, make friends, let 'em see how smart you are, and organized and efficient and never stop expressing your interests and goals. Editors have helped me a lot. They evaluate your work very critically because your notes facilitate their work. And make friends with directors...often the choice of script supervisor is left to them.

What do you like best about your job?

Variety; every day is different. Autonomy; very seldom does anyone tell me how to do my job. Witnessing the creative process.

Chapter 4 **WEDNESDAY...**
         REHEARSAL/NETWORK RUN-THRU

In this chapter:

Wednesday is about refining! Just as a writer edits what he writes, an actor refines his performance as he rehearses. At the very least, this means learning the text and getting "off book." At its very finest, refining means honing a performance so that every moment is believable, every joke pops, and all this work looks effortless.

This seemingly effortless performance will be for the network at the end of the workday. That's why the food is better today! Everyone is trying very hard to make the network enjoy this run-thru. A tasty nibble from the **craft service**[1] table may put the suits in a better mood after a long day. It also demarcates the office from the stage. Hopefully, the stage feels more like a place to be entertained rather than a place to work. The goal is for the network executives to sit back and enjoy the show!

When the actors arrive on Wednesday, the crew has already been busy. Most of the sets and props are in place. Costumes have been bought or rented.[2] The script has undergone another revision. The actor is responsible for noting all these changes just as he did for the previous rewrite...and more!

Occasionally, Wednesday will begin with a table read if the script has changed

> **SITCOM RULE**
> *Faster is funnier.* Pace and energy cause *dramatic material to be more comedic.*

---

[1] "Craft service," usually one or two people, provides snacks and (sometimes meals) for the crew working on stage.

[2] On the groundbreaking sitcom *Soap*, Judy Evans designed and constructed much of the wardrobe for each episode.

significantly and the writers want to hear it aloud. Otherwise, everyone leaps into rehearsal. Scene by scene, the director will convey any performance notes that the producers requested after the Tuesday run-thru. Each scene will be rehearsed a number of times. The scenes with few changes will take very little time and others may take an hour or more per scene. The stand-ins are present, writing down blocking as they watch the actors rehearse. With most of the props and sets completed, everyone gets a real sense of how this episode will actually look. Repetition is the actor's friend. It not only gives the actor a chance to mold his performance, it allows the other actors to know what to expect from their fellow scene mates. It also allows the crew to know how to plan appropriately.

On many sitcoms, the level of acting expertise varies. Producer Peter Engel talks about how to get the most out of an actor. "We'd give them boundaries and stretch them within the boundaries. We never asked more of an actor than he or she could do." There is an excellent opportunity for the sitcom novice to learn from rehearsing or watching. We believe that recognizing types of jokes is the key. In the previous chapters, we looked at the construction of jokes and how they are divided into a setup and a punchline. We identified the easy-to-spot jokes that have *K* sounds or patterns of three. Now we want to look at the overall structure of a script and talk about other specific kinds of jokes common to sitcoms.

SITCOM STRUCTURE

Sitcoms classically are two-act teleplays.[3] A short scene called the **teaser** precedes the first act. This scene introduces the theme of the episode. If it appears before the opening credits to entice or tease the audience into not changing the channel and watching the entire episode, it is called a **cold open.** The networks try to get the viewing audience to continue to watch their channel without switching after the previous program ends. They sometimes make the teaser so "cold" or unanticipated that it may start immediately after the other show ends, without even a station break to separate them. The advertisers use the time after the teaser to air their first commercial break.

Next is the first act, which introduces the A and B stories. Sitcoms have usually two stories going on simultaneously. The A story is the main plot, always involving the lead character, usually introduced in the teaser. The B story is the secondary plot, often involving a secondary character, which may or may not echo the theme of the A story. The number of scenes in the first act varies from episode to episode. Some writers like the energy derived from many short scenes. Others will write three or fewer scenes per act.[4] Most scenes end with

---

[3] Very occasionally, sitcoms have three acts to allow for another commercial break.

[4] Peter Tolan's brilliant pilot script for *Style and Substance*, starring Jean Smart, actually only had two scenes in the first act. Shows with fewer (and therefore longer) scenes are more dependent on the strength of the writing and the ensemble cast for pacing and performance. *Style and Substance* had no problem filling these shoes.

a final joke called the **blow** (big joke) or **button**[5] (smaller joke). If an actor is not giving enough energy to a blow or button, he is instructed to **"punch it up."** To punch it up means to give a joke greater emphasis or to hit it harder. The blow or button must be punched up to let the audience know that the scene is over and that the story is moving on. The added energy or emphasis also helps bring out the FUNNY. Of course, going too far can kill the joke. Developing skill means knowing the difference.

The first act concludes with an **act break**: the dividing point in the story. It is usually punctuated by a twist in the plot that makes the audience want to come back after the second commercial break. It is also a moment that should be a major dilemma for the lead character and at the same time be very funny. It occurs about halfway through the show.[6] The number of scenes in the second act also varies. Writer Michael Langworthy (*Drew Carey, 8 Simple Rules*) simplifies it: "Sitcoms build to a strong act break. The dilemma gets worse in the middle of Act 2." This intensifying of the dilemma is often referred to as the **wrinkle.** Everything gets solved and the second act winds up the A and usually the B stories.

There is a third commercial break after the second act. The show concludes with the **tag**: a short, final scene before or during the end credits. Since the story has already concluded, the tag is icing or a confection. Although it may be a place to conclude the almost forgotten B story, its main purpose is to leave the audience laughing! Sometimes it has been used just to show outtakes from the filming or as a place to revisit a very funny joke that occurred during the show. For example: In "The Helmet" episode of *According to Jim* written by David Feeney, Jim (Jim Belushi) says he doesn't know what he did to deserve his wife, Cheryl (Courtney Thorne-Smith).

```
                    JIM
     The only thing I can come up with is when I was ten,
     I gave a hobo half a hot dog. I mean, I guess I've
     done other good stuff, but that's the one that
     really stands out.
```

In the tag, this incident is revisited.

```
                    TAG
FADE IN:

INT. LIVING ROOOM/FRONT DOOR - NEXT DAY (DAY 6)

(JIM, OLDER MAN)
```

---

[5] "Button" can also refer to some verbal or physical emphasis given to the end of any joke.

[6] Not counting the opening and closing credits, there is roughly about 20 minutes of actual script per episode.

SPFX: DOORBELL.

JIM CROSSES AND OPENS THE DOOR REVEALING AN OLDER, SOPHISTICATED MAN.

> JIM
> Hi.

> OLDER MAN
> Hello. You probably don't remember me, but years ago when I was down on my luck, you saw it in your heart to give a poor hobo half a hot dog.

> JIM
> Oh, my God. That was you!

> OLDER MAN
> Yes. And because of that single act of kindness I turned my life around and now stand before you a benevolent millionaire.

> JIM
> And you're here to reward me.

> OLDER MAN
> Why sir, your reward is the joy of knowing you helped a fellow human being. And no amount of money could ever—

JIM SLAMS THE DOOR AND TURNS AROUND.

> JIM
> (CALLING) Hey, Cheryl, when's dinner?

AND WE:

FADE OUT.

END OF SHOW[7]

Many experts understand the reasons why comedy makes people laugh. They range from Dr. Jonathan Miller, a comic and physician who performed with Dudley Moore and Peter Cook on English TV in the 1960s. He has actually

---

[7] Used by permission of Touchstone Television. All Rights Reserved.

lectured on the medical and brainwave functions that apply to comedy. Others may simply say, "I know it when I see it." It helps everyone working on a sitcom to have some basic understanding of how jokes work.

TWO CATEGORIES OF JOKES: PHYSICAL AND VERBAL

The specific kinds of jokes common in sitcoms can be divided into two broad categories: physical jokes and verbal jokes. Both are steeped in history. Physical jokes date back to vaudeville where performers were known for slapstick[8] routines. These silly antics took great physical discipline and timing. Verbal jokes still emulate the rhythm and style of the Borsht Belt comics that performed in the primarily Jewish resorts in the Catskills. Producer Peter Engel would say, "Take a wasp kid, teach him Jewish rhythms and you've got a star." He sites Mary Tyler Moore and Cary Grant as prime examples of people who understood this rhythm." Rob Reiner echoed the same idea to Elaine Dutka of the *Los Angles Times*: "My dad [Carl Reiner] filtered Jewish neurosis through a goyish personality with Dick Van Dyke and came up with a hybird that worked." Sitcom legend Dick Van Dyke elaborated on that when he told us, "Carl had a unique ability to pick up the cadence and personality of each actor. He immediately found Morey's [Amsterdam] and Rosey's [Rose Marie] pattern and he ended up making Rob [Van Dyke] Midwestern...all with the Jewish neuroses."

Sitcoms were one of the first forms that filled the fledgling medium of television when it began coming into thousands of households in the 1950s. TV tapped the established writers and performers of that day, who had developed their rhythms through their many live performances. After all the decades since, audiences may have no connection to the beginnings but still respond to the style. It is now the style and rhythm of the sitcom. The language and rhythm slowly evolves with every new show, but the emphasis is on "slowly." If an actor is having a particularly difficult time finding the rhythm of a sitcom line, a simple trick is to say the line aloud in a thick Yiddish accent. It will often reveal the writer's intention for the joke. Imitate the rhythms used by the late Henny Youngman in his signature phrase: "Take my wife...please." After the actor has a feel for it, it's simple to just drop the accent. Van Dyke echoed a similar idea, quoting writer Bill Persky, "Think British, write Yiddish."

> *On Home Improvement we invited a small audience of 20 regular people (usually gotten from the Universal Tour) to give the actors a feel for a live audience's reaction, and also to give them energy. It's always more fun to perform in front of real people.*
>
> Carmen Finestra, Co-creator and Executive Producer, *Home Improvement*

Rhythm is essential especially in **patter**[9] between two actors. Take this example from "Daddy's Lil' Girl" episode of the *The Hughleys* written by John D.

---

[8] Two hinged paddles were slapped together off-stage to emphasize a physical hit.

[9] Patter is glib or rapid talk used to attract attention or entertain. The word derives from praying the paternoster (The Lord's Prayer) or praying mechanically.

Beck and Ron Hart from the series *The Hughleys*, created by D. L. Hughley and Matt Wickline.

                          SALLY
          Who is Little Romeo, anyway?

                          YVONNE
          Not little. Lil'.

                          SALLY
          Little.

                          YVONNE
          Lil'.

                          SALLY
          Little.

                          YVONNE
          Lil'.

                          SALLY
          I don't really care anymore.[10]

PHYSICAL JOKES

There are many great comics and some are great physical comics.

Some physical comedy is as simple as turning your head. Here are three physical jokes that all involve turning your head. They are the **slow burn,** the **double take,** and the **spit take.** They are all a type of **sight gag.** This means you have to see it (as opposed to hear it) to get the joke. For example, in a slow burn, Character A is looking away from Character B. Character A hears Character B say something Character A doesn't like or agree with. Character A slowly turns his head until his eyes land on Character B. Think of the *Honeymooners.* Jackie Gleason, playing Ralph, would hear yet another inane comment from Art Carney, playing Norton. Ralph would slowly turn his head until his eyes landed on Norton. Norton would react appropriately—shamed or ignorant of his stupidity. Jackie Gleason was a master of the slow burn. Art Carney completed the joke with his reaction to it.

The double take and the spit take both require a quick turn of the head. With a double take, Character A is not focused on Character B. Character A turns toward Character B (for any number of reasons) and sees something that doesn't immediately register. Character A begins to turn away and go about his normal routine, then quickly whips his head back to stare at Character B. These two turns of the head constitute a double take.[11] A double take can also be done when Character B is an animate object. Imagine a character walking into his bedroom to get ready for bed. When he left the room this morning it looked normal. He walks in the door yawning, glances at the room, and then looks down as he begins to unbutton his shirt. Suddenly he registers that all the furniture is gone. His head shoots back to the room he just glanced at and stares at the empty room. He has just done a double take to the room. Surprise is key to making an audience laugh. In this example, the audience is waiting to see the character's reaction. The first part of the take shows no reaction. The quick timing of the second turn is what catches the audience.

A spit take involves…well…spitting. Similar to the two previous kinds of take, in a spit take a character is dissatisfied, unhappy, or surprised with what he sees or hears. His reaction is so violent that he spits out what he has just put in his mouth as the information registers. This works better for everyone (including the audience's sensibilities) if it involves coffee or some other liquid. Regardless, the wardrobe department must be prepared with two or more copies of the same clothing. This is called **doubling.** Spit takes are so big a reaction that they don't often find their way into sitcoms. They are much more common to sketch comedians, like the late Milton Berle.

Many sight gags are not specifically written in the script. But through script analysis, you can find opportunities to use physical business. Here is the beginning of the same episode of *The Hughleys*:

Fade in:

INT. DARRYL AND YVONNE'S BEDROOM - MORNING (DAY 1)

(DARRYL, YVONNE, SYDNEY, MICHAEL)

DARRYL IS ASLEEP. SYDNEY THROWS OPEN THE BEDROOM DOOR.

                         SYDNEY
         Dad!

DARRYL'S EYES POP OPEN.[12]

Both D. L. Hughley and Ashley Monique Clark, who played Sydney, seized their opportunities. Clark by emphatically throwing the door open and loudly screaming her line; Hughley by bolting up, not knowing what hit him.

Dick Van Dyke shared with us that occasionally the writers would just add the stage direction "Dick does what he does" and leave it to Dick's physical

---

[11] Again we site Michael Richards' physical comedy. He could make a triple take work!

[12] *The Hughleys* ©2003 Twentieth Century Fox Film Corporation. All Rights Reserved.

creativity and tenacity to invent a piece of physical business. Van Dyke told us, "I often went to the set on Saturdays to work with the props and furniture to find ways to create physical humor. Other times I would just find things at the spur of the moment. Carl Reiner saw my love for physical comedy, so Rob Petry became a klutz."

Actors worry about going "over the top" in trying to get laughs. It is all a matter of commitment to character choices and levels. Real life is not generally entertaining enough to put on television.[13] If an actor's energy is strong enough, his dialogue becomes dramatic. Amp it up a little more and it will become funny, especially if the line has sitcom construction. When you go too far, then it becomes "sketchy" or over the top.[14]

Situations can also border on going over the top. One of the more famous episodes of *The Mary Tyler Moore Show* was the Chuckles the Clown funeral. You would think that it is tough to get laughs at a funeral. However, the very tension of the event leads an audience to want to relieve this by laughing. The very last episode of *9 to 5* centered on a funeral and again there were big laughs. Actors, directors, and writers all have to walk the line to find the right level that keeps this in the arena of situation comedy and not slip into sketch comedy. A *Girlfriends* episode dealt with Jennifer Lewis falling off the wagon. Her drunken portrayal had the perfect balance needed for the necessary pathos without losing the humor.

There are plenty of other sight gags: a character walking into a door, a blender exploding, an oven billowing smoke, or a garbage disposal spitting back at you. All of these depend on the element of surprise. One of the most famous sight gags comes from the *I Love Lucy* episode[15] where Ball did a TV commercial for "Vitameatavegamin." Every time she had another spoonful, she would react accordingly to the bad taste or to the alcohol content that was rapidly affecting her. Using the element of surprise, another sight gag from that same episode was Lucy's talking head appearing in the empty TV console's "screen." The sequence ends with sparks flying and smoke billowing from a TV, another sight gag.

VERBAL JOKES

Verbal comedy tends to be more intellectual than physical comedy. It can be as simple as the use of alliteration (Lucy's "happy peppy people" or "poop out at parties"), a pun "especially if it's pun-expected," or simply funny-sounding words ("big booty"). These jokes depend on sound. Desi Arnaz would often rapidly vent his frustration with Lucy in Spanish or mispronounce a word such as "experience" as "sperience." These were sure laughs for Desi.

---

[13] So-called reality shows are carefully presented in an entertaining way. They don't resemble our lives.

[14] There was a dueling scene with umbrellas in a sitcom entitled *Over the Top* performed quite brilliantly by Tim Curry and John Ritter. Staged by Michael Lembeck, it was brilliantly funny and not "over the top."

[15] This *I Love Lucy* episode and others are available through CBS Broadcasting Inc.

One of the most common verbal jokes used on sitcoms is a **mislead,** which takes the audience in one direction with information or an idea and then surprises them by going in another direction. The point between the setup and punchline when the information goes in the other direction is called the **turn.** A turn can be accompanied by a physical turn, change of vocal pace, or change of body position. This physicalization accentuates the turn and enhances the comedy. In the "I've Got Friends I Haven't Used Yet" episode of *Becker*, Ted Danson (Becker) reunites with Kelsey Grammer who plays Becker's old friend Rick Cooper. Grammer flawlessly executes not only one but two turns within a single speech:

> BECKER
>
> Any more surprises?
>
> RICK
>
> No, no, no...oh wait a minute. There was...oh no, that wasn't you. That's it.[16]

Aided by Danson's sarcastic setup, Grammer does his first mislead with "No, no, no." He immediately does a turn on "oh wait a minute. There was...." This serves as another mislead so that Grammer can do his second turn on "oh no, that wasn't you...." He then punctuates it with "That's it." Watch these skilled professionals. Their light, yet skilled, touch with comedy is a joy to behold.

Another popular joke in a sitcom is a **callback**[17], which is a reference to previously mentioned material or piece of business. Sometimes whole jokes are repeated. Sometimes a specific word or piece of business is repeated. Every time Lucille Ball had another taste of the "Vitameatavegamin," either by spoon of swig from the bottle, it was a callback. Callbacks give the audience a chance to enjoy a joke again. Sometimes they occur within the same scene, sometimes in a later scene. The key for a callback that occurs in a later scene is that the first time the information is mentioned, it must be big enough to be memorable. The following example is from the episode "Invasion of the Gold Digger," written by Keith Josef Adkins from the series *Girlfriends*, created by Mara Brock Akil. The girls are trying to come up with a plan to get even with William's (Reggie Hayes) gold digger girlfriend Monica (Keesha Sharp). After Joan (Tracee Ellis Ross) suggests that they need to get rid of her, Lynn (Persia White) suggests her idea for doing away with Monica.

> LYNN
>
> "Officer, I don't know how that radio fell in the hot tub."

---

[16] From the episode "I Have Friends I Haven't Used Yet," written by Ian Gurvitz, from the series *Becker*, created by Dave Hackel. Paramount Pictures Corporation. All rights reserved.

[17] This is different from the callback an actor gets after an audition.

White not only gets her laugh on this joke but memorably sets up a callback for the tag where Monica is in the hot tub sitting across from Lynn. Monica wears an eye mask so she can't see Lynn's hand inching toward the radio. The show ends with another huge laugh as Monica reminds Lynn.

                    MONICA
    (WITHOUT REMOVING THE MASK) Lynn, you're in the hot
    tub, too.

ON LYNN'S "DAMN SHE'S RIGHT" LOOK, WE:

                                    FADE OUT[18]

Here is another example of a callback from "The Helmet" episode written by David Feeney from the series *According to Jim* where Cheryl (Courtney Thorne-Smith) and Dana (Kimberly Williams) are discussing an Internet auction where Cheryl is posing as a man:

ACT ONE

SCENE C

INT. KITCHEN - DAYS LATER (DAY 3)

(CHERYL, DANA)

CHERYL SITS AT THE COMPUTER. <u>DANA ENTERS</u> AND READS THE SCREEN. THEY AD-LIB HELLOS.

                    DANA
    (READING) "I hear that, my man. You marry them right
    away they try to change you." (TO CHERYL) You're
    still writing SPIFFYTOOL405?

                    CHERYL
    Yeah. That helmet's as good as mine. Men are so
    stupid.

                    DANA
    So you guys are becoming friends.

                    CHERYL
    How could we not? We both could stand to lose a

CHERYL (cont'd)

little weight, we've both been thrown out of Bulls
games for mooning the ref, and our favorite beer is
"the next one."

DANA

You're not going to go out cruising chicks together
are you?

CHERYL

It's fascinating being a guy. He tells me stuff he'd
never tell his wife.

DANA

Like what?

CHERYL

Get this...he buys sports stuff off the Internet and
hides it from her in a tool cabinet in his garage.

DANA

That poor woman.

CHERYL

Please, she's a sap. You can't feel sorry for women
like that, Dana. They bring it on themselves. (OFF
WATCH) Oh, it's twelve-thirty. I gotta go meet Jim.
(THEN TYPING AND READING) "Well, the ol' ball and
chain is calling. Nag nag nag."

DANA

Hey, tell him an off color joke. Guys love those.

CHERYL

I don't know any.

DANA GRABS THE COMPUTER AND PULLS IT IN FRONT OF HER. SHE STARTS
TO TYPE.

DANA

You don't know any? You're married to an off-color
joke. Check this out. It's about a sailor and a parrot
who meet the Pope. I heard it at a gas station.

CHERYL LOOKS AT IT, THEN CHUCKLES.

> CHERYL
>
> I get it. The parrot's Jewish.

> DANA
>
> What? No.

> CHERYL
>
> Oh. I don't get it then.

AND WE:

CUT TO:

The Jewish parrot returns at the act break:

> JIM (O.S.)
>
> Hey, Cheryl, I heard a great joke today about a sailor and a parrot meeting the Pope.

CHERYL REACTS AS <u>JIM ENTERS,</u> PUTTING ON HIS JACKET.

> JIM (cont'd)
>
> Wanna hear it?

> CHERYL
>
> Oh, un...no. I've already heard that one.

> JIM
>
> Oh.

AS THEY HEAD OUT.

> JIM (cont'd)
>
> The parrot's Jewish, right?

FADE OUT:

<u>END OF ACT ONE</u>[19]

An exact and immediate callback is called an **echo.** Mocking someone is an echo. Jane Leeves, of *Fraiser* fame, got great mileage from her English accent in an earlier series *Throb.* While discussing an automobile with Diana Canova, Jane simply repeated the word "car" in Diana's American accent and got a big

---

[19]

laugh. Like a callback, when a writer uses an echo, he has to be sure the audience has registered the information the first time that information is mentioned. The echo may be in the same scene or many scenes later on in the script. If the audience doesn't remember it, in either case, we say, "The callback is too far away."

The previously sited episode of *Girlfriends* begins with this echo:

> WILLIAM
> Joan, guess who got the Thatcher-Dunwoody case?
> Three hints. He's tall. He's devilishly handsome.
> And he's not you.

> JOAN
> William, every junior partner in the firm has been
> fiending for that case. How did you get it?

> WILLIAM
> I told you. I'm tall. I'm devilishly handsome and
> most importantly, I'm not you.[20]

In this case, Hayes echoed himself.

Writers often employ **irony** in sitcoms. An example that *Webster's New World Dictionary* gives to illustrate irony is "calling a stupid man 'clever'" or saying that "the firehouse burned." These jokes are usually very straightforward and depend on the audience's intelligence. Punching these kinds of jokes is not advised. Irony is very specific because the meaning of the words used is the opposite of their usual sense. *Fraiser* is known for its "smart humor" in the way it uses irony. Literary reference, the use of alliteration, or personification in constructing the language of jokes adds to this style. In the hot tub, Keesha Sharp accentuated the comedy accentuating the alliteration and using the *T*s in "hot tub too."

The two final types of jokes we'll discuss are the **understatement** and the **twist.** Understatement employs irony. It deliberately states the truth inaccurately or too weakly in order to make the audience laugh. Most jokes that are understatements are accompanied by the **subtext** "Duh!" Subtext[21] is what an actor is thinking while he says the line. It is his silent or hidden message. Subtext is an important tool for an actor not only when understating something but also whenever a character is thinking something different from, or more complex than, what his actual words (or lack of words) allow him to say. A **dichotomy** is another literary tool employed, as part of an understatement, to evoke humor. It divides an idea into separate classes, thereby bringing out

---

[20] From the episode "Invasion of the Gold Digger," written by Keith Josef Adkins from the series *Girlfriends,* created by Mara Brock Akil. Paramount Pictures Corporation. All Rights Reserved.

[21] Sub meaning "under" and text meaning "wording." Duh!

the funny in the comparison. These jokes are usually delivered very straight-forward and depend on the audience's intelligence. Punching these kinds of jokes is also not advised.

Many jokes are entirely based in character, for example, insults. An insult is based on information that one character feels about another. A running joke on *The Hughleys* was to see which ethnic or social group Darryl could insult that week. Over the course of four seasons, he insulted gays, the physically challenged, Little People, Republicans, Democrats, Asians, Hispanics, and many more. Every time he got a laugh!

Since much of comedy is based in insult humor, much care needs to be taken in assuring that the joke-tellers are still likeable. An audience will not laugh at real pain. They have to know that everyone will be all right. It is a hard line to walk at times. Insult standup comics, like Don Rickles, have always used phrases like "I kid" throughout their performances. Dabney Coleman (*9 to 5*, *Buffalo Bill*), Ted Knight (*Mary Tyler Moore Show*, *Too Close for Comfort*), and Ed Asner (*Mary Tyler Moore Show*, *Lou Grant*) were always actors that could play the part of the curmudgeon but still be likeable. Every writer, producer, director, and actor tries to create characters that the audience will care about. Even main-character villains must have human qualities that can be understood, so that they are somehow sympathetic. It is much more critical with comedy.

Some jokes are word-based like a pun or play on words. Other jokes build on a previous punchline. This is called a **topper**. If the topper is not funnier than the original joke, it is not worth doing.

Some jokes are based in story such as a **twist** or a surprise. It usually is an unexpected plot point. It is much the same as a turn, but not in the classic sense. Turns must have an immediate setup. Twists often do not. The following twist, a play on words, was delivered by Elise Neal on an episode of *The Hughleys*.

> YVONNE
> I know. I heard your version of "The old woman who lived in a show, who only had two children because a career is important too."[22]

Twists sometimes merely steer the story in another direction. When Bret Butler's character, Grace, in *Grace under Fire* saw her father-in-law in a bar during one episode, it got a small reaction. When Grace and the audience realized that it was a gay bar, the laugh was big. Classic act break material!

---

[22] *The Hughleys* ©2001 Twentieth Century Fox Film Corporation. All Rights Reserved.

Sitcom Exercise

Read these scenes and find the jokes. Next, identify the type of joke it is (turn, run of three, K sound, call back, echo, understatement, twist, pun, etc.). Here are two scenes. The first from the Home Improvement *pilot based on the stand-up comedy of Tim Allen. Wilson was played in the series by Earl Hindman.*

HOME IMPROVEMENT

"PILOT"

ACT TWO

SCENE 2

EXT. BACKYARD-DUSK (DAY 2)

SPFX: BARBEQUE SMOKE FROM WILSON'S YARD

(WE SEE WILSON BARBEQUING. TIM SEARCHES FOR THE DISHWASHER PARTS)

> TIM

What a mess.

> WILSON

Hi, ya, Tim.

> TIM

Hi Wilson. Mmm. Smell good. What are you cooking?
Baby back ribs?

> WILSON

Squirrel.

> TIM

Squirrel. What's that taste like?

> WILSON

Sort of like chipmunk. By the way, a couple of those
bolts landed in the birdbath.

> TIM

I was a little surprised by the torque on that
compressor.

> WILSON

I tell you, Tim, this is what it's all about. Catch
of the day cooking, sun setting, men standing around
the campfire telling stories.

                    TIM
Can I tell you one?

                    WILSON
Campfire's lit, good neighbor.

                    TIM
Jill didn't get the job she wanted. I tell her not
to feel bad and she gets angry at me.

                    WILSON
Hmm.

                    TIM
And then I tell her what to do, she gets all bent
out of shape and storms out of the room.

                    WILSON
Sounds like you were having an asymmetrical
conversation.

                    TIM
Asymmetrical. How do you spell that?

                    WILSON
Let's just say one-sided.

(TIM DOES A KNOWING GRUNT)
                    WILSON (CONT'D)
You see, Tim, by nature, men are problem solvers.
But Jill didn't want you to solve her problem.

                    TIM
She didn't?

                    WILSON
No. She just wanted you to listen while she shared
her feelings.

                    TIM
Just stand there and listen? That's like doing
nothing.

                    WILSON
Sometimes the best thing you can do is nothing.

(TIM DOES AN UNDESTANDING GRUNT)
                    TIM
I get it. Jill got mad at me because I didn't listen
to her.

                    WILSON
No, she got mad at you because you blew up the damn
dishwasher.[23]

Here is another scene from the Style and Substance *pilot. The character of Mr.*
John was played by Joseph Maher. Trudy was Linda Kash.

                STYLE AND SUBSTANCE
                    "PILOT"
                    ACT ONE
                      (A)

FADE IN:

INT. OUTER LOBBY - MORNING (D-1)

(Jane)

CAMERA STARTS IN CLOSE ON A BEAUTIFUL FLORAL ARRANGEMENT ON A
TABLE IN THE OUTER LOBBY (THE SHOW TITLE WILL BE SEEN HERE).
CAMERA PANS UP AND WE SEE THE SIGN ON THE WALL: "CHELSEA STEVENS,
A DIVISION OF FERBER COMMUNICATIONS." WE FIND JANE TALKING ON HER
CELLULAR PHONE.

                    JANE
Everything's under control, Mr. Ferber. You sent me
to run things here, that's what I'm doing. No,
Chelsea hasn't signed the budget agreement yet. Yes,
I did promise I'd have that signed by the end of my
first week. Yes, that would be tomorrow. Yes, I'm
aware I'm saying yes a lot. Yes. Mr. Ferber, I've

---

[23] From the pilot episode of *Home Improvement*, created by Matt Williams, David McFadzean, and
Carmen Finestra. Used by permission of Touchstone Television. All Rights Reserved.

                    JANE (cont'd)
just had a little trouble pinning Chelsea down, but I
will pin her. Consider her pinned. Yes. Thank you sir.

JANE CLICKS OFF, GROWLS AND EXITS INTO THE OFFICES.

INT. PRODUCTION OFFICES - CONTINUOUS (D-1)

(Chelsea, Jane, Trudy, Mr. John, Terry, Office Extras)

JANE ENTERS AND CROSSES OVER TO WHERE TRUDY IS MAKING HERSELF A
CUP OF COFFEE.

                    JANE
Hi, Trudy. Have you seen Chelsea?

                    TRUDY
Not yet. She hasn't signed your budget thing, huh?

                    JANE
I'm getting desperate.

                    TRUDY
Jane, let me give you some advice. When you deal
with Chelsea, you always, always have to remember
one important thing.

                    JANE
What's that?

                    TRUDY
She's a freak.

                    JANE
She's not a freak.

                    TRUDY
Oh, yes, she is. Last Christmas, she made a
gingerbread house? It was built to code. There was a
guest gingerbread house in the back.

                    JANE
Okay, she's a little obsessive, but she's built a

JANE (cont'd)
very successful business. The magazine, the
television show...

TRUDY
It's a great big freakdom.

JANE
Then why are you here?

TRUDY
Because I'm the best food stylist in the world and
Chelsea knows it.

TRUDY OPENS HER PORTFOLIO AND FLIPS THROUGH IT.

TRUDY (cont'd)
My award-winning chocolate sundae.

JANE
That ice cream looks delicious.

TRUDY
Thank you. It's lard. I can recreate any dish for
photographic purposes. I use whatever it takes. That
chocolate sauce?

JANE
It looks good.

TRUDY
Quaker State motor oil. That's thirty weight, if
memory serves. (TURNING THE PAGE) This is my
fettuccine alfredo.

JANE
The noodles look real.

TRUDY
Oh, they are.

JANE
How about the sauce?

TRUDY

Sears Weatherbeater house paint. And that's one coat, Jane.

MR. JOHN CROSSES OVER. HE'S A DAPPER MAN IN HIS FIFTIES.

TRUDY (cont'd)

Perhaps we should ask Mr. John.

MR. JOHN

Ask me what?

TRUDY

Do you think Chelsea's a freak?

MR. JOHN

No, I don't. I've been designing for Chelsea Stevens for ten wonderful years, and I believe her to be the apotheosis of taste and style.

TRUDY

She's not in yet.

MR. JOHN

She's a freak. (TO TRUDY) Let's tell her about the gingerbread house.

TRUDY

I already did.

MR. JOHN

(TO JANE) It had plumbing. Guy and I still talk about it.

JANE

Guy?

MR. JOHN

My life partner. I'm sorry if my frankness shocks you, Jane, but I'm proud of my relationship and I don't hide the fact.

JANE

I'm fine.

                    MR. JOHN
Well. I know you've come from the Midwest...so if I
do say anything that makes you uncomfortable, I hope
you'll speak up.

                    JANE
It's not a problem. I am an adult.

                    MR. JOHN
Thank you, Jane. It's like I was saying to Guy
in the shower this morning as we were lathering
up...

                    JANE
Oh, dear.

                    MR. JOHN
Too much?

CHELSEA STEVENS, THE JUGGERNAUT OF STYLE AND TASTE, ENTERS FROM
THE OUTER LOBBY. SHE CARRIES A SMALL WICKER BASKET COVERED WITH A
RED-CHECKERED NAPKIN.

                    CHELSEA
Good morning, everyone!

STAFFERS ADLIB GREETINGS.

                    CHELSEA (cont'd)
This morning before breakfast while I was restocking
my trout pond and shearing my lamb, I realized
I wanted to tell you all how much I appreciate the
hard work you do. But then later, while I was
airing out my quilts and making prosciutto jerky,
I reminded myself that we can always work harder.
I guess what I'm trying to say is...be more like
me. And one more thing. In the magazine, on the
show...no more kiwi. Kiwi is over. If I could talk
to a kiwi, do you know what I'd say? I'd say "Get
out, get a shave, you're through." No kiwi. Let's
all say it.

                    ALL
No kiwi.

                          CHELSEA
Thank you. And the big news. My divorce becomes final
today, so I think we all know what that means.

A BEAT, THEN SHE PUTS THE BASKET ON THE TABLE.

                          CHELSEA (cont'd)
That's right. I made scones!

CHELSEA DISAPPEARS INTO HER OFFICE.

                          MR. JOHN
She seems down today.[24]

PLAYING A JOKE

Recognizing a joke and playing a joke are two different skills. Many an actor is born with an innate sense of comedy. He may be able to deliver any of the jokes we mentioned above without being able to identify them. He may simply feel them. He may be funny without knowing why he's funny. Some actors feel that overanalyzing may trip them up in performing because they begin to "over-think" the material. A person, who has an analytical approach to comedy but without the mastery of how to perform it, may be better suited to writing or directing than to acting. Our advice is to go with whatever works for you. Actor/director/playwright Carlos Lacamara (*Brothers Garcia*) advises:

> Keep it real. We've all seen examples of big, wacky acting on sit-coms, but the best actors keep their performances honest. Create your character and be true to it. Forget about being funny. One of the easiest traps to fall into is trying to repeat a laugh. If you get a laugh in a rehearsal, then you imitate your line reading to get that laugh again, you often get rewarded with silence. Forget about the laugh. Be true to the character and the teleplay. Listen and react. The laugh will take care of itself. And bring a sweater. Those stages are cold.

We think Lacamara's advice is good…for SOME actors. If being conscious of the comedic requirements takes you out of the scene, you won't get laughs. We're not trying to confuse you. Sitcom acting requires a light touch. You must understand the inherent rhythm, feel the timing, and hear the music of the words but not punch them too hard. If the audience sees the joke coming a mile away, you have lost the element of surprise, which is what causes their laughter. Find the level that works for you. For example, jokes that have funny words, alliteration, or *K*s and *P*s play themselves.

---

[24] Used by permission of Touchstone Television. All Rights Reserved.

TRAPS TO AVOID

It is easy to fall into some traps. Lacamara pointed out the most fatal one: repeating. EVERYTIME AN ACTOR SAYS HIS WORDS, IT SHOULD HAVE THE ILLUSION OF THE FIRST TIME. Be present! Listen! Good actors know that this means staying in the moment. Watch Ted Danson, Michael J. Fox, Kelsey Grammer, Mary Tyler Moore. They are brilliant comic actors with huge bodies of work that can teach you volumes.

Other traps are specific to comedy because comedy uses the element of surprise. The first trap is called **tipping the joke.** Tipping the joke is giving away prematurely what is about to come. It's also called **telegraphing** or **giving it away.** Actors often tip the joke by laughing before the punchline or reacting to a line before replying to the line. This robs the audience of the surprise, which the punchline will reveal. This may seem like you're robbing the character of his natural reaction. We suggest building into the character that he hears the information but waits to reveal his feelings with dialogue. Let the line be funny. The writer will appreciate it! That being said, there are exceptions to this. Sometimes the simple reaction that occurs when an actor is listening is funnier than the line that the writer wrote.

So many jokes are character based. Lacamara mentions creating a character and being true to it. Most sitcoms have characters whose jokes are based on the same premise. For example, on *Cheers*, Nicholas Colasanto created the Coach character who always misunderstood information. Woody Harrelson's character trait of naïveté, worked the same way when he replaced Colasanto after his untimely passing. Choose well when creating a character. Know what will best serve the comedy.

In Chapter 1 we talked about the SITCOM rule **COMEDY COMES IN THREES.** To play a joke that is a run, the secret is to not telegraph that the joke is coming. List the first two items and then make sure they hear the third because that's the funny part.

Another comedy trap is leaving too much air between lines. The SITCOM rule at the beginning of this chapter states that **FASTER IS FUNNIER.** An easy way to keep the pacing fast is to **cue bite** or take out the pauses between the lines. It is also called **picking up the cues** or **dovetailing** the lines. The only time an actor shouldn't cue bite is after a punchline, when he should be holding for a laugh. After two days of learning staging and memorizing cues and lines, it is easy to forget that this stuff is funny. The goal is to pace up and energize the dialogue but stop to wait for the laughs.

THE DIFFERENCE BETWEEN TUESDAY AND WEDNESDAY

The Wednesday rehearsal will be different from the Tuesday rehearsal; It will probably be more fun because more things are working. This is due to the writers' pinpointing places in the script where they could help with the writing. Another factor is the actors and director are now more familiar with the material as they incorporate the changes and refinements. If a particular scene is still proving problematic, the director might ask the showrunner to come to the set. The problem scene or section will be shown to the writer. Writing changes may be done on the spot[25] or the writer may go back to his office and send down new pages as soon as the rewriting is done.

Every cast has a different relationship with the writers. Some are adversarial, some are collaborative. Writer Michael Kaplan (*Girlfriends*) says, "All too often, scripts are changed and not always for the better." Director James Burrows (*Cheers, News Radio, Will & Grace*) suggests that the most important function a director has is to break down the barriers between actors and writers. On shows where an actor holds a writing title or executive producer title, that actor may be more vocal about rewrites. The ultimate goal is to create the best show possible. Ideally, this is done within a respectful, creative environment.

Many sitcom casts do a **speed-thru** of the lines before the run-thru begins or before a scene begins. In a speed-thru, an actor recites his dialogue at a quicker speed than normal (sometimes devoid of meaning). This serves two purposes. First, it refreshes and reviews the dialogue (especially if there have been changes) and it lets the actors discover that simply saying a line faster enhances the comedy.

On that last funeral episode of *9 to 5*, executive producer Michael Kagan was cast[26] as a minister and for the first time joined the actors in rehearsals. Just before a run-thru, the cast wanted to play a gag on him by telling him that they always do a speed-thru at that time. They then proceeded to run the lines at a speed that was so lightning-fast that Michael had trouble just keeping up. After a good laugh, everyone realized that the one thing that the show had been missing was extra pace. The run-thru and the show played much better, when they split the difference between how they had been doing the lines and the newfound energy. Let us repeat once more **FASTER IS FUNNIER!**

THE NETWORK RUN-THRU

Besides pacing the show, an actor must also pace himself. The goal for Wednesday is doing an excellent network run-thru. The suits are the buyers of our product. Whether an actor is in every scene or just one, he must time his day so that his energy is peaking for this performance. For some actors this means "saving it" for run-thru. For others, it means attacking every scene at performance level all day so they can see what that feels like. Most casts will get a short break before run-thru. This is a good time for an actor to close his eyes and regroup or focus. Another actor may have that afternoon tea or coffee to bolster his energy. Others may seek out the script supervisor or dialogue coach to run lines. Another actor may find that visiting[27] with producers or studio and network people, who are arriving for the run-thru, clears his mind for a good performance.

---

[27] Better known as "kissing ass."

[25] The script supervisor will be noting all the changes made.

[26] Michael must have liked acting so much that he now acts full time.

This break between rehearsal and run-thru is when the rest of the crew is getting ready for the run-thru. The on-set crew is doing everything possible to make the run-thru flow as smoothly as possible. The on-set crews are the people who are there to support the daily rehearsals. It includes the assistant directors, or stage managers, the script supervisor, the onstage prop person, the onstage decorator, and the dialogue coach. The rest of the department heads are winding up whatever they're doing so they can attend the run-thru.

The network run-thru begins the moment the last network executive arrives. The AD or stage manager quiets everyone down. Some people will be standing; some people will be sitting in chairs right in front of the set. Crew members will either be "on the floor" or in the audience bleachers. Someone from the lighting crew will usually bring up basic show lights[28] in each of the sets as they are used. This is different! All week we have been using fluorescent work lights.

The script supervisor will be timing the scene in order to answer the first question that usually is asked after run-thru: "How long are we?" The lighting director is noting what areas of the set are specifically being used. As soon as run-thru is over, his crew led by the **gaffer**[29] will do the **hanging** of extra lighting instruments in those areas noted for this episode.

In order to facilitate a smooth run-thru, actors must anticipate where they need to be. The show is run in order from top to bottom so there are no surprises. While the network execs on the soundstage floor are walking to the next set and stagehands move their chairs, the prop master is distributing hand props and doing last-minute adjustments for the next scene. The AD or stage manager is reviewing his or her checklist to see that everyone is in place for their first entrance to the next scene. Actors, DON'T make the AD or stage manager have to look for you! Delays in the run-thru, due to anyone not being ready, is unacceptable. It ruins the flow of the show for everyone.

After the run-thru, the showrunner meets with the network and studio executives to get notes. Their opinions count. Usually the rest of the writing staff returns to the writers' room and begins work on the obvious fixes. The set crew immediately gets to work on finishing the set. After notes, the actors sign out and get their call times for the next day. There may be some preshooting done on Thursday. The actors and the crew will be told Thursday's schedule, which scenes will be camera blocked, and which scenes will be preshot.

With luck, the note session with the network will be brief. If their notes from Monday have been addressed, they may have a few additional requests, praise the work that has been done thus far, and leave. That is the best-case scenario. The worst-case scenario may involve a massive rewrite or recasting a guest star. Yes, this means someone may get FIRED!

---

[28] Show lights are instruments hung especially to light the set as opposed to general fluorescent lighting that exists in the soundstage for everyday use. Show lights are hotter and more concentrated.

[29] The gaffer is in charge of hanging and focusing the lighting instruments. He is an expert electrician.

GETTING FIRED, NO, WAIT, NOT GETTING FIRED

Getting fired is the actor's worst nightmare.[30] It happens often enough on sitcoms that actors live in fear until they get their new script on Wednesday night and check to see that their name is still there. In our experience, there are two main reasons for getting fired: miscasting and not being very good. Miscasting is NEVER the fault of the actor. In fact, an actor that gets miscast must have been pretty darn good to get the part in the first place.

Not being very good is trickier. It doesn't necessarily mean the actor is a bad actor. It just means that something isn't clicking. Maybe the actor can't handle the constant and sometimes on-the-spot rewriting that goes on in a sitcom. Another actor may simply not be funny. To be able to apply funny rhythms and rules and still be naturalistic in a scene is a special acting gift. Not everyone has that gift. Some less than funny actors have had the luxury of learning their craft on the job. If you watch their shows in syndication, you can tell the early episodes from the later ones by their comedic improvement. Remember, dying is easy, comedy is hard! The important thing is for an actor not to let getting fired destroy his confidence. With this major disappointment is also an upside. An actor that gets fired still gets paid!

If a massive rewrite is required, then all the writers go to the writers' room, order dinner[31] and get to work. Scripts will be delivered as soon as they have been rewritten, proofed, and copied. This probably won't happen until after dark. This is the job of the night runner Production Assistant who comes in after the normal workday. His duties include copying and labeling the scripts for delivery. Actors should leave a light on for the PA delivering the script because he might not arrive until the middle of the night. The PA will not ring your doorbell unless he or she knows you have requested that he do so. Actors should get a good night's sleep, especially if they are going to be preshooting.

Sitcom Vocabulary Quick Review

Read these sentences. If the director gave you these notes, would you instantly know what he meant? If not, go back and review the explanation in this chapter.

*We need a **blow** for the **act break**.*

*Replace the **button**.*

*The **callback** is too far from the setup.*

*Let's start with the **cold open**.*

*Keep it down at **craft service!***

*If we **cue bite**, we could knock a minute off the show.*

---

[30] Not remembering lines is traditionally the actors' most common nightmare.

[31] One of the perks of writing sitcoms is that you are well fed and do not have to pay for it.

That's the **dichotomy,** the character doesn't get it either.

The **double take** is too big for this show.

We'll be **doubling** the shirt but not the pants.

Dovetail those two lines.

It's an **echo,** so make it sound like the first one!

Is the **gaffer** done **hanging?**

Don't **give it away!**

It's not funny if they don't understand the **irony.**

The **mislead** has to be more sincere.

Make sure you are **off book** for the run-thru.

Pace up the **patter** in that section.

Pick up the cues!

Say it as written; the writers will **punch it up.**

Save the **sight gag** for the second take.

The **slow burn** can go a little faster.

We'll do a **speed-thru** before each scene.

Don't do the **spit take** until we're shooting.

We have to rethink her **subtext.**

We'll rehearse the **tag** just before run-thru.

The **teaser** is running too long.

You're **telegraphing** the joke.

The smile is **tipping** the blow.

Did you notice, they give your character a **topper** for everything he says?

Can you turn as you do the **turn?**

That's a great **twist!**

The humor will come from the **understatement.**

The **wrinkle** made the audience gasp.

Sitcom Insider

MY WRITERS' ROOM

A good writing room is about collaboration. A bad writing room is about competition. The worst thing that can happen in a writers' room is for someone to offer an idea and someone else to shoot it down with "that sucks." Cruelty and bad manners aside, ridiculing an idea only makes the room grind to a halt.

Also, the person who offered the idea won't be heard from again for a long time. People who curtly dismiss others may claim they don't have time to listen to bad ideas, but I maintain there are no bad ideas. Any producer who runs a successful writers' room knows that the end product (whether it's a story, a line, or a joke) often comes from an idea that's 180 degrees opposite it.

By encouraging all ideas, you give writers the freedom to build on what each person says. In the best writing rooms, a good joke is like building a house. Once it's standing, no one cares who put in which nail and board. Everyone just enjoys living in it, and feels good they had a part in building it.

Matt Williams, my co-creator on Home Improvement *(along with Dave McFadzean) says, "There are infinite possibilities with the word 'yes,' and very limiting ones with the word 'no'."*

Here are some tips for writers' room etiquette:

1. *Be on time. If someone says, "Let's take a 10 minute break," be back in 10 minutes. Nothing is more draining than sitting around waiting for someone else. It also establishes a bad precedent. "He said 10 minutes, but he probably means 20." Soon you're wasting time trying to corral everyone.*

2. *Don't veer off the track. I've seen writers' rooms waste hours as people discuss "the trades," movies, or TV they've seen, etc! Good producers nip these diversions in the bud. People may hate to write, but they'll hate it more if they're doing it at midnight. Also in bad writing rooms, people waste time criticizing the actors for ruining the jokes. (Bad writers don't know that actors can't play jokes, they can only play emotion and motivation. If you write that well, it will be funny.) Writers also waste time talking about "what idiots" they feel are running the studios and networks, and not giving them a chance to shine.*

3. *If you disagree with an idea, don't dismiss it, but instead offer an alternative. Say something positive like, "That could work, but I was thinking…" or, "That's one way to go, but another way is…." Whenever you hear an idea you like, always, always, always acknowledge it, and compliment the person who said it. If you honestly can't think of an alternative to an idea you don't like, simply say you're not sure. Ask everyone else what they think. If it's a good writers' room, constructive criticism will be offered, or an alternative you can use.*

4. *Last, but not least, when ordering a meal in, stay away from heavy food. Your eyes will be drooping, and you'll be no help to anyone.*

Carmen Finestra,
Co-creator and Executive Producer, *Home Improvement*

Sitcom Career Profile

BRUCE FINN
DIRECTOR OF PHOTOGRAPHY

Bruce is a gregarious, focused, hardworking, and creative guy. We first met him working on the Hughleys. He not only designed but was published, and had developed innovative lighting equipment known as the Gambox, Topbox, and Maxilight. Bruce always does more than you ask. It's very clear he loves what he's doing.

What shows have you worked on?

My last few show include *8 Simple Rules for Dating My Teenage Daughter, The Hughleys, One on One, Style and Substance,* and *Leap of Faith.*

What are your responsibilities?

I design the lighting and supervise the electricians and grips during prelighting and shooting to achieve the best possible photographic look.

DIRECTORS OF PHOTOGRAPHY
Union: IATSE Local 600
Typical Weekly Salary: $3500–$5000
Hours Per Week: 31

Did you have specific training in this field?

I was interested in photography from an early age. I studied at Antioch College and after dropping out struggled my way up the ladder starting as an intern. I always try to excel at whatever task I'm asked to perform, no matter how basic. I was a great PA. I made the best coffee!

How did you get your first job?

Michael Petok (a wonderful producer and person) vouched for me after working on single-camera projects together.

What advice would you give someone who wants to do what you do?

Befriend and call huge volumes of business-potential clients. Persevere and shoot as much as possible. Develop your own style; learn from other's talents and flaws. Develop a positive attitude. Be helpful to others. Try to make every person on the set think you're happy, reasonable, responsible, hardworking, and a talented co-worker.

What do you like best about your job?

Performing my art and craft. Inventing and manufacturing innovative equipment that improves the selection of good tools cinematographers have to work with. Making money to support my family.

Chapter 5 THURSDAY…CAMERA BLOCKING

In this chapter:

What happens on stage before an actor arrives

The steps in camera blocking

Camera tips for actors

The importance of the stand-in

Why Lucy and Desi were trailblazers

Recording on film, tape, and 24P

The responsibilities of a camera operator

Career profile of a sitcom technical coordinator/associate director

Sometimes things must get worse before they get better. Thursday is the day that happens. After 3 days of refining both the writing and the performances, now things may seem a bit chaotic as we add the recording elements (cameras and sound) that make it a TV show. Lots of people have lots of questions or simply must talk aloud to do their job at the same time an actor is performing. *Home Improvement*'s Carmen Finestra describes Thursday:

> The camera persons and the regular crew work with the director and actors to "camera block" the entire show. This requires a lot of work. There may be hundreds of camera shots to block and rehearse and the actors are pretty fried by the end of the day.

This phenomenon of the stage show getting worse is also common in the theatre. After weeks of just rehearsing the play, performances always suffer during "tech" when lighting and sound cues are added. In television, the challenges grow exponentially because of the myriad decisions involved in filming or taping with multiple cameras and microphones. However, with a great crew and a *lot* of cooperation, the work gets accomplished.

BEFORE REHEARSAL

As the actors arrive at their call time, there are many more people from the technical crew already on stage. They are setting up

SITCOM RULE

Say the line, then move. Movement distracts from the important material. It causes the camera to widen, further distancing the viewer from the information.

cameras and microphones often referred to, on a tape set, as **ESU**[1] or engineering setup. The art department is finishing some paint details and adding more artificial and potted greenery to the set. Additional wardrobe personnel are bringing clothing into some on-stage dressing rooms that have been constructed using plain black flats booked together behind one of the sets. The makeup room has been opened, waiting for makeup artists for any preshoots that will be done later that day.

Everyone seems to know each other and a guest actor may feel like a stranger in this extended family. The regular cast and crew are catching up with the technical crew on details of their week. You, as a guest, are left out. Everyone needs to study the newest edition of the script and see what changes have been made. Few rewrites for this show will be done on Thursday. Nancylee Myatt describes the writers' room today: "Most of the time you'll be worrying about what you'll be eating for lunch or dinner—then after that is settled you'll spend a little time cutting the script for time and trying to replace jokes that were funny on Monday and now on Thursday aren't making you laugh anymore." All glibness aside, the writers are probably taking a pass at next week's episode in between all that eating. No matter what your job category, for questions about substantial script changes, you should quickly seek out the director. The day is already jammed full so there is no time set aside for reblocking or reworking anything new.

DRY BLOCKING

When the stage is ready, guest actors might[2] finally be introduced to the tech crew. The director or AD will announce your name, or maybe only your character's name, to everyone. This is what the crew has been getting ready for. The camera department has prepped their cameras. The lighting crew is standing by to adjust levels. The audio team is setting up their microphones either on giant stands called **booms** or on the catwalk above.

Long-time boom operator Ed Valfre talks about camera-blocking day from the sound department's point of view:

> By the day the actors are in front of the cameras, the sound department should have been notified of any unusual situations from sound effects and music playbacks to placement of an actor delivering dialogue in places that no microphone will go. In general, this notification is rare but it does give the job that fly-by-the-seat-of-your-pants kind of excitement.

Dry blocking begins with the crew watching the actors perform one scene at a time for its visual and audio content. The crew needs to see where the actors

---

[1]   Seeing ESU on the schedule for Thursday and Friday is usually a clue that the show is to be taped and not filmed.

[2]   Some shows (or stars) are better hosts than others!

move and listen to what the actors say. The first scene to be blocked is not necessarily the teaser. Like every other day this week, the order of scene rehearsal
is determined by many factors such as the star's and children's availabilities.
One more scheduling factor is added on this day: the time it takes the cameras
and booms to be positioned in front of each set. This makes it efficient to block
every scene that takes place on one set before the crew moves the cameras and
booms on to another.

SOME BACKGROUND

This is a good time to talk about the different kinds of recording mediums and
what they mean to your process. One view is that no matter how the images
are recorded, they all end up being displayed on the TV screen in people's
homes, so they all look like TV. Getting from the stage to the television screen
in your home has taken many different routes. Sitcoms were one of the types
of programs on early live television. Radio had these kinds of shows starting in
1929 with *The Goldbergs*, and it was only natural for the form to make the jump
to TV. In fact, *The Goldbergs* was the fourth sitcom to premiere on TV. The first
sitcoms, like all other live shows, were displays of 30[3] frames per second of
black-and-white electronic images. There were not very many camera shots and
almost no special effects.

The only editing was the **live cutting,** and occasional **dissolve,** between cameras on the stage. Live cutting means editing on the fly. A dissolve is a specific
kind of transitional edit. Thirty-nine episodes made up the season's show
order. The only way to have a repeat broadcast from these nonfilmed sitcoms
was to have a film shot off of a monitor, called a kinescope, at the time of
broadcast. Because of their cost and poor quality, these kinescopes were not
commonly made by the average weekly show. There would be a different
summer series in that time slot for the other thirteen weeks and then the new
season would begin.

As videotape technology was developing, Hollywood with its rich film history
had a more difficult time getting into the television arena because film is more
expensive to produce. Reuse of "B" movies, movie shorts,[4] and "serial" action
series[5] was all that was in demand. In 1951, when television wanted to make a
sitcom pilot[6] with Lucille Ball and Desi Arnaz, film came to sitcoms. Film
actress Lucy did not want to move to New York to the live TV stages of 1950s
television. Desi created Desilu Studios where they thought that they could
approximate the multiple-camera techniques of live TV. With the help of inno-
vator Al Simon, they placed sets side by side. They planned for a live audience.

---

[3] It is technically a fraction less than 30 so that there is room for the sync signal which also contains things like captioning.

[4] *Laurel and Hardy, Our Gang,* and *The Three Stooges* are still airing.

[5] *Flash Gordon* and *Junior G-Men* are good examples.

[6] At this time, called an audition.

They used three film cameras and had to have the film processed, edited, and transferred before it could be aired. This was a more expensive process but resulted in a product of such quality that episodes are still being aired to this day. Maybe the added input of an editor and the ability to repeat performance "takes" is partly responsible, but the biggest reason for the show's success was Lucy herself.

When tape came into usage as a recording medium in the 1960s, the networks had the ability to easily repeat episodes that had the technical quality of the original live telecast. By then, color cameras were being used. Videotape and film reruns resulted in reduced episode orders to 25 or 26. Today, orders are even more reduced. A full season of 22 episodes is a major accomplishment for most shows. Many times shows will get a network order for six to thirteen episodes until they are a rating's success.

In the early days, the economic savings from 39 shows to 26 allowed them to add a fourth camera. This meant a few more camera shots were possible during the visually "swinging 60s." There was not much postproduction editing done on those tapes because it required that the two-inch-wide videotape be sliced with a razor and sticky-taped back together.

Whenever feature motion pictures add a second camera for a setup, the cameras are referred to as the "A" and "B" cameras. Therefore, the film sitcoms started with A, B, and C rather than the video's cameras 1, 2, and 3 numbering system. In time, video added camera 4. It was so rare for film shows to be able to afford extra film stock that their occasional use of an "extra" camera was always called X. Now, all sitcoms use four cameras regardless if they are shot using film or videotape. The cameras are lined up from left to right from the audience's perspective: A, B, C, X or 1, 2, 3, 4. It is opposite from the actor's perspective.

It is much more difficult to break into comedy or dramatic television today than it was even 10 years ago. The learning curve is steeper and there is less margin for error. Typically, they still look for someone who is comfortable operating a camera and has the basic mechanical skills down already. These skills encompass the areas of framing and composition of shots, smooth zooming, panning and tilting skills along with the ability to work well with others. Confidence, the ability to collaborate, a good sense of humor and an ability to deliver the goods when necessary are all "must have" attributes for a successful multi-camera operator. A person who fits in and isn't threatening or overbearing will get farther than all the talent in the world.

Once you manage to get on an actual set; watch, listen, soak up the atmosphere and learn as much as you can as fast as you can. An opportunity will eventually present itself. I think everybody in the business has bluffed their way into a situation at least once in their career; the successful ones grabbed the opportunity and made the most of it. Others weren't prepared and they lost out.

Randy Baer (Camera Operator)

FILM

There are two recording forms: film and tape. They both continue to evolve with some separate techniques and terminology. Film cameras move on dollies. Think of a wagon with a mast for the camera...only much more sophisticated. This wagon is usually pushed but can also be pulled. It can operate on the floor or on tracks. The film camera operator is riding on the wagon. It can be levered up or down changing the camera's height from the ground.

The camera operator is framing the picture by looking through a telescope-like portal. At the same time, he is using his right and left hands to turn little wheels with tiny handles to tilt the camera up or down and right or left. Since the camera operator is operating the camera, a dolly requires a dolly grip[7] to move it and a focus puller to adjust the lens. Film focus is calculated by running a measuring tape between the subject's eyes and the focal plane mark on the film camera. The focus puller, also known as the first assistant camera, makes this measurement and then pulls (sets) the focus during the performances. Precise marks need to be put on the stage floor to see that the distance between the actor and the lens is always consistent; otherwise, the image will be out of focus. This three-man team (camera operator, first assistant camera, and dolly grip) tries to blend shots from position to position so that as much footage as possible is usable by the editor. The whole system is completely reliant on teamwork and trust. It is amazing to watch a good team do their job well. That job is to tell the story by photographing the actors. This three-man team may work for years together as a unit. There is no reliance on shot numbers in this system. Depending of each show's routine, a technical coordinator[8] may, or may not, be on headset with the team reminding them of their moves. The dolly grips have put many marks on the floor marking the dolly's path.

Technical Coordinator Dan Fendel tells us about the origin of his position:

> When multi-camera filmed sitcom TV was born more or less with Desi and Lucy, somebody figured out that the show needed someone to coordinate the camera crews of operators, assistants and dolly grips and the job was originally known as "Camera Coordinator." This ended when, as the result of a jurisdictional dispute between the camera union and the DGA. The Director's Guild won the job and didn't want the word "camera" anywhere near it. Of course, the Director's didn't want their position diluted terminologically speaking by adding "Director" to it anywhere either, so this vague, complex, and obscure term "technical coordinator" was born in contract language as a compromise. When I was doing *Major Dad* and people would see my name go by VERY fast in the closing credits, what they THOUGHT they were seeing was "technical advisor" which led to some confusion that I was or had been a Marine.
>
> The way I usually describe the job is that I am the director's creative executive officer the way the First AD is his/her production

---

[7] Jobs with the term *grip* require the person to grip things whether it is a light, scenery, or a camera dolly.

[8] A Directors Guild position.

one, that I am the editor's advance scout and protector and, especially on shows which play "musical directors" week after week, a guarantee of continuity in shooting style for the producers, too. I'm also there to help the camera crews use their talents and, where possible, help make the actors' best work actually get transmitted to the audience—as such, the TC/Associate Director really bridges the ravine between the artistic and the technical and, in a pinch, also helps the AD/UPM staff get the practical side of things moving and happening efficiently, too. Of course, that's how I do it, which some people LIKE and others are bothered by. If you want to play it safe, you take notes from the director and call cues, period. And the show isn't as good. Period. Smart producers, directors, Ad's and UPM's and camera folks know this.

TAPE

Tape, the second form, is developed from a video system. Tape camera operators are a one-man band: a single operator pushes, focuses, and frames each shot. The **pedestal dolly** or ped for short is like nothing you've ever seen. Think of a heavy-duty microphone stand on wheels…only, in this case, the mic is a camera with extended arms to control the panning, tilting, focus, and the zoom lens. The ped also has a pneumatic assist to raise or lower the camera's height and "wheels" to help it glide. Instead of the telescopelike eyepiece of a film camera, the pedestal dolly's viewfinder looks like a little TV screen. It allows the operator to use his vision both for what's in the viewfinder and what he can see peripherally on stage. It is a complex piece of equipment that the operator must know intimately. Cameraman Martin Goldstein paints this picture:

> The camera and dolly is the operator's dance partner and the actors are the music. When it is otherwise, it's a walk uphill. Understanding and using the pedestal dolly is even more important than use of the camera. If one is clumsy with the dolly, it can slow down the operator and get the operator negative attention from others on the stage floor. Although the shot may be there for the director when needed, it may have been a painful chore getting it. If the pedestal is balanced and the camera head is balanced properly in the morning when the stage is cold, the dolly will remain in control. Struggling with the hardware on top of dealing with the "software" of the show can be exhausting. Remembering that the dolly is the operator's dance partner, one can look as though he is an accomplished ballet dancer with the Bolshoi or flail about like a hard core dancer at a punk rock concert.

Tape camera operators rarely drop a mark on the floor because they have to concentrate on getting the image without the assistants. Because the video camera's viewfinder is actually a TV monitor, he can see the accurate results.

The camera operator frames a shot and then the **tally light**[9] comes on his camera when the shot is used live. When the light goes out, he goes to the next shot. Martin Goldstein advises:

> The operator should have his zoom and focus controls properly mounted in such a way that is second nature using them. If an operator has to think about which direction his controls work, it's already too late. The shot can be lost. Speed is equally important as accuracy.

The camera operator has an additional tool at his disposal. Goldstein describes it.

> The cameras are usually given an external feed showing the output of all four cameras. This is usually referred to as the **quad split.**[10] An operator should use it liberally. It's a great tool for matching an opposing camera's over the shoulder shot, avoiding duplicate coverage, or to find **iso coverage**[11] not given by the other cameras.

THE HYBRID

A third hybrid form was developed in the early 1980s and first used on a show called *Harry and the Hendersons.* This is a film camera on a tape pedestal. It has been continually refined since then and is still in use because it gives the show the quality of film with some of the economy of tape: One tape operator is cheaper than the three-person film team.

24P—IS IT FILM OR TAPE?

In this period of digital innovation, new cameras have been developed that gather pictures electronically just as video cameras always have but are recorded at 24 individual frames per second, like film cameras. They are referred to as **24P** cameras. The recording can be on tape or on computer hard drives and recently on optical drives.

The fact that these new cameras use film's frame-scanning technique, but keep the economic savings of recording on tape, accounts for their popularity.

So, does the use of 24P cameras give filmlike quality? The element of film that remains superior to video is its ability to handle a wider range of light levels. Live television needed very bright lights at its inception.[12] As the years

---

[9] A light (usually red) on the camera that comes on when that camera is on-line.

[10] The monitors on stage will be showing either the switched pattern of camera shots (line feed) or this simple four-way output showing each of the cameras.

[11] The cameras that are not on-line as the active camera of the switched feed are also being recorded or "isolated" for use during post-production.

[12] At one time, every call sheet for Thursday had the admonishment "Do not wear white or yellow." It is still a good idea not to wear small stripes or checks because they interact with the electronic scanning to cause a distracting moiré, or "worming" effect.

have gone by, the tubes, and now chips, in the cameras have steadily improved and have allowed light levels to drop. Today's video cameras are much closer to film in light-handling ability. DP Bruce Finn discusses 24P.

> Being one of the first DP's to work with 24P for sitcoms has allowed me years of in-depth experience to evaluate this fascinating new medium. 24P isn't instant film but it's getting close. For a sitcom that is being broadcast, the quality of the image is very compelling. The shooting advantages include a high-quality picture from each camera on a monitor for purposes of lighting, framing, and aesthetic decisions. These decisions include production design, wardrobe, makeup, playback to check technical or performance issues. Some very valuable attributes along with time and money saved.

Most of the digital video cameras used in the 24P setup are new **hi-def,** high-definition TV format. Since most viewers do not yet have hi-def television sets, this is another challenge for camera operators. They have to frame for two separate and different formats at the same time. High-definition TV has a different ratio for its wider shape. It is 16 units wide by 9 units tall. Normal TV is 4 by 3. The wide-screen hi-def image has more space on the sides. So, what does this mean for a cameraman framing? If he frames too tight, TV viewers might lose part of a face. If he frames too big, he might be **shooting off** the set or shooting where there is no set.

Since 24P cameras have come to the marketplace, video in general has improved. Adding the same frame rate as film causes most executives to marvel at the filmlike quality of the 24P cameras, especially when they see the cost savings of eliminating film stock and processing. Technology always changes but storytelling stays the same.

WRITING SHOTS

Tape shows and film shows have different operating procedures on camera-blocking day. In tape, the AD and director spend at least a couple of hours on Wednesday night camera blocking (on paper) by waiting for the final draft of the script and then selecting and writing cameras shots in each of their scripts. After that session, the AD has to prepare another copy of the script for the technical director. The technical director is the person who physically switches between the cameras and acts as the crew chief of the camera and sound teams on a tape show.

As directors, we're big believers in the "don't agonize" theory when it comes to these camera-blocking-on-paper sessions. You may be describing 200 to 300 sequential shots on paper.[13] The key is that the shots are written in pencil. They can always be changed. While sitting in an office or on the empty stage,

---

[13] Director Paul Bogart would use as few as 70 shots while directing *All in the Family*. Asaad Kelada had used close to 400 while directing *The Facts of Life*.

it is a little abstract to envision the way that the actors were positioned and what the important focus should be. The next day watching the monitor, it is easier to see if the selected shot is the angle and framing that the director really wants to see in order to tell the story. If the original choice wasn't right, it takes less than a minute to change it. Actor/director Scott Baio was a seasoned performer from his years on *Happy Days* and his spinoff *Joanie Loves Chachi* before he came to direct many episodes of his next long-running success *Charles in Charge*.[14] Baio described his challenge writing down the shots for the first time:

> I sat there for the longest time not knowing what to write down. I was completely dumbfounded. Then I pretended I was sitting there watching my show on TV. I just described what I was seeing shot to shot and it was easy.

The "don't agonize" theory, when doing camera blocking on paper, was repeated to us by director Peter Baldwin (*Andy Griffith*, *Mary Tyler Moore*, and *The Bob Newhart Show*) and associate director Mikki Capparelli (*Living Single*, *227*). They both had the wisdom to know that the shots were a preliminary blueprint. Since it's a visual medium, the choice becomes apparent once a director is looking at the show rather than *pretending* he is looking at the show.

GETTING SHOTS—TAPE

On tape shows, camera operators have an early meeting with the associate director where they are told the camera shot descriptions with sequential camera shot numbers. The number of shots depends on the story and the director's style, but usually number anywhere from 150 to 250. The operators know nothing of the new characters or the show's plot, but they know descriptions of 50 to 100 shots that each of the four cameras are expected to compose today. They mark them on large index cards and keep them on their cameras. Martin Goldstein talks about taking shot notes.

> Operators write their notes to be read quickly and on the fly. Any note is a good note if it can be read fast. All sorts of shorthand have been used...Dick Harwood, the associate director who basically set the form for Tandem's[15] revival of sitcoms on tape, would use something like this for an over-the-shoulder shot (using a name or the initial of a name): ArchieX2Edith or AX2E. The first name is the character (Archie) the camera is looking at; the second (Edith) is whose shoulder it is over. The reason for the second name is that it is not always readily apparent in a fast-moving scene with multiple

---

[14] Baio went on to star in other series as well as direct many shows in which he doesn't act.

[15] Norman Lear and Bud Yorkin created the Tandem production company (1970–1982) for *All in the Family*. Lear went on to form T.A.T. (1975–1982), an abbreviation of a Yiddish phrase meaning "putting one's butt on the line." His other sitcom companies were P*I*T*S and TOY.

characters just how the shot should be built. So a little extra help, as to whom to include or exclude in the shot, helps.

The associate director calls the shot numbers aloud on stage during the camera dry blocking. This is the guy talking during your line. First-time sitcom actors may worry that the crew is not finding many jokes funny when actually they are missing the punchline while listening for their numbers. These same numbers are called on the headset system during every subsequent camera rehearsal and the taping.

GETTING SHOTS—FILM

This process is completely different on film shows. The film team receives no prior instruction before they watch each scene the first time, so no one is calling out numbers while the actors are performing. Possibly more distracting, though, are the extra people who join the scene. Various people from the camera department, beginning with the second assistant camera operator[16] and loader,[17] follow every actor and put a tape mark down on the floor whenever that actor stops. Each character is assigned a different color tape. The secret for the actor is not to trip on the person laying down tape in front of him. Actors (**first team**) are replaced by the stand-ins (**second team**) for the camera-blocking process. The film camera team marks their shots on index cards as they go. Rather than following one sequential numbering system, each camera operator keeps his own numbers. Shots change when actors move. Cameras consistently follow just one character or follow one character on a move to another.

GETTING SHOTS—24P

24P uses either film or tape style with many variations. On tape shows, operators used to move from shot to shot. If they weren't on-line, their camera was not being recorded. It wasn't until *All in the Family* was being taped at CBS in Hollywood that a tape engineer named Marco Zappia[18] started doing

Sitcom is a purely television form. You can't see a sitcom anywhere else. You could take an episode of NYPD Blue *or* Law and Order *and show it in a movie theater but you'd find it's hard to watch a sitcom on the big screen. It's really a small screen creature. Part of the reason is that it is all auditory. It's the words more than the business. No one had ever looked at a sitcom and said, "This is the funniest 2-shot I have ever seen." You can close your eyes and listen to a sitcom, and get it. If you close your eyes during a film or* Law and Order, *you won't know what is going on.*

Television comedy owes a lot to theater. On a sitcom, the lenses of the camera are the audience. There is even someone laughing along with you. Both the theater and television audience are outside the fourth wall. It is much more theatrical than a single camera style show where the lens is inside the fourth wall and the viewer has a sense of aloneness and intimacy.

Steve Zuckerman, *Everybody Loves Raymond, Friends, Murphy Brown,* Series Director *Empty Nest*

---

[16] This individual also claps the slate at the beginning of every scene when filming.

[17] This individual loads the film into the camera.

[18] Marco was the award-winning editor on countless shows including *Roseanne, Home Improvement,* and *8 Simple Rules.*

sophisticated editing on videotape. Now tape, film, or 24P...all cameras are recording all of the time.

DIRECTOR OPTIONS—CONTROL ROOM, VIDEO VILLAGE, OR AMONGST THEM
During camera blocking, the director can be found in the control room, at a bank of TVs near the set, or walking amongst the cameras directly in front of the set. Every director has his own style.

CONTROL ROOM
A director and his team in the control room or booth wear headsets to communicate with the stage manager, also wearing a headset, on "the floor." The stage manager is the director's main line of communication to the actors. The director communicates with other crew members on different channels of the headset system. In the control room are TV screens, called monitors, showing what each camera is seeing as well as a screen showing the show as it is edited live. This is another difference between tape and film. A tape show will do a live edit called a **line cut** during an actual taping. The technical director who is cued by a snap of the director or AD's fingers switches this edit. They often save finger fatigue by using a small tin cricket toy to click during rehearsal. The booth is the hub. Newscasts, daytime dramas, game shows, and sports broadcasts use the booth.

VIDEO VILLAGE
The hub on the stage floor is the bank of monitors where the director, TC, and script supervisor can sit with their rolling podiums and canvas director's chairs. This station, often nicknamed **video village**,[19] can be moved around the stage to facilitate equipment placement as well as easy proximity to the set. Since 24P, this hub is used most often. How can film that requires developing be seen on video monitors? Film cameras have an electronic pickup off the viewfinder that will give a somewhat dim, but serviceable image of what is being exposed to the film. These videotapes of film cameras are fed to monitors so that their shots can be monitored just like video cameras. Even on some taped sitcoms, the director will choose to stay "on the floor" and let his associate director work with the technical director to cut between the cameras in the control room. On film shows, an audience switcher performs this same function. The reason for giving up the technical superiority and comfort of the booth is that the director likes to be in close range to give adjustments to the actors. When he is in a control room, his messages have to be relayed by the stage manager or via a booming speaker above the stage.[20]

AMONGST THEM
Some directors choose not to look at any monitors while camera blocking. If

---

[19] We believe TC Tom Doak came up with this name.

[20] Some directors like the "God-like" quality of this studio address speaker. Others think it is impersonal.

they want to see exactly what a film camera will be recording, they will simply climb on or next to the camera and look through the eyepiece or viewfinder. The advantage to being amongst them is the proximity to the cameramen for direct communication.

CAMERA BLOCKING

Each scene of the sitcom teleplay may take up to one hour for dry blocking, working out each camera's exact framing on every shot, and a final camera rehearsal to see if everything works. Lighting adjustments and the planning of how each microphone will be deployed during the scene is happening simultaneously. Soundman Ed Valfre explains:

> Traditionally, in the sitcom world, dialogue is picked up by two boom microphones on pedestals from the floor or a series of booms hanging above the lighting grid in what is called, a **green bed.** When the actors go through their blocking with dialogue for the first time, the sound mixer and boom operators watch and take copious notes on how the booms will divide the scene. These notes will most likely change many times before the scene is recorded causing their scripts to resemble the abstract expressionist work of Jackson Pollack. Division of which microphone picks up what dialogue is based on several factors…distance between actors, pace of dialogue, lighting and at times, just laziness.

TIPS FOR ACTORS

The camera-blocking process requires the director to review every shot as the scene is rehearsed. The action is stopped constantly for a slight camera or actor reposition or for a complete change of a shot pattern sequence. Actors don't ever get a chance to really play the scene because of the interruptions. On film sets, the actors will perform the dry blocking and then the second team or B team will come in to do the actual shot-by-shot blocking. The B team is the stand-ins who have watched the dry blocking or yesterday's run-thru, copied down the actors' physical positions, and then represent each character during this laborious process. Any blocking changes that affect their character must be noted and reported to each actor by their stand-in. Steve Zuckerman likes using the second team:

> The actors go away. The second team is there and sometimes I have to move them. They might have to cross a little later. When the first team comes back, I don't have to tell them their changes. Their stand-ins do. What is amazing is that no one has ever objected. No one has said, "All week I have been doing it this way." They must appreciate their time off. They must say, "He had all this to do and I'm not going to bust his chops."

Videotaped sitcoms evolved without using the B team concept. It is common, however, for there to be one stand-in available on tape sets to fill in for child actors who are in the schoolroom during a scene or when the extracurricular demands on the show's star are so great that relief is in order.

Camera blocking can be tedious for the actor. It is hard for the actor to appreciate all that is being done while repeating a section of the scene for the umpteenth time or standing still on his mark. Actual physical tape marks are rarely used for the actor's position on tape shows. Standing on a mark merely refers to stopping dialogue in position while cameras line up shots. On film shows, the marks are snipped so they are very tiny. There are also plenty of marks on stage for each piece of furniture that needs to be moved during the episode. Lighting sometimes lays actor's marks until the actors are familiar with them. The mark for the actor to hit will be left on stage only with an extremely critical position for a hard-to-get camera shot. Hitting that mark takes some skill in being able to see it from your peripheral vision.

This is a good time for the actor to make an impression on the director. Whether you are a stand-in, a guest actor, or a member of the regular cast, you can help make camera blocking easier. When you notice that you are casting a shadow on another actor that a slight lean or physical adjustment will correct, you are saving the director time and money.[21] Actors will often hear a director say, "Get me two eyes." When a camera has run out of room trying to get a view of you that sees both of your eyes, you can again make some slight adjustments to help.

An actor should keep these important things in mind on camera-blocking day. Try to be consistent. If you haven't locked into your blocking or the way that you will handle a prop...NOW IS THE TIME TO DO SO! What you do now affects many other people. For example, if a camera is shooting an insert shot of a woman's hand holding a ring box, and the actress decides to switch hands, a different camera might be needed to get a better look at the ring. If that better angle is from a camera that has the previous shot, the director has to juggle all of his **coverage** in order to get that new shot. Coverage is all the camera shots. If a show has many characters, the producers may want you to "cover" all the actors with close-ups. Even with four cameras, this is sometimes a challenge. Reverse angle walls or moving of set furniture might be needed. To minimize the length of time required or the number of times an audience would have to watch the same scene, a director may choose to preshoot the whole scene without the audience. If the choice of camera is switched, the boom operator may have to switch which boom is recording the actor's line. It's a huge domino effect.

---

[21] It is not the director's money, but his reputation is partially based on getting the show done in the time allotted. Money-saving efficiency that does not come at the cost of quality has been the hallmark of many successful directors. This, of course, means more jobs and more m-o-n-e-y. Okay, so it kind of is his money.

Actress and USC Instructor Marilyn McIntryre believes, "An actor should know which camera(s) are on the 2-shots and/or group shots and which one is yours at any given time. And ask the cameraperson what the shot sizes are. This will all become second nature and give you the freedom as an actor and save a lot of time and energy on the set. By the way, this is the way so many actors learn about directing."[22]

Another actor choice that affects camera blocking is handling a **practical** prop. An example of this is a functioning appliance or a light switch. Do you really switch the light on or do you just put your hand on the switch and wait for the lighting board operator to switch on the new illumination? This choice will be made for you depending on how many lighting instruments are involved in this lighting effect. Faucets, stoves, vacuum cleaners, and blenders are just a few of the props that may or may not be practical. In one episode of the *The Hughleys*, D. L. Hughley was using a practical leaf blower inside a kitchen. It became apparent that no dialogue could be heard over the blower especially when the baby in the scene heard the noise and began crying during the dialogue as well. Camera blocking is the time when all these matters get worked out. In the case of the leaf blower it was decided to have the baby leave the scene earlier and that the sound of the blower could be put in during postproduction.

Here's another thing an actor should keep in mind: If you can't see a camera, it can't see you! Camera blocking is the perfect time for an actor to sneak out of character and peek at which camera is pointed at him at any given time. A camera operator noticing this effort from an actor will go that extra mile to make sure the actor is seen in the best possible manner. You are showing respect to him as part of the creative team to collaborate with him. At the same time, these "peeks" should be *very brief* just to get your bearings. Remember, the director is looking at the overall picture in order to line up coverage and wants to see the actor looking at his scene partner, not into a camera lens.

When playing a scene with another actor who then crosses to the other side of you, you should **counter** his move. This means to readjust your position so that you are still 50/50 (both equally visible) if the conversation is to continue. This will allow the cameras that were set to get each close-up to just switch to the other person.

The director sees all of your adjustments and observations. He is watching the monitors, sees the same shadows, and sees the same camera problems. If you fix it before he has a chance to stop things, you are a hero. Moving a light or repositioning a wall to fix the problems takes a lot of time. If you are asked to hold your position, DO IT. Remain looking at the actor with whom you have your dialogue. There is a reason for this. It is likely that two cameras are simultaneously trying to line up or match opposing shots. Your positions are critical. Director Madeline Cripe remarks:

---

[22] Ron Howard, Michael J. Fox, Tom Hanks, Robbie Benson, Michael Lembeck, James Widdoes, Sam Weisman, Peter Bonerz, Scott Baio, Amanda Bearse, Dorothy Lyman…to name a few.

> It is always surprising to me that actors don't understand "upstage" from "downstage." I can understand not being camera savvy ("camera right" vs. "stage right"), but understanding the stage and your position on it should be a priority. The most commonplace problem is "upstaging" a fellow actor. By making them look upstage. This pulls their look away from the camera. Typically, as unnatural as it may feel, two actors will be asked to stay on a 50/50 plane so the camera can see both their faces.

It may not be said aloud, but the director is going to remember your help-fulness if you get a chance to audition for him on another episode or show. You will also gain the respect of your fellow technical artists, if they know you are camera savvy!

Depending on your job function, it is not necessary to be completely versed in the technical aspects of shooting a sitcom, but an awareness of the process is helpful. Audrey Meadows, famous for playing Alice on *The Honeymooners* was guest-starring on a sitcom episode late in her career. She came to one of us just before a scene was to be camera blocked and asked if it was okay to take the gloves from her purse during a certain line of dialogue. It was obvious that she knew that we would be on a master shot rather than a close-up at that time and, thus, the action would be seen on camera. She only asked in order to defer to the director's position of authority. She learned a lot in her career and was a joy to work with.

The basics of camera angles and camera positions are not hard to learn. An actor can absorb volumes by just sitting in the audience and watching a monitor during the camera blocking of a scene he's not in.

Television has a much smaller screen than motion pictures, so big panoramic shots don't read as well. Therefore, those master shots are kept to a minimum.[23] Those shots are used only for "geography" at the beginning and end of scenes and to establish location and the physical relationship of the characters. Almost all of the setups and punchlines are delivered in close-up. Close-ups are the staple of the television visual language. When someone is entering or exiting a scene or moving across the room, this is a good time for more geography. As soon as the movement is over, it's back to close-ups or small group shots.

When you are aware of which of the two center cameras is on you during camera blocking, it is another chance to check if you and your scene partner are 50/50 to that camera. Remember the new proscenium that you are lining up with is the camera that is shooting your master. For a short exchange between two characters, it may be the only angle. The proscenium that was assumed to be the setline might be slightly different as the cameras vie for

---

[23] The outside cameras have the best angles for close-ups. Therefore, cameras 1 and 4 have the most shots.

position. Again, a simple small position adjustment or shift of weight will help the camera operator frame the shot.

In Chapter 3, you learned **DON'T MOVE ON THE JOKE.** Now that the scene is on camera, the close-ups actually accentuate the setups and the jokes. The camera cuts between them help give the structure and rhythmic precision to sitcom jokes. Everyone who works on sitcoms gets used to this. Now you must refine your movement even more. The rule from this chapter, **SAY THE LINE, THEN MOVE,** asks you to feel the rhythm of the setups and punchlines and the audience's laugh. You have an indication from each run-thru of how big the laugh will be. A full audience will laugh even longer. As a performer, you now have to decide whether to deliver the joke and beat it *or* stay for the laugh and the ensuing reaction shots that will follow. There is no hard and fast rule here. Each choice is dependent on the character's point of view.

Take this example: Lisa Kudrow on *Friends* delivers a joke that her character doesn't know is funny but her scene partner (or the audience) does know is funny. If she went on about her business, the audience would not be able to see her face, especially her eyes, to know her character was oblivious to her funniness. This would rob the audience. We have to know what her character is thinking (or not thinking). In a case such as this, the actor should not move to his next position until all three elements (the setup, punchline, and laugh) are completed. The director will bounce between the close-ups of the person who delivered the punchline *and* the reaction of the person who delivered the setup until the anticipated laugh is finished.

Conversely, other jokes will work better if the character delivers the punchline and immediately hightails it out of there. This leaves the camera with only one reaction shot: the person left standing still in the scene. This type of delivery is very effective when one character is knowingly zinging the unsuspecting scene partner with an insult. It leaves the insulted character mulling over the insult. In a case such as this, the actor delivering the punchline should move immediately after the punchline while the audience is laughing. The director can show enough geography that the audience will know that the insulter walked away. The "funny" will be the insulted person's reaction shot.

GETTING NOTES

Different people have differing opinions on what makes and sells funny. For example, many network executives are fond of close-ups: the more, the better. They have been known to even ask for close-ups as characters enter at the beginning of a scene. Directors struggle with this kind of note. The director wants to be true to telling the audience the story and use a master shot to have the audience know what kind of room and where the character has just entered but must also service the requests of the network executives.

It is important for everyone to realize that any note from the producers or the network comes from a desire by that person to see the story slightly different from the way the actor is playing it or the way the director is directing it. Getting to the root of that need is what can help your working relationships and ultimately help the show. The director, using a shorter time on the master shot or slightly different framing, might satisfy the network's note for an entry close-up. Actors can try performance adjustments as they respond to notes. Don't write off a challenge as "just another stupid note."

Sitcom Exercise

Choose a two-character scene from the Appendix. With a partner, stage (or block) yourselves as if four cameras were filming you. Remember to stay 50/50 with your scene partner when you are standing or sitting in close proximity. Try opening up to the camera. Remember that if you can't see your imaginary cameras, they can't see you. Be very specific how you handle props, especially practical ones. Practice countering your partner when he crosses in front of you. Remember to lean on your upstage leg if you are casting a shadow on your partner's face. And, of course, say the line, then move, making your choices on what serves the joke better from your character's point of view.

AFTER CAMERA BLOCKING

When all of the scenes have been camera blocked, three things can happen: the actors and most of the crew can go home, everyone gets ready for a run-thru, or preshooting will begin.

CAMERA RUN-THRU

Carmen Finestra explains the second scenario.

> At day's end, a camera rehearsal is held for the producers and writers. Obviously, everyone is just looking to give notes on the camera work, knowing the actors won't be at peak performing levels. Any tweaks to the scripts hopefully will happen now.

This camera run-thru is the first time the episode will look like a television show and not a theatrical experience. It usually takes a minimum of 15 minutes for the stage to be readied for the run-thru. The camera and sound equipment are positioned in front of the first scene because the show will be run in order. Actors are studying the scripts because no one should be **carrying**.[24] The very occasional actor that still has a script in his hand during the camera blocking tends to make the script supervisor and director nervous that he won't have a solid grasp of the lines when the audience comes in tomorrow. This actor is robbing himself and his fellow actors of a valuable chance to see how the material plays.

The writers have been in **the room** all day working on the next script. The

---

[24] Most actors have the scripts out of their hands by Wednesday. By Thursday, it's crucial that lines are memorized.

show runner might have taken a break from this to watch closed-circuit views of the camera blocking on a scene that was shaky at last night's rehearsal. He might even be called down to the stage to watch the dry blocking of a scene that had a major rewrite last night.

All the writers are called down for the camera run-thru. Actors are in wardrobe and all working props and effects are "live." For this run-thru, the writers and other office personnel will watch the switched feed monitors from the audience bleachers. The show runner and network executives will watch from a viewing booth often located above the last row of the audience area. On sets where the director is working at a video village, the show runner will usually be next to the director giving notes as they go along. The bulk of these notes will address camera work and not performance.

Now is when the play finally looks better. There might be a few camera or actor missteps, but it is now close to a real television show. As directors, we always like to make a videocassette copy of this run-thru to review at home this evening. Without the need to pay attention to every camera move and cue, it is easier to see if the story is being told clearly and if all of the acting subtleties and camera coverage is working.

PRESHOOTING

After, or in lieu of a run-thru, if any scenes need to be preshot everyone involved prepares for that. Actors not involved in the preshoot scenes are released for the day. It is becoming common practice to preshoot some scenes on camera-blocking day; some shows do more than others depending on each individual script. Some examples of scenes that may be preshot are exterior scenes that need to be shot on location, scenes with special effects, scenes that eliminate lengthy waits for the audience during complicated makeup or costume changes, scenes that may require a lot of extra coverage, or scenes that are playing in a swing set so far away from the audience that it's easier to preshoot and replay them the next day.

Those actors staying for preshoots get into hair, makeup, and wardrobe and get ready to perform. Network and studio executives may or may not be around for preshooting. The editor may show up to see what he has to quickly edit for the audience playback the next day. The script supervisor is recording every piece of information imaginable from keeping the takes straight to continuity and time code to find the takes later. The show runner and director do multiple takes until they are satisfied with both performance and cameras.

Preshooting is challenging; everyone is tired from camera blocking, but this is the *only* opportunity to tape or film these scenes. To compound the difficulties, the actors don't have the benefit of a full audience. The crew may be so tired that they aren't the willing audience they were at the beginning of the day. Some show runners bring in several people to sit in the audience and be professional laughers. This helps but is no substitute for a real audience. Everyone has to rise to the occasion and find that extra energy. The sooner the preshoots are completed, the sooner everyone gets to go home and rest up for show day!

FINAL PREPARATIONS FOR SHOW DAY

After any preshoots, the rest of the cast is released and the crew will push the equipment aside for the set dressers and painters to put any final touches on the set for tomorrow. Lighting may stay and tweak a few instruments. Wardrobe may have to do some last-minute alterations.

Tonight is the last time that the writing staff will have hours to work on changes to fine-tune the script. Ideally, the script won't need major changes or restructuring. Just as when the script was first read at the table by the actors, seeing it on camera for the first time makes the story more alive. This day was important for that reason. Reading a script takes some imagination to envision the show itself. Watching the actors rehearse makes it easier. Seeing it on a monitor is the closest thing yet to a real television show. For all the interruptions and time that the actors have spent working on technical considerations rather than concentrating on the script, everyone can tell that all the elements are starting to come together. The only thing missing now is the audience. Everyone feels great in anticipation for tomorrow!

Sitcom Vocabulary Quick Review

Read these sentences. If the director gave you these notes, would you instantly know what he meant? If not, go back and review the explanation in this chapter.

*Cameras are in place; we're waiting on the **booms.***

*The network is powwowing in the **booth.***

*No one should be **carrying** during network run-thru.*

*You need to **counter** her move.*

*We can't get the **coverage.***

*We'll do a **dissolve** there rather than a cut.*

*We'll start **dry blocking** with "A."*

*The **dolly's** coming your way.*

*We'll start as soon as **ESU** is done.*

*We'll get **first team** into wardrobe while we dry block with **second team.***

*Say good morning to the guys dripping coffee on you from the **green bed.***

*Take a step closer so we can frame for **hi-def.***

*We're on you with the **iso.***

*We'll show the audience the **line feed.***

*The **live cutting** will be tricky until we get a feel for the audience reaction.*

*Keep the **monitors** turned away from the actors.*

*The **ped** can't get in there.*

Is the stove **practical?**

Look at the **quad split!**

Please take a step upstage because we're **shooting off.**

Who knows what goes on in **the room!**

We're shooting on **24P.**

Look for the **tally light.**

Video village is moving.

Script Supervisor's Thursday Tasks

✓ Read new shooting draft.

✓ Repeat Tuesday/Wednesday duties.

✓ Create Scene/Page Count Breakdown and give to the 1st AD.

✓ Create Daily Progress Report for any pre-shoots.

✓ Mark script for take numbers.

✓ Log time code, audio loads, film loads, takes, camera descriptions in script.

✓ Log any notes for specific takes, mistakes, wardrobe, prop, lighting, boom shadows, etc.

Sitcom Insider

RESPONSIBILITIES OF A CAMERA OPERATOR

The responsibilities of a camera operator come in varying degrees and in all shades of colors depending on the producing company, the director, the associate director, or camera coordinator of the episode. That said, however, I think they fall into three main categories. First, is the ability to work well with others, i.e., the relationship with the other operators on the set, the craft people, and the production staff. Secondly, technical/mechanical i.e., knowing one's equipment well. Thirdly, the application of the operator's own talents, physical ability, intuition, and patience.

There is a short learning curve to understand how each director likes to work—in effect finding his/her shooting "style." The "style" or manner of photographing the show can be quite different between directors. For example, some directors like closeups while others prefer to shoot their actors loosely at the hip. Some use the zoom lens liberally and like to make dolly moves on air, others not. Some prefer extensive coverage options offered to them while others prefer to adhere to their existing schedule of shots.

Today, in film and now in digital tape, each camera is recording its own coverage continuously. The responsibility for a camera operator has grown enormously since decisions are now generally deferred to the editing room. Consequently, difficulties lie with the producer's expectation of a usable shot during the entire length of the scene when that is not always possible. Moreover, the director may not make it known to the operator when he expects the operator's camera to be on the air, or the director's staging may be at cross-purposes to the operator's need for a usable angle. In today's production environment, if it is not clear, it is the operator's responsibility to "speak up" and elicit from the director or camera coordinator what shot is expected and when during the course of the scene.

On the other hand, with the production staff working mainly from the stage floor rather than a control room, the operator can get directions from all sorts of sources. The director, the associate director, camera coordinators, even producers have whispered in my ear in the heat of battle. It can be unclear which master to serve. So it's a responsibility (as simple as it seems) to remain relaxed and patient (accepting of eccentric personalities); yet, in the end, listen only to the director. That can keep the operator's career from getting bruised.

From an operator's perspective, goodness flows from the top. At any given camera angle, if the director has staged the scene well, it will make sense and it will be extremely easy to shoot. It is very easy to pick up on the rhythm of the scene, and the operator's shots, numbered or not, seem to flow into another.

It's a camera operator's responsibility to not only pay attention to his own work but to the needs of his fellow operators (camera and boom) on the floor. It can, at times, get very crowded when the cameras and sound booms are competing for floor space in a busy scene. In today's production environment, operators tend to use shorter lenses to protect their depth of field. Consequently, they work more closely to the proscenium line. When operating a center camera, one can play back farther, for example, in order to let the other cameras cross-shoot more easily. So, an operator, while watching his finder, is peering alongside the camera to see where others are positioned.

Martin Goldstein, Camera Operator

Script Career Profile

DAN FENDEL
TECHNICAL COORDINATOR/ASSOCIATE DIRECTOR
Dan is the kind of guy who does his job...and more. He is a passionate story-teller and loves collaborating with the director.

What shows have you worked on?

I've done about 2,000 episodes of many, many series. The longest runs have been *Family Matters* and *Major Dad* but I've done the famous (*Seinfeld, Friends, Fraiser*) and the relatively unknown (*Pig Sty, The Marshall Chronicles*) and everything in-between.

What are your responsibilities?

The Technical Coordinator assists the director in planning and executing camera coverage.

Did you have specific training in this field?

I attended USC's School of Cinema but got too busy working in the "biz" to formally graduate.

How did you get your first job?

As for getting into being a TC, a good friend from USC was doing it, had a schedule conflict, and needed someone to take over a show he was doing and could no longer do. He helped me get the gig and let me sit in with him for a few weeks to see how the routine went before he departed for his other show. They hired me for one week, more or less on probation, and that was many years and shows ago.

What advice would you give someone who would like to do what you do someday?

No matter what other experience you have (and certainly some camera and directing and production work is essential) you really need to try to do some hands-on editing if you can.

What do you like best about your job?

The variety—the three days are totally different, the creative rewards of doing the various tasks are wide-ranging, and it's just plain fun to "watch TV" (at least on the booth monitors) for a living.

Technical Coordinator/
Associate Director
Union: DGA
Typical Weekly Salary: $3000
Hours Per Week: Until it's done

Chapter 6 FRIDAY...SHOW DAY

In this chapter:

Overcoming nerves

How show days differ on each series

Where to get tickets to be the live audience at a sitcom

Advice to an aspiring camera operator

The role of the warm-up guy

Pickups and why they are necessary

The importance of the audience

Career profile of a camera operator

Today is the day that we all get to the finish line. Finally, we are going to reap the reward that we have been working toward all week...the audience's laughs. Certain calmness is evident on stage as you arrive on show day. There is no mystery to what needs to be done today. To be sure, there is a set of changed pages waiting for you. Most of the changes are small things like a different **handle** at the beginning of some lines. A handle is one or more incidental words that lead in a sentence. It gives dialogue a conversational tone.[1] In addition, there might be yet another punchline to a joke that has changed every day this week.

Unless the episode is the pilot for a series, the personality and operating style of the regular characters have long been worked out. Because the lead characters have the most lines, they usually have the most small changes. Guest actors might have only one change, but it can be a major adjustment for their characters. In some instances, there might be a complete change of attitude and purpose for some characters that are in only one or two scenes. It is always a challenge for guest actors. The characters that have been created just for this episode are there only to serve the plot and to present challenges to the regular characters.

Sometimes rewrites happen during the filming of the show if the scene does not get

> **SITCOM RULE**
>
> *Make sure you set it up.* The audience will not laugh if they don't clearly understand the premise or setup of the joke.

---

[1] The most famous handle is the Valley Girl expression, "Like, you know...."

the expected audience response. Character actor Charlie Dougherty tells about a rewrite when he was guesting on *Drew Carey*.

> I had been playing this strict, officious supervisor all week. There had been minor rewrites every day. Come show night, we did two takes of the scene in front of the audience and the actors were told to stand by while the writers huddled in front of the set. After a few minutes, I was handed the rewrites that we would shoot immediately. After reading the handwritten page, I walked up to the show runner and said, "So I'm gay now, right?" I wasn't joking. The character's dialogue had been altered so much that the character was completely changed.

The show runner just laughed at Dougherty's question, but that was the confirmation of the new direction.[2]

Years earlier, legendary show runner Mort Lachman (*All in the Family, Gimme a Break, Kate and Allie*) was approached by an actor who said, "My character wouldn't say this." Mort, showing all the toughness of his many years of writing for Bob Hope, replied, "Yes he would. The script has your character's name right above those very words." The actor would have certainly gotten more help with a less challenging approach.

SHOW DAY REHEARSAL

A few different things can happen on show day. Rehearsal can be just a few hours, then actors will get into hair and makeup before doing the audience show. Other shows prefer blocking and taping the entire show prior to the audience's arrival. Still others will rehearse and do a run-thru.

In all these cases, the director may have changes before any work begins. He may have taken home a quad split tape of the scenes that were camera blocked yesterday to review and come in with a list of shot changes for the technical coordinator or associate director. These notes are usually given to the camera crew before you go "on camera."

Carmen Finestra explains the block and shoot option.

> On *Home Improvement* we blocked and taped all day without an audience, to make sure we had the scenes right and in the can. Certain producers sat in the booth with the director to make sure everyone agreed on how a scene should look.... Having the security of the scenes in the can from the afternoon helps make the taping pressure-free, and allows the actors "to run with the material," i.e., perform at a high level.

---

[2] Finally, the actor decided that his new character was actually not gay but flamboyant. That take was never used in the version that aired.

In both rehearsal cases, every scene that wasn't preshot yesterday is reviewed on camera with the attention going to any changes that require new blocking or new shots. Before moving on to the next scene, it is run again just to sharpen the pace and energy. The cast gets used to cue biting. Makeup and hair can be scheduled around each scene. Second ADs or 2nd stage managers are adding **background artists.**[3] Lighting is **tweaking** or adjusting the lights. Tweaking or adjusting can be many things: moving a black flag in rectangular frame that purposely partially shadows the light, opening or closing the barn doors that fit into the front of the lighting instruments, adjusting the focus of the light, or adding or deleting an instrument.

If the show runner wants to see a run-thru, it happens immediately after the scene rehearsal. The show will be performed from top to bottom (in show order) with cameras. The emphasis is on finding the performance energy again. By now, the cameras and sound should be fully integrated so there should be no stopping or adjusting for them. Notes will either be given after each scene or at the end of the whole show. The secret is now to build up everyone's confidence for the audience.

Rehearsal often ends with a full script speed-thru of lines. After all, louder and faster is funnier.

Sitcom Exercise

Record an episode of two different sitcoms. Watch the first one. Turn off the sound.

Watch it again while you stop and start as needed so that you can write down a description of the shots used. Start simple. Use the following notation:

E: Establishing shot that sets up location

M: Master shot that tells geography

G: Group shot with three or more characters featured

T: Two shot with two characters featured or one character featured over the shoulder of another

S: Single shot with one person in the frame

Note the patterns of shots. Compare the shooting style of one show to the other.

DRESS SHOW

Traditional videotaped shows would break after the rehearsal and get everyone into makeup and wardrobe while they brought the first audience in for the **dress show.** This name came from live television's final dress rehearsal.[4] This

---

[3]   Extras.

[4]   Red Skelton was known for off-color dress rehearsals of his CBS variety show.

show would be taped and serve as the first of at least two performance choices for the editor. The dress show would be performed in about an hour. There would be no **retakes**[5] because things that went wrong could be fixed at the next performance. The decision whether to have a dress show (or not) lies with the show runner. Carmen Finestra explains:

> Some sitcoms tape two shows on Friday, one early (around 4 or 4:30) and one late (around 7 or 7:30). They then edit the best of both versions. Generally though, the early show lacks energy and much of it never gets used. Sitcom actors come alive at night. That's when it feels like real theater.

GETTING READY

Everyone who works on a sitcom has a special routine for the hour before show time. The audience is being loaded into their seats, so it has to be quiet on stage. Department heads are going over their preshow setup checklist, and reviewing with their crew the assignments for each scene, or catching up on paperwork. Some wardrobe is being given last-minute pressing or steaming.

On a tape show, the AD is running shot numbers with the TD and camera crew. Since there have been two days of changes, he is making sure everyone has eliminated the same shot numbers and added the same A and B subnumbers between other shots. On film shows, the camera operators may be reviewing notes they scribbled and may approach the director for clarification. As directors, we like to give a last-minute check with the show runner, and then pay a quick visit to each department to see if there are any unanswered questions. Finally, a visit to the makeup room and a moment to stand behind the last row to observe the audience really gets the adrenaline pumping because we know this is show time!

Actors each have their own final preparation routine. Some like to run their lines, one last time, with the stage manager, stand-in, dialogue coach, or another actor. Others walk through all of their positions on the set, if the set is screened from audience view. Some use a meditative quiet time in their dressing room. Others smoke a cigar. A few like to hang out backstage amidst all of the preshow activity.

THE AUDIENCE

Getting an audience for the dress show is somewhat of a challenge. One reason is the 4 or 5 o'clock in the afternoon start time. The audience is asked to arrive and wait in line more than an hour before. Most of the hardcore fans of the series would not be available this early. The show contracts[6] with a service such as Audiences Unlimited or Audience Associates, which guaran-

---

[5] Doing a scene over.

[6] For a negotiated fee.

tees filling the approximately 200 seats of the audience bleachers. These services give away "free" show tickets. According to Steve Sheets of Audiences Unlimited, "We are hired by producers. We currently have about 30 to 40 shows that we are presently servicing that cover all of the networks. Our group department books tour groups, seniors groups and school and college groups. We also have a website[7] where individual tickets can be ordered online." This website gives *very* detailed information about their service as well as fun information about current TV shows.

Other audience service groups hand out hundreds of tickets at popular Hollywood tourist locations. At one memorable taping, we were stunned when most of the jokes did not get any laughs. When we noticed that the audience was predominantly foreign-speaking tourists, the mystery was solved. Even if they speak English, the audience starts getting hungry and thinking about dinner just as we are starting the second act.

THE WARM-UP GUY

A stand-up comic is hired to be the official host for the audience. Sometimes one of the show's writers fits neatly into this added job. Director Alan Rafkin[8] used to warm up his audience before putting on his director's hat. The **warm-up** performer serves two very important functions: keeping the audience pumped and at the same time keeping them focused.

First, he gets the audience in a comfortable and joyous mood. Remember, there are approximately 200 seats. The reason for that is the hope that someone will always find every joke funny enough to start laughing and the group then follows without thinking. Group dynamics dictates that a happy crowd will laugh out loud at things that they might only smile about at home. Often a previous episode is shown to the audience to familiarize them with the show. There are no lights flashing "laugh," but there are microphones over the audiences' heads specifically recording their responses.

The second important function for the warm-up performer is to keep the audience keyed into the show's storyline. Between scenes, the equipment needs to reposition to the next set and the actors might need to change their wardrobe for any scene that is not played as continuous action. Warm-up guy Mark Maxwell Smith would play challenging guessing games with the audience to keep them alert. Some shows have been known to have a live musical combo to play light jazz during longer **resets**.[9] Others use a DJ. Blas Lorenzo of Klassic ProDukShuns and DJ Interactive Entertainment explains:

---

[7] See Appendix.

[8] Alan Rafkin was a dry-witted director of hundreds of sitcoms including *Coach*. He was a curmudgeon with a heart of gold! His contributions reached beyond Hollywood to his alma mater, the University of Syracuse, where he gave his time and financial support to mentor students interested in sitcoms.

[9] Stopping a scene at a certain point; moving props, walls, or cameras; and then starting from that point. This can also refer to going BACK to a certain point and starting again.

Music is a big factor in raising the enthusiasm level for any sit-com. Desi Arnaz utilized music like ammunition to a soldier. He had so much talent that he could entertain an audience as long as it took to finish shooting an entire episode. Music helps in uplifting the environment of a set into something memorable. Music communicates in every language. A good DJ can be a key part in celebrating the accomplishment of weeks of work.

In addition to being a DJ, Lorenzo is a warm-up guy. He is an actor that comes from an improv background. Lorenzo describes the job the way he sees it:

> Warming up an audience is fun! If you're not having fun, how do you expect the audience to have fun? The cast and crew have worked all week long to put together the best possible show. The warm-up should create an environment that celebrates their talent and effort, and makes the audience members feel like they're a part of the party…which they are. Without them, there is no party.

During the 10 to 15 minutes or longer for costume changes, the audience might forget an important plot point. They are sure not to remember the last line of a scene that serves as a setup for the punchline that starts the next scene. The last thing that the warm-up performer says before the scene starts is a reminder of what is happening in the show. During a short **hiccup**,[10] the warm-up always has to repeat the last line for the audience. Sometimes the director will ask the actors to **overlap** the last lines as the scene starts again.

Great warm-up guys can make all the difference in the flow of the show. Some go on to much greater fame and fortune. Actor Bob Saget worked as a warm-up guy early in his career, but he went on to star in the hit series *Full House* and to host the popular *America's Funniest Home Videos*. Saget continues to perform live as a stand-up. He has had his own HBO Comedy Hour and directed both television and feature films.

There have been many very funny comics who have not been invited back to warm up more episodes because they forgot the most important part of the job: keeping the audience aware of what's happening in the show. Others don't understand that they should use all of their "A" material before the show starts and then just be a good host during the taping. It is not good when the audience wants the scenes to end so that they can go back to enjoying the warm-up person.

ELIMINATING THE DRESS SHOW

In these days of film and 24P camera crews, the dress show is becoming almost nonexistent. Film shows could never afford the amount of film stock

---

[10] A reset of 30 seconds or less in the middle of a scene. The cameras continue to roll and the delay is edited out later.

necessary to shoot two full audience performances. 24P is scheduled just like film at many studios. Even with this savings, most show runners make the decision *not* to do a dress show. Some believe that the air show is always better and that the dress show is a waste of time.

What is missed by the lack of a dress is the chance to remind the actors where all of the laughs are in the show. Four days ago, at the table, the show was very funny. Each day after that, the comedy was improved by the staging and the performance tuning. It came even more alive and funny once on camera. Don't forget the SITCOM RULE: **MAKE SURE YOU SET IT UP.** The audience will not laugh if they don't clearly understand the premise or setup of the joke. It is common that one character may set up a joke and someone else **pays it off** (delivers the punchline). A considerate actor is aware of this fact. He makes sure that he doesn't bury the feed.

BETWEEN PERFORMANCES

Today we were working on pace and energy. We have been working so hard on the pace that there are a dozen jokes that we forgot are funny. The audience tells us where. During the catered meal between the dress and **air shows,** reminders of jumped laughs dominate the acting notes. Jumping a laugh is continuing with dialogue when the audience wants to laugh. Jumping causes a problem by shortening the laugh and causes the audience not to hear dialogue that follows. In effect, it kills two jokes with one misstep. Both the actors and whoever is cutting the cameras can be guilty of a jumped laugh. If the camera is prematurely switched to a shot of someone who was not involved in the joke, the audience will stop laughing to get some new information. This is because the audience came to experience a live show, but their eyes immediately look up at the monitors above them as the scene starts. We found this to be true even if the actors are right in front of them. The flickering images of television are that appealing.

If there has been a dress show, the meal break gives the writers an hour to come up with alternate punchlines for the jokes that were heard properly, but were not appreciated by the audience. The catered meal for the cast and crew is either between shows, if there is a dress performance, or it is after rehearsal when there is only one show. The meal is often called lunch, even though it is served closer to the dinner hour. Actors are touched up for hair and makeup after the meal, while the air show audience is loaded into their seats. The director will often meet with the cast to give final notes, do a speed-thru, or simply to remind them to "hold for laughs."

On a bad sitcom, massive rewrites are done Friday between the first and second show. No actor can possibly give his best if he's having new material flung at him (or her) at the very last minute. These shows tend to be written "joke to joke" instead of "moment to moment," so they don't engage you when you watch them on the air, no matter how great the jokes are.

Carmen Finestra, Co-creator and Executive Producer *Home Improvement*

THE REASON FOR AN AUDIENCE

The air show is scheduled at about 7 P.M. It

is a lot of work to load in, entertain, and present the filming or taping as a polished total performance. Then why do shows bother? The laughs are that important! Situation comedy uses the laughs as a main ingredient of its mix. When every element is clicking, there is a rhythm (of three, of course). Setup. Punchline. Laugh. Setup. Punchline. Laugh. Setup. Punchline. Laugh.

The radio comedies of decades ago such as *The Burns and Allen Show, Fred Allen*, and *The Jack Benny Show* always had live audiences. Television kept that tradition. There has always been a fear that if you tried comedy without the audience, it would sound as if nothing was funny. This is especially true now with the way society has more things going on in the room than just the TV. Families no longer gather around the set with rapt attention. Now, the TV is more likely to be on in the background as dinner is being prepared. Hearing laughs might actually cue someone to look up at the screen.

Larry Gelbart (*Danny Kaye Show, Your Show of Shows*) always thought it strange that the network insisted on adding laughs to *M*A*S*H* since it was set in the battlegrounds of Korea.[11] He was allowed to make only a few episodes without the laughs. About the same time, Jay Tarses (*Bob Newhart Show, Mary, Buffalo Bill*) was successful at making *The Days and Nights of Molly Dodd* without an audience or canned laughs. It was so unusual for newspaper critics not to hear laughs, that this show was described as a **dramedy.** *Ally McBeal* followed this tradition with an hour-long show. Although the line was now blurred, we don't think that *Ally* was a sitcom. It was a drama with many comedic scenes.

In recent years, some true half-hour sitcoms have used a single-camera movie style and not used an audience. *Malcolm in the Middle, Scrubs*, and *Bernie Mac* are good examples. These single-camera shows follow an entirely different rehearsal schedule; often there is none. This type of show is more reliant on its film style and the taste of the individual director's single point of view to convey the timing of the comedy. Even though it is animated, we consider *The Simpsons* one of our favorite sitcoms. It has no laugh track.[12]

Whether a show needs a laugh track or not, the harsh reality is that audiences are accustomed to the track and usually miss it when it's not there. There are two examples of shows where lack of a laugh track was thought critical by their networks. *Police Squad*, a fast-paced gag and non-sequitur–oriented show, lasted only six episodes. It went on to become a very successful movie series as *The Naked Gun*. In the movie theaters, the group dynamic took effect and there were many laughs. Before the recent *Watching Ellie* series was invited back by NBC, a laugh track was added.

THE AIR SHOW

The air show often begins with cast introductions. Only the regular cast is

---

[11]   Filmed in Malibu Canyon State Park.

[12]   *The Flintstones*, the first prime-time animated sitcom, did use a laugh track.

introduced with the star coming on last. Often the star (especially if he is a stand-up comic) will take the warm-up microphone to thank everyone for coming, then tell a few jokes.

The audience for the air show has many fans of the show that wrote in for tickets. Also in the audience are friends of the cast and staff. The fans are always good laughers. Agents and managers of actors on the show are not considered the best audience. They have been known to only nod to each other and mouth "that's funny" rather than actually laughing out loud. This kind of silence does not help the actor's performance.

The air show is really energy charged. It can be nerve-racking for an actor. The late John Ritter (*8 Simple Rules for Dating My Teenage Daughter, Three's Company*) told James Brady from *Parade Magazine*, "We tape before a live audience. And I still get butterflies. I'm nervous for about the first five minutes, then I'll make some little mistake, and after that I can relax." Actress and USC instructor Marilyn McIntyre talks about her first sitcom experience:

> I was a theatre person, accustomed to performing in front of a live audience but there was insanity on the floor—the studio audience, the warm-up guy! It was somewhere between a carnival and being thrown to the lions at the Coliseum. I was one of four women guest stars that week...all theatre people. We played a women's therapy group that Tony Danza had to join. I sat and watched Tony in the scene before ours. He did something that was so brilliant: he went out and made the first mistake. I'd seen him do this scene all week. He knew it cold. I knew that his flub was a fake. He did this to lift the load from everybody else. How smart was that? Our scene came off flawlessly!

Emmy-winning director Will Mackenzie (*Reba, Scrubs, Moonlighting*) loves the energy that only an audience can bring:

> My attitude towards a single-camera sitcom like *Scrubs* and a four-camera sitcom in front of an audience is the same. What the single-camera show doesn't get is the fever pitch that two hours in front of an audience gives. At times, it borders on too silly and the actors can get carried away. Sometimes I have to keep the lid on, but the audience's influence is mostly good.
>
> Shooting single camera for twelve to fourteen hours a day over a five-day week means that the actors can't keep up that kind of hyper pace they have in front of an audience. The shots look better but you can't get the same comedy. As a result, the comedy tends to be more sophisticated.
>
> I love them both. The four-camera lifestyle is great. You can have a life and can even go to the theater at night. When I look at the final

product though, nothing looks as good as the single-camera show. But the people who watch don't care about a great moving dolly or steadycam shot. The viewers only care about what happens to the characters, the situations they get in, and the humor.

Directing single camera makes your multi-camera stuff look better because you get used to taking the extra effort with each shot. After doing a single-camera show and going back to four-camera, I don't want to settle for not seeing the actors. I'll cut a hole or open a door to get the camera in for a better shot, especially if the star is new and can't cheat for the camera well. I end up moving the cameras up into the set more.

Each scene begins with a loud bell or buzzer going off. This is a traditional signal, on studio lots, that film is rolling and everyone needs to be quiet. It is the Pavlovian signal to tell the audience to settle down. Tape shows then roll videotape and sound backup tape. When both are running at speed, the stage manager loudly counts down beginning with "5" and ending with a silent "1." The cast begins speaking off the countdown. On a film show, the procedure is a little different. Sound tape is rolled. Every individual cameraman turns on his own camera. When sound is up to speed, the second camera assistant will slate the scene. He will turn to each camera so that the letter of the scene and take number is clearly photographed. Then he claps his slate. The clap is a visual and sound cue that helps to synchronize film and audiotape in editing. At this point, the director calls "Action" and the actors begin.

Actress Nancy Travis (*Becker, Three Men and a Baby*) who is equally accomplished on stage, screen, or television gives her insight into working in front of four cameras:

> I have been on three sitcoms thus far in my career and I have found that perhaps the greatest misconception about acting on a sitcom is that one needs to try harder or "push" to be funny and sell the jokes. It is important to be relaxed and remember that even though an audience is present, there are also four cameras to capture your every nuance. "Bigger is not better." Concentrate on your relationship with the other actor and your objective in the scene. The jokes will either work or they won't. Ted Danson is a master to watch. He seems as though he is barely working—his acting looks effortless—but in the finished product his performance is fully realized, detailed and every joke works. I have had a great time working with him on *Becker.*

After the scene is over the director calls "cut" or "clear." The cast waits for notes. The show runner, network, studio, and director are now extremely critical about getting every beat[13] and every laugh "just right." They keep a running tabulation of what "worked" in each scene. After the scene is finished, they quickly confer and decide what notes need to be given before it is done again. This resembles a huddle.

These decision made in the huddle are critical. The audience can get worn out by the end of the night if everything is done more than ttwice. In that case, the quality of the laughs will not match from the first act to the second act. If the shooting runs too long, the audience may simply leave, giving the cast NO RESPONSE to their work.

If a certain joke was delivered well and still received a less than anticipated audience reaction, the actor will probably be given a new punchline just before starting the scene again. Most show runners will have anticipated a few of these situations and had the writing staff prepare several alternative lines. If not, they will come up with one on the spot.

The director gives all acting notes. The script supervisor is standing by to go over the exact words of the rewrite. Actors have to be loose enough to be able to remember and deliver new lines with no rehearsal. This acting challenge is NORMAL for a sitcom. The ability to adjust will result in more jobs but the immediate reward is that the actor does not have to go through the scene again with egg on his face because of a failed joke. Most of the audience thinks that the actor ad-libbed this funnier line and will laugh even louder. Again, surprise is the key ingredient that causes laughs. The prop crew resets the scene, makeup and hair people run in to give a quick check to make sure everyone looks the same as in the first **take** and the scene is redone. Each time a scene is done, it is assigned a take number for keeping things straight during editing.

It is of utmost importance that each actor match all of his actions exactly with the first take. This allows for the editing to use the best of both scenes. This matching will be second nature to the actor, if he has been using his rehearsal time effectively. Teenage actress Ashley Monique Clark who played Sydney on *The Hughleys* had to match in this department store scene:

> SYDNEY
> Why don't you go, I just need a belt and some
> socks...(OFF DARRYL'S LOOK) C'mon, Dad, you can
> trust me.

> DARRYL
> Okay, here's my credit card. Daddy needs to get out
> of here before he has to pay the two-drink minimum.

---

[13] *Beat* came from famous method-acting teacher Constantin Stanislavsky's pronunciation of the word "bit." Actors kept the term because it suggested that performances are like music.

DARRYL EXITS. WHEN SHE'S SURE HE'S GONE, SYDNEY BEGINS GRABBING CLOTHING OFF THE RACKS AND TURNS TO THE SALESGIRL.

                         SYDNEY
        Okay, I want this, but tighter, I want this but
        shorter. Oh, and I want this with the matching
        thong.[14]

Clark repeatedly rehearsed the order in which she pulled clothes off the rack. She knew she had to maintain continuity. Although her actions seemed random, they were actually carefully planned.

If any of the changes require new action or positions, actors must confirm this with the director. In the interest of not wearing out the audience, the director will usually yell out to the crew "Moving on!" after the second take. However, the scene may not be done, just done for now. The director should take a minute now to ask the script supervisor to circle his selection of the better take for each part of the scene. This saves many hours of viewing each scene later in editing.

Moving through the entire show in this manner takes two to three hours[15]. The scenes that were preshot yesterday are shown to the audience on the monitors that hang above the bleachers. This way they do not miss any crucial scenes that move the story along. The editor has made a preliminary edit in order to show the audience these scenes.

After working on your standup craft, one knows when to move on while the audience is laughing and when not to. Acting is a whole other universe. Obviously, in TV, in front of a live audience it's sort of similar to stand-up as you must hold for the laughs before continuing—not too unlike the stage—and yet I don't believe in hard fast rules but for sure, in film acting, with no feedback in a comedy, it's easier to play the reality—the moment to moment, and although you know it will get laughs in the cinema, you have a choice to take a beat and realize that if you move on too swiftly they (the audience) won't hear the next line—or not. Eventually—the great ones find a great combo of all these variables that works for them. The most important thing though is the believability—be it as a comedian, a TV or film actor—and the laughs—if they come, should come from a truthful place.

Richard Lewis, Actor/Writer/Comedian and author of *The Other Great Depression*

CURTAIN CALL AND PICKUPS

When the show is completed for the audience, the warm-up performer will reintroduce each cast member for curtain call applause. Make sure you check with the AD or stage manager to find out what the etiquette is for this show. It might be, for example, that guest actors always come out from the wings beside the set and the star makes an entrance from an upstage door.

The audience now leaves, but we're not done...**pickups!** During the evening, as each scene was evaluated, the moments that still weren't performed as well as expected were marked. Now the show runner and director compare their

---

[14] *The Hughleys* © 2001 Twentieth Century Fox Film Corporation, All Rights Reserved.

[15] Sometimes four or five. We've both worked on a few episodes that finished past midnight.

notes and decide which scenes or portions of scenes need to be done again. This time it will be without an audience. The AD is given the list and he informs the crew and the actors the order of the pickup scenes.

This is when the crew goes into hyperdrive. Remember that the show was filmed in order so that the audience would understand the story. The pickups are scheduled out of order for many different reasons. The first concern is getting the minors who are guarded by child labor laws to be through by the legal hour. The second is convenience. Wardrobe, hair, set, set dressing, and makeup changes take a *lot* of time. The AD may suggest the most efficient order to get the pickups done in the least amount of time.

To be successful, actors need to know two things about pickups. The first is that it is easy to match the physical position they were in at that point in the scene that is picked up. The script supervisor has taken extensive notes logging time code, takes, camera descriptions, and any incorrect lines. The script supervisor is the authority on matching blocking, wardrobe, hair, makeup, and everything else. At any given time during a scene a script supervisor can tell an actor which hand was holding which prop while noting what shoulder an actress's hair was or was not draped over. Trust a good script supervisor. Continuity is their specialty!

Perhaps the harder part for an actor is matching the energy level he had in front of the audience. It is the end of a long day and everyone is tired. The kind of focus that an actor unconsciously gives to work an audience for a laugh is difficult to duplicate. That is another good reason why it was important to shoot sitcoms in front of an audience. There is something in almost every actor that drives him to make that extra effort when an audience is present. That extra effort, whether conscious or not, gives the scene just enough to make it even funnier. Comedy is all about levels of loud and fast. A pickup energy level that might seem "too big for the room" is usually slightly less than what was given during the air show.

If the AD and director decide that you won't be needed for a pickup of a small portion of a scene you were in, they will release you to go home. Here's our tip: stick around! It has happened more than once that, as the pickup is being done, there was a decision to change something in the scene that required an unplanned expansion of the moment. If you are still there, you may save the day. This tip will work for directors and ADs as well. Never release any actor that was in a scene that is not finished.

There is also another reason to stay after being released after a show. Crew and actors share a special camaraderie after a successful week of work together. Everyone generally lets his hair down and the stage is released from the tension of "getting it right." Carmen Finestra told us, "After the taping, everyone usually goes to a designated restaurant to party. You've earned it." The sad part of this is that certain crew members are still working. The cameras are being put away, film is being labeled and sent to the lab. On a show that is starting a new episode the next morning, sets are being struck for the next morning's load-in.

Pickups are done and, except for the crew that needs to strike equipment and swing sets, now everyone is finished. The AD or stage manager calls in a loud voice for everyone to hear, "That's a wrap!" We have a good feeling about all the hard work we did this week. We hope that as we get this show into post-production, it will be as funny and look as sharp as it seemed tonight.

Sitcom Vocabulary Quick Review

Read these sentences. If the director gave you these notes, would you instantly know what he meant? If not, go back and review the explanations in this chapter.

*We're saving the stunt for the **air show**.*

*The **background artists** are upstaging the principals.*

*This isn't a **dramedy**. Punch the joke!*

*The **dress show** came in five minutes long so we need to pace it up.*

*Don't put a **handle** on that line. It hurts the joke.*

*Come through the door again after the **hiccup**.*

*We had too many **jumped laughs** in that scene.*

*Set it up so we can **pay it off**.*

*There are no **pickups!***

*Roll **playback!***

*Keep the energy going after the **reset**.*

*We'll need to do a **retake**.*

*Match the action of the first **take**.*

*Let's take a five while they're **tweaking** the lights.*

*The **warm-up** guy is really great!*

***Overlap** the setup when we restart the scene.*

Script Supervisor's Friday Tasks

✓ *Read revised shooting script (or revised pages only).*

✓ *Transfer blocking notes. Stay on book in order to prompt actors.*

✓ *Advise actors of dialogue if they are having difficulty.*

✓ *Do scene/page count breakdown and give it to the 1st AD.*

✓ *Prepare for show.*

✓ *Mark script for take numbers, etc.*

✓ Log time code.

✓ Log information regarding audio loads and film loads.

✓ Log all takes, camera descriptions, etc., in script.

✓ Log any and all notes given that pertain to that take.

✓ Log any mistakes, i.e., incorrect line reading, wardrobe, prop, lighting, boom shadows, etc.

✓ Turn in completed, neat script to production office. Have copy made for yourself. The original goes to editing.

✓ Do Daily Progress Report. Turn it in to 1st AD.

Sitcom Insider

ADVICE TO AN ASPIRING CAMERA OPERATOR

I can't think of anything better than the timeless advice that still stands strong—"Get Experience!" Any type of experience that involves photography, video production, and working collaboratively will be of benefit for the rest of your career. The type of experience you obtain really doesn't matter in the long run. What does matter is that you are working on projects from which you can learn. Small-scale productions such as wedding videos, demo/audition tapes, homegrown music videos all give you hands-on experience that give you a foundation to build on. In fact, I feel that the larger variety of experience one has, the better they end up being in their final area of expertise. Experience gives you empathy with all of the fields that make up production, and experience gives you a broader range of contacts to network with as you move through your career.

A secondary, yet silent partner to this advice is to "Listen!" Listen to what others are doing while they are working and learn through osmosis. Listen to actors, listen to directors, and listen to writers, editors, and producers. There is a wealth of experience to be gained through observation and it is free for the taking. All you have to do is be aware enough to take advantage of the situation and learn from it. A day in which you do not learn at least one thing new is a day that has been wasted!

The best piece of advice I can give is to take any opportunity that presents itself to observe or participate and go for it! The more familiar you are and the more comfortable you are with a given situation, the better you will be able to perform when your opportunity arises. Everybody has butterflies in their stomach when their turn comes but those that rise to the occasion are the ones who are able to use those feelings to their best advantage.

Randy Baer, Camera Operator

Sitcom Career Profile

RANDY BAER
CAMERA OPERATOR

Randy is a camera operator who has never wanted for a job. He is a great craftsman! We think that the secret to Randy's success is, in addition to being a great guy, he is also no maintenance. Randy is a problem solver who is experienced enough to figure out a solution without drawing attention to himself.

What are your responsibilities?

At its most basic level my key responsibility is to be the human interface between the director's vision of how a shot should be composed and the mechanical operation of the camera itself. Realistically though, I feel that I am an integral part of the visually creative side of the production since so much of the job depends on my judgment and interpretation of events. There are dozens if not hundreds of small decisions that have to be made during the filming of even a short, three-minute scene.

Did you have specific training in this field?

I started my professional career at local TV stations in Tucson, Arizona, working as a general crew member. It was there that I had the opportunity to work in nearly all of the areas of television production. I learned set construction, lighting, audio, camera, stage managing, makeup, editing, and graphics. After moving to Los Angeles, I started to focus my career more on camera operating and worked for ABC Network and various sporting event producers before moving full time into freelance camerawork (meaning no specific affiliation with any one production entity). Each time the opportunity arose to try something new I took it, feeling somewhat assured that my experience and behind-the-scene observation skills would give me the confidence to rise to the occasion.

> **CAMERA OPERATORS**
> Union: IATSE Local 600
> NABET Local 53/57, IBEW
> Typical Weekly Salary: $800–$4000
> Hours Per Week: Varies whether you work one or two shows. 10- to 14-hour days

How did you get your first job?

When I first started working in sitcoms there were still the remnants of the old studio apprentice system which allowed you to observe, learn, and then eventually move into being a full-time sitcom operator. Even though I was already an experienced camera operator with hundreds of hours behind the camera, I was still required to "observe" sitcoms and prove my skills before I was allowed to be a member of the team. Fortunately it didn't take much more than a week or two to learn the idiosyncrasies of situation comedy which led to my being an often requested "observer" by several experienced camera operators.

The win-win situation being that I would do the work and gain some more experience while they would get paid for having little else to do besides hanging around and having fun (and maybe having a drink or two at the dinner break).

What do you like best about your job?

Truthfully, I have got to have one of the best jobs in the world! In what other line of work do you get to judge the quality of your day by how much fun you have had? I love working with actors and I love working with the type of "show biz" people that make up my professional life.

Chapter 7 **POSTPRODUCTION, GETTING THE NEXT JOB (AND ANYTHING ELSE WE FORGOT)**

In this chapter:

Why actors get a hiatus but writers don't

The editing process

The importance of matching

Sweetening the sitcom

The reel as a selling tool

How to contact the authors

Advice and inspiration from sitcom pros

Career profile of a sitcom editor

The episode is filmed or taped, but it is far from finished. In fact, some members of the team are now just getting into the game. In Chapter 1, we talked about all the preparation that comprises preproduction including the audition, the script evolution, and putting a staff and crew together. In this chapter, we will discuss the one- to three-week process that completes the episode. For those of you who are not going to be working on the next episode, we will cover how to parlay your experience into more sitcom work.

Sitcoms usually shoot three weeks in a row and then take a hiatus week. Clever scheduling will make sure that the hiatus weeks fall on weeks that have holidays[1] and avoid scheduling conflicts that would otherwise interfere with the time needed to produce each episode. Scheduling conflicts may include the show's star having a personal appearance on talk shows during a rating's sweeps week, giving birth, guest starring on another sitcom or television movie, or a comedy club date. A television movie commitment with the series star benefits both the actor and the network that airs this series. It broadens that star's audience. If he or she is the lead in the movie, a longer hiatus is necessary. An

> **SITCOM RULE**
>
> *Gotta be clean for comedy. There is a rhythm and subliminal signals that an actor gives an audience that indicates the end of the joke. Any extraneous word or movements that distracts from this hurts the comedy.*

---

[1] Most crews work under union contracts that guarantee higher pay for holidays. Producers try to avoid working on holidays to avoid that added cost.

important comedy club booking, Las Vegas performance, or talk show appearance more neatly falls into these single weeks off. When a star appears on another show (sometimes playing his character from his show), it is called a crossover. Kelsey Grammer played Ted Danson's old friend (not Frasier) in that very funny episode of *Becker*. This is an example of stunt casting but not a crossover. Either way, this is done to boost the ratings. Grammer probably shot *Becker* during a hiatus week from *Frasier*.

NO HIATUS FOR THE WRITERS

For the writers, the hiatus week gives them time to catch up on scripts. Although the season started with about a six-week lead time on scripts, by the end of the 20- to 22-episode season, some shows barely get to each table reading with a complete script.[2] Television is so voracious in its appetite for product that those who can meet the demand get the power. The incredible amount of work and hours spent on each episode is used up in one half hour of the television schedule. This is why the head writer becomes the person in power. No one else can go to work without the scripts.

Executive Producer-Writer Al Burton (*Charles in Charge, All in the Family*) participated in writing every episode but was not the head writer. He exemplifies the former system of a producer–show runner rather than a writer creator–show runner. He said:

> That change in power came about because of economic reasons. Warner Bros. and the other studios started paying big money for new scripts. When they reached the money limit, they had to start offering a bump up in credit to reward these writers. The cost of the pilot scripts had to be amortized over the entire series. They couldn't justify also paying a separate executive producer who wasn't the creator.
>
> Norman Lear and Grant Tinker knew how to make shows really good without being the head writers. They have a 360-degree eye and know all facets of the show including casting. Some head writers can do this well but not all of them. Some know how to write funny stuff but can't execute well. It is helpful if the producer–show runner can get along well with the head writer. I think that it's an error not to have a separate executive producer but that error is one that no bookkeeper would agree with.

Ambitious writers who want to get their own pilot produced, or are moonlighting writing a feature film, have to find some spare time to write. Hiatus weeks may be the only time they leave the studio a little earlier and have time to write on their own. This is quite a challenge for any writer who has already spent the day writing "on staff." Nancylee Myatt has been in the sitcom

---

2   The writers' brains are tired from dealing with notes!

trenches for 15 years—where she was often the *only* woman on the writing staff. Myatt had to leave prime time and go to animation to finally get her Emmy. She has a very realistic view of the sitcom world. She echoes writer Michael Kaplan's view (see SITCOM INSIDER, Chapter 3) that writing for a sitcom can be frustrating. She advises:

> If there's anything that you love doing and are good at other than writing for television, do it. Go, have a normal life. Don't sell your soul or get your heart broken by show business. Creating a hit, or even working on one is like winning the lottery. Everyone thinks they can write, and the market is flooded with the talented and untalented. And these days, even the film community is coming to the small screen and taking the television jobs. The competition is fierce. But it pays better than just about every job in America. So if you decide to throw your hat or spec script into the ring and get lucky enough to get hired, SAVE YOUR MONEY.

We have to concur with Nancylee's opinion. Of course, we wouldn't have written this book and you wouldn't be reading it if there was no hope for employment. Veteran sitcom writer Ian Praiser offers a different piece of advice:

> When things aren't happening the way you want, it's easy to sink into a hole. Just know it only takes one "yes" to change your life. Look for the "yes." If you're going to give up because you haven't heard the "yes" maybe you haven't worked hard enough.

There are many sitcom jobs and the sitcom form will always exist. New people are getting their start on sitcoms constantly. Ignore the odds of how many people are seeking the same jobs. The main frustration will be that talent is not the final arbiter of getting the next job.[3] Especially in the wake of reality TV's popularity, we have seen *so many* exceptionally talented (previously working) writers unemployed. Likewise, we see this waste of great talent in the acting and directing fields as well!

Touchstone Television's Steve McPherson purposely plans his "end of the season wrap party" before the next season is announced. He laments the reality of television, "Things that you love don't get picked up; things that you don't like get made." He wants every individual involved on a sitcom to celebrate "just being part of the process" where they can say, "I created that, I was a part of that."

But back to the lucky employed sitcom writer's routine. Monday morning of a hiatus week means the writing staff can work hard on completing the scripts in progress. Writer/producer Jamie Wooten (*Half and Half*) describes what happens in his writers' room.

---

[3] Did someone say nepotism?

The day starts with about an hour of pop culture discussion: what we watched on TV the night before, what movie we just saw, what restaurant we ate at, and if it's Monday morning we read through the tabloids, especially the *Star*. Then it's plunging into the rewrite for the day, the story breaking, or the notes. No breaks, no phone calls, working through lunch. Writers come and go when they need to, but mostly the focus is on the task at hand. Some producers say they don't feel creative until after the sun sets. I say that's bullshit. They just don't have a home life they enjoy and want to get back to. There is no excuse on having insane hours. If you're organized and use your time to get the work done, then go home. How can you reflect life if you never take the time to live it? My responsibility as the person who runs the writers' room is to get the job done, but also to treat my writers as human beings and to respect that they have a life that is not sitcom only. I don't trust anyone who wants to work all the time. Repeat after me: IT'S JUST TELEVISION.

All writers' rooms have a different tone. Michael Langworthy (*8 Simple Rules*) who was both a lawyer and stand-up comic before his sitcom-writing career, quips about the advantage of sitcom writing, "You get to swap jokes and not have to entertain drunk people."[4] Writer Keith Josef Adkins paints a great picture:

The writers' room is a very sacred place. Ten to twelve writers spend 9 hours a day, 5 days a week, 44 weeks out of the year, with each other. Whew! That's a lot of time, yes, but it's what helps build the bond that creates the comfort that allows writers to feel free to be funny. We share our fears, lunacy, secrets, and our joys…we share everything. AND IT NEVER LEAVES THE ROOM. Well, except when it shows up in a script. In a nutshell, the writers' room is the family room. Lots of eating, arguing, politics, teasing, sibling rivalry, and sometimes a little discipline from Ma and Pa. And every now and then, the youngest sibling has to scream to be heard. And that's just family. There's a real special bond that happens in the writers' room. And the better the bond, the better the show.

Some shows habitually work *very* long hours. It is not unusual for a **page 1 rewrite** to take until 2 or 3 A.M. during a production week. Usually hiatus weeks are not as gruesome.

BEFORE EDITING
Like the writers, the postproduction team does not get a hiatus. Over the

---

[4] We hope Michael is talking about the drunks being from his stand-up experience, not the time he spent as a lawyer.

weekend, or overnight after the show is shot, the footage is transferred as digital computer information. For shows that are filmed, this means that the negative needs to be processed and then transferred to electronic form.

For 24P digital tape or conventional tape, the process is easier. All of the material is digitized onto an array of computer hard drives. This is done by the assistant editor who logs all the information. Gone are the days of physically cutting film from work print copies or assembling rough cuts of videotapes from cassette copies. We live in an age of nonlinear editing; the times of linear editing are long gone. Linear editing meant the show was assembled from teaser to tag without going back. Each subsequent change to an edited assembly had to wait until the next complete cut of the show. There was usually time for only about three or four versions before the show had to be finalized for airing. The postproduction supervisor makes sure the material is transferred and that the editor is ready to begin assembling the first cut of the episode.

ASSEMBLING THE FIRST CUT

On a videotaped show, the camera's output was recorded as well as the switched feed dictated by the director that serves as the basis of this first cut. A technical director or an audience switcher who chooses among the four camera feeds generated a switched cut manually. He operates a machine called a switcher that edits instantly. It looks like live TV for the studio audience watching the filming or taping.

On filmed shows and film-style digital shows, the editor may only have some notes from the director as to how the shots fit together. Many editors and directors prefer to let the editor make a rough assembly of the shots before the director gets involved with the process. Some directors, in the interest of time (and probably control), want to work with the editor from the beginning.

MAKING THE ACTOR LOOK GOOD

Getting to the best take of each line of dialogue is the main objective of this first cut. This is where it is easy to see how technically proficient an actor is. If

Here is what new sitcom actors have to face up to:

1. *It is fast.*

2. *Be prepared each day.*

3. *Come to work with some conclusions drawn about the scene and particularly about your character.*

4. *Be prepared to change, as the script is rewritten every day, frequently between shows on the day of filming.*

5. *Bring a pencil or two and write the blocking in the margins in order that you may keep going in run-thru.*

6. *Learn your lines as quickly as possible.*

7. *Be prepared to drop lines and learn new ones.*

8. *Be completely off the script when it is time for run-thru.*

9. *Timing is everything—in the delivery of a line and playing the scene overall.*

10. *Take criticism and use it to your advantage.*

Katherine Helmond, Actress, *Who's the Boss?, Coach, Soap, Everybody Loves Raymond*

I often refer to show biz people as circus people because we all seem to be the ones that don't particularly fit into the ordinary 9-5 life. All of us have egos and most of us seem to be the only members of our families that broke away from our childhood homes. We're thick skinned, self-deprecating professionals that do our jobs well and take pride in doing our individual part to make someone else look good.

But to me, the best part of the day is the laughter. We laugh at the writers' jokes, we laugh at each other and we laugh at ourselves. If I've been caught in an embarrassing position I have been known to say, "If I can do just one thing to make somebody laugh today then I have served my purpose".

At this point in my career, it is taken for granted that I do my job well and do my part to make the production better because of my participation in it. These are my base level expectations that aren't even considered a variable any more. I work hard, I have a good time doing it and I get a great sense of satisfaction out of my contribution to the end product. I enjoy being a member of the circus family and find it hard to visualize another field that would offer half the rewards this one does.

Randy Baer, Camera Operator

the actor matched his physical movement and even more importantly his energy level from take to take, it is easy for the editor to navigate between performances. It is common to hear cuss-words used in an edit bay when an attempt to get to a good performance is stymied by non-**matching action.**[5] We like to occasionally invite an actor into the process for a couple of hours[6] for them to see how easy or hard this is. After a short time, some actors have been known to swear at their own images when they realize their best performance cannot be used because of a mismatch.

Mismatching and energy level are not the editors' only concerns. Editor Mike Cole (*One World*) once compiled a tape for an actress on a series he was editing, showing her a consistent clicking sound she unconsciously made with her tongue. So many takes had been unusable because of this nervous habit. Seeing was believing for that actress. There was never a problem again.

Editors also run into problems when actors have not held for jokes. If an actor is speaking while the audience is laughing, there is a chance that the editor can get that line clean by moving the audience track covering the line. Just as the cameras are isolated, the audience's mics and the booms are recorded separately on spare audio tracks. But often, the laugh is so loud that it bleeds into the actor's mic so it renders a piece of dialogue unusable. Cameraman Martin Goldstein acknowledges the importance of audience awareness. "Operators need to pay attention to the audience behind them. If the writers are lucky enough to get a great laugh on a joke, don't forget to hold long enough to give the editor some footage to work with."

In postproduction, the editor is limited to what has been already committed to tape. The better the actual the performance, the easier the edit. *Home Improvement*'s Carmen Finestra tells us "90 percent of the show you see on the

---

[5] Starting in Chapter 3, we warned you that you have to be able to reproduce the same performance and action each time. Once it is recorded on tape, it becomes very critical.

[6] Danger! The length of time to complete an edit is proportional to the number of people in the room.

air comes from the evening performance." Certainly, a show can be cleaned up in editing, but a marginal performance can never be made great. During a show, a producer might say, "We will fix it in post." That solution only goes so far. Sometimes a small movement or pause interfered with a good joke and it did not score a big response from the audience. They were distracted slightly. This is where the sitcom rule **"GOTTA BE CLEAN FOR COMEDY"** applies. Any extraneous word or movements that distracts, hurts the comedy. One crisp gesture is better than a muddy movement. Director Bonnie Franklin[7] would demonstrate a useful technique to young actors who tended to wander around on stage. She would begin at Point A and walk with purpose to Point B. The moment she arrived at Point B, she would ground herself by touching a piece of the set. For example, she would firmly put a hand on the back of a chair. It was a clean movement. It had no extraneous, distracting gestures. We have passed this technique on to you. If a musician were trying to illustrate our **"GOTTA BE CLEAN FOR COMEDY"** rule, he would say staccato is better than legato. Remember that comedy has innate rhythm to it. It is a sharp rhythm, not a smooth one. That's why people are instructed to punch a joke, as opposed to stroking it. We gave a good example earlier of *Girlfriends* Tracee Ellis Ross breaking the spaghetti over the boiling pasta pot.[8] Ross wisely chose one clean sharp movement to punctuate the joke.

Editing can help performance timing. The audience is an impartial judge of what is funny. The editor and director are using their experience to second-guess some of this. If the performers didn't make it clean, they might get some help after the fact. A producer may instruct an editor to "tighten up the jokes." Tenths of seconds are removed between lines[9] to help increase the pace. As much as 1 minute of time is removed from the show at this time. This is without cutting out any dialogue. It is ideal for most shows to come in about 2 minutes long as shot. By the time the **director's cut**[10] is complete, it might be less than 1 minute long.

Sitcom Exercise

Without watching, record a scene from two different sitcoms. Turn off the sound. Play back the first one. See if you can tell what the scene is about just from the visual storytelling. Write down the plot in one sentence. Watch and listen to the scene. See how accurate you were.

---

[7] Franklin is even better known as an actress from starring on the long-running hit comedy series *One Day at a Time.*

[8] Kudos also go to the prop department who had the pot steaming (for many takes) on a nonpractical stove!

[9] Time is never removed from the laughs.

[10] The DGA contract stipulates that directors get to edit their show first…or at least give notes on the first assembly.

> *Next, turn on the sound. Play back the scene from the second episode. This time, turn away from the TV. See if you can tell what the scene is about just from the audio storytelling. Write down the plot in one sentence. Watch and listen to the scene. See how accurate you were.*

Besides cutting together the **first assembly**[11] of a show, postproduction is going concurrently on *many* episodes. Editor Timothy Mozer describes a normal editing week:

> Our show (*Girlfriends*) shoots in front of a live audience on Tuesday night. So, on the preceding Monday, the producers preshoot some scenes. I get the dailies on Tuesday morning and edit the scenes for playback in front of the audience when they film the remainder of the episode that night. My assistant digitizes the dailies on Wednesday morning. I edit the new episode beginning that afternoon, and finish it by Friday night. At that time, I make a VHS tape of the show and send it to the director. I get notes back from the director on Monday morning and make those changes. I run the show with the producers on Monday afternoon and they give me more change notes. On Tuesday, we shoot another episode, so I am tied up with another preshoot. On Wednesday, I show the producers their changes on episode #1 and the show then goes out to the studio and network for even more notes. While we wait for those notes, I continue editing episode #2. After we address studio notes on Thursday and network notes on Friday, episode #1 is locked and I hand it off to my assistant and jump back to episode #2. And so it continues, all the way to episode #22.

The director's contractual control and obligation to the episode is complete after he does his cut. If he is working on the next episode already, he has worked with the editor during lunch hours or after rehearsal during Monday and Tuesday of the week after filming or viewed a copy of the assembly and given notes to the editor. The show runner now gets to make his changes. He might go back and look at some other performance options, but mostly he is cutting out the jokes that didn't work as well as others. The trick always is to remove them without hurting the story continuity.

THE PRODUCER AND NETWORK CUTS

With a strong show, that got even longer laughs than expected, it becomes a problem to get the program down to time. This is the time that network is allowing for this program including opening titles and end credits. It does not include commercial time. Opening titles are the opening of the show, sometimes accompanied by the theme song. It always gives the name of the show,

---

[11] The director's cut.

the names of the lead actors, and often the names of the show's creators. End credits are the end of the show where the names of the crew spin by (so fast that you can hardly read them).

As we said in an earlier chapter, sitcoms usually run about 22 minutes. The easiest scene to cut is the tag. The tag of the "No Fat" episode of *Everybody Loves Raymond*, as we say in the business, "landed on the cutting room floor." Sometimes it is necessary to cut out another entire subplot rather than butcher the "A" story through heavy-handed cutting. This is why actors who have been involved in a successful cameo-length performance will view the show on the air with friends and family only to find that they were eliminated from the episode. It is not necessarily their fault. It might have been the only option. Then again, it might have been the least humorous part of a very funny episode.

The **producer's cut** is now within a couple of seconds of the length required by the time slot. The network executives view this. Knowing their target audience for this show's slot, they may ask about a performance of a joke they think plays better from another take. Understanding that the show is now on time and needs to be delivered very soon, they have fewer notes than at any other stage of the project. The editor now works with the show runner to make any of these last changes, finds the frames[12] necessary to bring the show in at exactly the right time, and transfers the show to an edited master.

> When things aren't happening for you the way you want, you can't seem to get anyone to read your stuff, you've done all you can, it's easy to sink into a hole. Been there, done that. Just know that "no, you haven't done all you can," you only think you have—I know this is true because it has happened to me three times (once when I was just making a call to borrow money from my mother). It only takes one "yes" to change your life. You can't predict when (which is the bitch). Somebody once said "If you give up, then what the fuck did you do all that work for?" Actually, I just said it, but it's true, isn't it? You either want it or you don't. I say, "Want it."
>
> Ian Praiser, Writer, *Tracey Ullman, Suddenly Susan, Caroline in the City*

THE ON-LINE ASSEMBLY AND SWEETENING

Although the show is now edited, postproduction is still far from over. The master must now be assembled[13] using the final edit decision list that was created during the last couple of days. Years ago, all the work cuts were made using 3/4-inch videocassettes. The time code from this edit decision list was then replicated using the master tapes. Similarly, in film, the original negative was conformed to the edge numbers from the work prints. Computerized editing has not only made the rough cuts easier with no loss of generation with each subsequent copy but the final "on-line" assembly is now

---

[12] Each frame is $1/30^{th}$ of a second regardless of whether it was shot originally on 24 frames per second film, 24P digital tape, or 30 FPS videotape. These small last-minute cuts or extensions can always be found in the transitions between scenes.

[13] The assistant editor will make the "on-line" final assembly of the episode to be sent to audio post-production.

just making sure that each source is properly set up as the master is rendered by the computer. Film no longer needs to be touched.

Work on the sound track is now the focus of getting the show ready to deliver. The editor did his best to smooth out the sound track at each edit point. Every editor knows that you can trick the eye of a viewer with a cut that happens on action. If the action is similar, the viewer might not be able to see slight mismatching. However, the moment that there is a mismatch in the sound, every person who watches the show will think that there is something wrong with an edit. This is regardless of their technical expertise because television pictures are flickering images with a change of angle at every camera cut. Sound is continuous. You can't fool the ear.

The music composer or coordinator has viewed the final cut to see what music cues are needed. The cut is also prelaid on a multi-channel audio recorder with any necessary sound effects. It is typical to add a light track of birds chirping for outdoor scenes that were shot on stage. Crickets replace birds for a faux outdoor night scene. If there was a lot of background action in some scenes, the "walla"[14] tracks are added. Room tone is prelaid for scenes with no background actors. Room tone is the sounds that go on in an empty room with no one moving. It may appear silent to the naked ear, but actually there is ambient sound. During pickups, it is common to record 45 seconds of room tone in a swing set used only on that episode.

These things are needed to make the scene sound as if there were no edits.

All of this is mixed together in a final session that lasts an hour or two. Any off-stage dialogue or lines that need to be looped[15] are done at this time. More

---

[14] Before leaving the set, the background actors were asked to recite 30 seconds of soft "walla, walla, walla," which sounds just like nondescript conversations when mixed in the sound track.

[15] Unlike location filming, very little dialogue that is recorded on stage needs replacement. Location film footage used to be made into loops that would repeat constantly until an actor could recreate the line perfectly while watching.

room tone needs to be added with any of this replacement dialogue. The biggest job at the final audio "sweetening" mix is smoothing out the laughs. Some of the jokes were edited from a pretaped performance with no audience. Others were from the second or third take in front of an audience and got a smaller laugh than the first time they saw it. If a show was taped in front of two different audiences, the quality of the laughs will be different. The editor tries to make this unnoticeable, but there is an insurance policy: the "laugh man."

There are a very few highly specialized people who "laugh" a show. Most viewers are aware that this is a process but usually for the wrong reason. They complain often about the "phony" laughs in some shows. The "laugh man's" job is not to put in bigger laughs but to smooth out the laughs that are already there. Two hundred people who attend the recording of a show laugh more often, much louder, and much harder than people in their living rooms. They were entertained before and during the event and might be attending because it is their favorite show. They are also well miked.

Charlie Douglass was a technical director when *I Love Lucy* was the first multi-camera sitcom being filmed. A couple of years before, *The Hank McCune Show* had spliced some audience laughter into their single-camera show. Since *Lucy* was trying to emulate a live television studio audience with their edited film studio audience, Charlie recognized a need. He developed a small box that had a series of laughs on tape. Using this tool like a typist uses a typewriter, he was able to select an appropriate laugh that would cover an edited laugh that needed smoothing. He could skillfully play the machine like a keyboard instrument. He was very protective of this invention and worked hard at getting cleanly recorded laughs from each subsequent show he **sweetened.**[16] When asked if the people inside his box "were still alive," he would just raise an eyebrow.

Soap operas were a good place to learn multiple cameras. You are shooting 80 pages a day. I did one for NBC and one for CBS. For NBC, you had to block the whole show in your head and write and number all the camera shots before any rehearsal. You would then get there at 6 o'clock in the morning and the actors would say "No!" When you don't know how to adjust, it is so hard. You have to turn your script into a scene. The good news was that, my first show, I was snapping my fingers away and the TD was taking it where it was right. All I could say was, "Thank you." At CBS, it was so much easier because it was a half hour show and I could rehearse and then hand my shots to the AD.

The transition from theater to television was a two-step process. I had a show Off-Broadway that got great reviews. The executive producer of Another World *asked if I would like to do an episode of his show. He said, "Come and observe." I knew people had observed for years and never gotten a shot. At that time, I had enough power, that I asked my agent to get me half of the directing fee upfront and the other half whenever I did the episode. I observed for six months, but not every day since I was still doing plays. I ended up doing only two episodes.*

John Whitesell ended up hiring me on Search for Tomorrow. *I actually hated soaps but would be their fill-in director for about two years That was a great job. Then*

(continued on next page)

---

[16] This can refer to adding laughs or to the entire process of audio postproduction.

(continued from previous page)
I wanted to move to L.A. and test the waters. I knew Chip Keyes, a producer of Valerie's Family. *So again, I went to observe. Peter Baldwin was directing a lot of episodes and was very gracious to me. I met all the executives and was still going back to New York and doing plays, which gave me some cache. Beth Uffner was their agent and decided she would represent me, which was the best thing that ever happened.*

Observing is helpful if you don't know how to do it. However, observing just to be seen is not helpful. You have to know somebody. Chip got me to Beth. Beth knew everybody in the business and was very good at starting people out. She said that I had to be here during pilot season. Barnett Kellman directed the pilot for Murphy Brown *and it sold. I was able to get an episode of* Throb *which he now could not do. That got me started.*

Steve Zuckerman, *Everybody Loves Raymond, Friends, Murphy Brown,* Series Director *Empty Nest*

Charlie's son Bobby followed in the same career and was in much demand as were the small crew of "laugh men" assembled by John and Carol Pratt. Their work is valuable because of their technical skill but more for their ability to know exactly how an audience would react to any joke. The beginning, middle, and ends of each laugh are very different, depending on the joke. These skilled artists can duplicate the natural sound of a studio audience.

Sure, some producers are tempted to use this process to bolster their weaker material, but very few producers will try to give a joke a bigger laugh than it deserves. The entire week of production was spent making sure each joke was properly written and properly delivered. If something still ended up not working, it should have been edited out of the final show. Now is not the time to betray all of this work.

The final mix is done and the show is now complete. It is delivered to the network for airing. Sometimes the entire process finished so close to deadline that it has to be fed to the New York network transmission center by satellite, but this is frowned upon.

GETTING THE NEXT JOB—THE ACTOR'S REEL

While all of this postproduction is being completed, the actors and director might be involved in another episode or trying to get a job on another show. Each of them should use their work on this episode as a tool in getting that next job. It is often joked, "You are only as good as your last job in Hollywood." This means that you should get a copy of this work. The director is given a copy as part of his contract. The actor needs to fend for himself.

You want the best quality possible so a dub of the master would be preferable. If you were the primary guest star of the episode, it might be possible for you to get the producer to make you a copy when the show is finished with postproduction. If this fails, knowing when the show will air means that you can tell your friends to watch and you can tape it at home or have a professional record it for you off the air.

Just how do you know the air schedule? The best way is if you became friendly with the line producer during the week. This person knows about the schedule better than anyone. It might be as simple as a call to him to get the right information. Sometimes the newspaper TV section will have a wrong listing or there could be a last-minute preemption. Networks have their own individual Web sites as well. There are a couple of companies, such as Phase-L Productions, that specialize in recording shows off the air. They do what they call an **air check.**[17] This term comes from radio, when advertisers wanted to be sure that they were getting the airtime they were paying for. These same companies, like Phase-L, help actors put their demo tapes together. Phase-L's Rick Fazel calls this "a necessary tool just like pictures and résumés." This copy of the episode (or scenes from the episode) needs to be on your reel. Just as you constantly need to update your headshot, you should also update your acting reel. Because casting directors and producers don't have the time or patience to watch an entire episode of your work, actors should only provide one short scene to show off their latest effort.

A few independent editors specialize in making slick presentation reels. They understand that less is more. The entire reel should be well under 10 minutes long. Five to seven minutes is ideal. You want to show the best moments of your work. You also want to show yourself in any scenes in which you are working with major stars on popular shows. It is only natural for the person seeing it to think that if you were good enough to work in that company, then you might be good enough to work with them.

Editing this type of reel is painstaking and time-consuming. Be clear about how much the editor will charge you for making your reel. Don't cut corners on this. A poorly designed or executed reel will reflect badly on you.

Directors are guaranteed a copy of the episodes they direct as part of the Director's Guild contract. Often a producer who is considering hiring a director will request a sample episode of that director's work. Director Steve Zuckerman comments:

> If you put together a reel or show someone an episode, it doesn't show too much about you. It looks the same as the other episodes of that show. What it doesn't show is how the week went. Did you do it on time? Did you do the shots or did the TD or AD do them? By the time it is edited, all sitcoms look the same. But my agent said I had to give them a reel so you try to give them something that they are looking for. They might be looking for a lot of physical comedy. That will help. If you are looking for a single-camera show, you might have an episode with some single-camera elements.

WRAPPING IT UP

We have tried to cover a broad spectrum of jobs in the sitcom world. We hope you will have an appreciation for the number of talented people who collaborate to make a sitcom. Since writing this book, we have a greater knowledge and appreciation of the intricacies and day-to-day details that every crew member attends to in order to do their job with ease and finesse. Just as there are great

---

[17] Recording a show off the air for purposes of archiving it or checking its content.

actors, who "make it look easy," there are great network and studio executives, writers, designers, set decorators, costumers, editors, script supervisors, prop masters, boom operators, cameramen, grips, gaffers, TCs, ADs, and SMs[18] who amaze us with their vast knowledge and expertise. We hope we have represented everyone as accurately as possible and would be receptive to any corrections, comments, or your funny sitcom stories. Contact us at sitcomcareer.com.

Director Linda Day was typical in that she didn't start with the sitcom job she has today,

> I went from office jobs in radio, television news, and talk shows, to 10 years on and off as a script supervisor. I spent 5 of those years as a script supervisor on various projects with Jay Sandrich. I was watching one of the best and getting paid for it, too. This was heaven.
>
> During one of my heavenly lulls, I took another office job, organizing the *Mary Hartman, Mary Hartman* headquarters. I had one stipulation: NO SECRETARIAL DUTIES. The first day, they sat me down with a Dictaphone to transcribe a writers' meeting. The second day, Norman Lear rightfully had me fired. The third day, Jay called with a pilot project: *Soap*. That was the last office job I had.
>
> A year later, I did the pilot of *WKRP*, again with Jay. When Jay went back to do *Soap*, Ted Kaye (the associate producer) asked me to stay with *WKRP* as their associate director. Big break!
>
> The end of the second season, Hugh Wilson gave me an offer I truly couldn't refuse; I got my first shot at directing. The particular script I directed happened to get special recognition for its content. In 1981, I was nominated for an Emmy for an episode of *Archie Bunker's Place*, a Norman Lear show. I didn't win. I think I was mainly disappointed because I didn't get the chance to get up and publicly and personally thank Norman Lear for firing me back on *Mary Hartman, Mary Hartman!*[19]

The people we interviewed agreed on two things. First, a sitcom career *is* fun. Second, a sitcom career *is not* glamorous. Camera Operator Randy Baer shares:

> My friends and I all laugh at the realization that at one time or another all of us thought that being a camera operator was a glamorous position. The thought of being right there in the action, working directly with actors and directors was just about as good as it could get. The reality of the situation though is that if you are good at what you do then you end up being intimately involved with everything that is happening on the stage. Every single element of production is geared to one thing and that is making an actor look good and appear funny on

---

[18]   Notice we ended with a run of three.

[19]   Linda, consider Norman thanked.

camera. It is my job to make that happen. Production days are often long and the mental concentration is constant—not to mention the physical toll it all can take on your body, standing all day. Cameras need to be moved, set and prop changes need to be double-checked, dialogue changes need to be processed and worked into the pattern of camera shots. None of this is especially glamorous at 2 in the morning after you have been up since 6 A.M. then driven cross-town for an hour so you could be at work by 8.

Some of our contributors praised the income and opportunity to have time with their families.[20] Director of Photography Bruce Finn tells us, "The hours are much less demanding than a single-camera episodic schedule." He says that one of the things he likes best about his job is "making money to support my family." Martin Goldstein agrees. "Sitcoms are attractive because they generally provide for a good base income. Additionally, and maybe more importantly, they tend to keep regular hours, leaving room for a family life and free weekends."

Writer Michael Langworthy (*8 Simple Rules*) reminds aspiring sitcom writers, "A career is a long-term process rather than a sprint." We think this is true of any sitcom career. We hope that this book will give everyone who reads it a greater respect for this very specialized form of television and the artists who toil every day[21] to bring it to the viewing public. Our basic philosophy when we began teaching a sitcom technique class was, the more you under-stand the style and structure and technical requirements of this medium, the better you will be at it. We believe that knowledge is power.

We also think that luck or good fortune plays a part in a successful career. In the Emmy nominee issue of *Daily Variety*, Sarah Jessica Parker and Jennifer Aniston both mention it. Parker is quoted, "The only time I ponder the good fortune that we've experienced is when interviewers ask what the ingredients are. I think it is just good fortune, really good writing, and smart producing." Aniston said, "Someone is watching out for me, or something. I wish I could say that I had all these options mapped out and that I made these smart choices. But I was really just lucky." Luck aside, there is no doubt that these women are gifted, dedicated artists who know their craft!

We hope that the information contained in these chapters will help you get a job, do it well, and enjoy it while it's going on. We know that working in sit-coms is a great job. Maybe you'll agree!

When interviewing people for this book, we asked industry professionals, "What advice would you give someone who would someday like to do what you do?" Richard Lewis had some thoughts on his route.

I'm in the class of Leno, Boosler, and Kaufman from the early

---

[20] This is in comparison to working on other forms of film and hour-long television, which work *much* longer hours.

[21] Except during weekends…and hiatus.

seventies. There were few comedians then and we worked from sheer passion. Anyone should work from that place regardless of what part of the arts you strive for. Sadly, many comedians in the 80s and 90s just used standup to be seen by casting directors. That's cool but to me, a half-assed attempt at standup is a waste for an actor. If you want to act then study, do plays, and be seen as an actor, not a comedian. It's that simple. Figure out what you want, go for it, be true to yourself and surround yourself with winners and people who believe in you and be able to trust their criticism and guidance.

Writer Ian Praiser advises:

> To find out the qualities that make you unique, first you have to find out who you are. Listen to the way you talk to people, how they talk to you, what things get you going and how does that lead into other things, your feelings on people, things, events, politics, your family, anything. Try to remember all emotional things, not the things in the middle, but the things in the extreme. Tragic, sad, ironic, funny, awkward. And try to remember the time in September...sorry, I love that song. Remember how all these things have changed in you over the years, because that gives you more perspective, objectivity, distance, maturity, and also puts you back to the little person inside you, you know, the honest one. The more you know who you are and how you react to things, the more you bring to the table. Each actor, writer, owns a treasure of life experience like the locket in *Titanic*. Don't throw it in the ocean like that stupid old woman, where it's no good to anybody.

This final piece of advice comes from script supervisor Ellen Deutsch:

> Look within. First and foremost, there must be passion deep within your soul. If you don't go within, you'll go without. You will not be successful in this industry. It is hard work, long hours, with very few "atta girls" along the way. You learn quickly that Hollywood and Show Business are NOT synonymous with "glamorous." But, if you love it, really, really love it, and can't imagine doing anything else but this, then yes, most definitely do it. As the lyrics go: "THERE'S NO BUSINESS LIKE SHOW BUSINESS." In my thirty years of being in this business, I have never once dreaded a Monday morning. Not many people can say that. There is a lot I have gone without in my life, but loving what I do every day leaves my soul at peace.

If there is anything that you wish we had included or a question you'd like to ask us, again, go to our Web site sitcomcareer.com and we'll try to get you an answer.

Sitcom Vocabulary Quick Review

Read these sentences. If the director gave you these notes, would you instantly know what he meant? If not, go back and review the explanation in this chapter.

You can edit it from the **air check.**

I swear it was in the **director's cut.**

We had to cut the scene to get **down to time.**

The editor should be done with the **first assembly** this afternoon.

It needs a **page 1 rewrite.**

The **producer's cut** is still ten seconds long.

We have to get **room tone** before we move on.

We'll **sweeten** it in post.

We need some **walla** for that scene.

I couldn't use that take because he didn't **match action.**

Sitcom Insider

When I ask my students, as I inevitably do at the beginning of any sitcom writing class I teach, why they want to write a sitcom spec script, I get answers like, "It's fun." Well, that won't get you to the end of your sitcom script because a lot about writing isn't so much fun. Or I hear, "To tell a story," or, "To make people laugh." I've even heard, "Because I really, really, really want to." All of those are good reasons to write something, but not a sitcom spec script. The only reason to write a sitcom spec script is **$$$.**

Let me explain. Every other format has a range of outlets, some of which you can actually control. If you write a play, it doesn't have to be done on Broadway for people to see it. A screenplay can be done low budget; you can even raise the funds and do it yourself as an independent. If you write a novel—even if it doesn't get published—you can self-publish and it's still legitimately a novel. Same with short stories and poetry. Everything else has a reason of its own to exist. And you can write it just the way you want to write it, even if nobody wants to buy it. But not a sitcom. You have to do a sitcom on commercial television. There's no other place for it.

What this means is you have to follow the rules. There is not a formula—formula is what leads to predictable dull scripts that nobody wants to read past page fifteen. However, there is form—quite a different thing. There is a very specific form and you must follow it. And it doesn't matter if you know how to do it better or funnier or fresher. That's not your job when you're writing a spec script. Your job is to do it exactly the way it's done and still be original.

So, how do you keep your original voice within the confines of a very rigid form?

By finding stories that have something emotionally meaningful to you (that's your original voice) and then translating that passion into the established sitcom character in the world of his show (and there's the form).

For example, when I was writing for Everybody Loves Raymond, I was looking for family relationship stories because that's what the show is about, and I thought about my relationship with my Dad. I loved painting and drawing, and my Dad, who was a salesman, could only relate to my artistic interest by having me decorate the windows of his store. I remembered how much I hated that the only way my father could see any value in my talent was if it was "useful" for his business. I still get upset just thinking about it.

So, I connected with that emotional current and translated it into the characters of Ray and Frank in the world of the show. The result was the script for "You Bet," an episode about Frank taking a surprising interest in Ray's sports writing. Ray cautiously starts to feel gratified and respected until he discovers that his father's interest in his work is only to get inside information so he can place sure-thing bets on sporting events. Ray's sense of betrayal and anger at his father's using him like this made for a strong emotional narrative and a script that I really wanted to write. Even though "You Bet" had no connection to the actual details of my life, the whole concept came from my personal connection to the emotional content, and that connection informed every decision I made in writing that script.

In order to bring your personal connection to a story, you need to find out why you want to tell that story. You already know why you want to sell the story (see $$$ above), but that's quite different than why you want to tell the story. Why you want to tell it is where "you" are in the story. Getting you into the story is what makes the difference between an okay script that follows the rules but doesn't seem special, and a great script that excites agents and makes producers want to meet you.

The best stories come from your own emotional life. Things you care about passionately. Things you hate, things that make you angry, things you're afraid of. They come from pain, humiliation, jealousy, embarrassment. Comedy goldmines, all.

And when you do find a story with a personal emotional connection, please do not give the story to an outside character. Find a way to tell the story through the character whose name is in the title of the show. If you're writing for Bernie Mac then the story starts on Bernie, it develops around what Bernie does, and it ends on Bernie. Bernie has the problem, the emotional current that drives the story, and he gets the big face-off. In addition, the conflict ought to be with another regular character, not a new character you've invented.

That is how you get your personal creativity inside the form. If you do that, you are well on your way to a fresh and original story that shows you have imagination and still know how to serve the needs of the show. That's on the money! About $17,000 an episode. Now tell me that's not why you want to write for sitcoms.

Ellen Sandler, Emmy-nominated Writer and Writing Consultant—
see Appendix Services/Resources

Sitcom Career Profile

TIMOTHY MOZER
EDITOR

Tim has two essential skills needed in this profession. He knows funny and works fast. Also, Tim is incredibly easygoing and a great guy. His reputation preceded him and he lived up to the hype!

What shows have you worked on?

I have worked as an editor on *Wings, Frasier, Men Behaving Badly, Jenny* (Jenny McCarthy's short-lived sitcom), *Encore, Encore* (Nathan Lane's even shorter-lived sitcom), *Stark Raving Mad, Girlfriends,* and *So Little Time.*

What are your responsibilities?

The editor has only one responsibility: Make it funny. If a bit didn't work in front of the audience, fix it. If you have to change the timing on a joke, do it. If you have to steal a reaction shot from another scene, or even another episode, do it. Just make it funny.

Did you have specific training in this field?

My only training for being a sitcom editor was spending five years as an assistant on *Wings*. *Wings* was a family. A generous family. The people there turned to me and said that I should make sure I didn't leave the show in the same capacity in which I began. In year three, the executive producers let me edit an episode. By the end of my fifth year, in addition to all my assistant editor responsibilities, I had edited 17 episodes of *Wings*, two episodes of *Frasier* (which was produced by the same team as *Wings*), and had received Emmy and ACE Eddy nominations for one of the *Frasier* episodes. At that point, I was able to get hired as an editor on *Men Behaving Badly*.

EDITORS
Union: IATSE local 700 (Editors Guild) and the DGA
Typical Weekly Salary: $2500
Hours Per Week: 40 to 50

How did you get your first job?

LaserEdit was being used on 99 percent of the sitcoms in Hollywood. And almost immediately after I got trained on it, I got called from Paramount Studios for the job on *Wings*.

What advice would you give someone who wants to do what you do?

Think it over carefully. I love what I do and am thankful for having the opportunity to do it. But, I know many people who are out of work and some who have been forced to sell their homes. The business is changing. More and more film work is leaving the country. And more and more students are graduating film school and moving to Los Angeles. Today, we have fewer jobs combined with more people looking to fill the ones that remain. That is not a situation to be entered into lightly.

What do you like best about your job?

If I am working on a good show, I get to laugh all day.

Unions and Professional Organizations

THE ACADEMY OF TELEVISION ARTS AND SCIENCES (ATAS)
Nonprofit corporation for the advancement of telecommunications arts and sciences. Very active in supporting newcomers to the business.
www.emmys.tv
5220 Lankershim Blvd.
North Hollywood, CA 91601
(818) 754-2800

ACTORS' FUND OF AMERICA
Nonprofit organization providing for the social welfare of entertainment professionals.
www.actorsfund.org

LOS ANGELES
5757 Wilshire Blvd., Suite 400
Los Angeles, CA 90036
(323) 933-9244

NEW YORK
729 Seventh Ave., 11th Fl.
NY, NY 10019
(212) 221-7300

CHICAGO
203 N. Wabash Ave., Suite 2104
Chicago, IL 60601
(312) 372-0989

AFMA
Trade association for the independent film and television industries.
www.afma.com
10850 Wilshire Blvd., 9th Fl.
Los Angeles, CA 90024-4321
(310) 446-1000

ALLIANCE OF MOTION PICTURE AND TELEVISION PRODUCERS
Trade association involved with labor issues within the motion picture and television industries.
www.amptp.org
15503 Ventura Blvd.
Encino, CA 91436
(818) 995-3600

AMERICAN FEDERATION OF TELEVISION AND RADIO ARTISTS/AFTRA
Labor organization representing actors in television and radio broadcasts.
www.aftra.org

LOS ANGELES
5757 Wilshire Blvd., Suite 900
Los Angeles, CA 90036
(323) 634-8100

NEW YORK
260 Madison Ave., 7th Fl.
NY, NY 10016
(212) 532-0800

AMERICAN SOCIETY OF CINEMATOGRAPHERS/ASC
Union representing professional cinematographers and dedicated to improving the quality of motion picture representation.
www.cinematographer.com
1728 N. Orange Dr.
Hollywood, CA 90028
(323) 969-4333

ASSOCIATION OF TALENT AGENTS/ATA
Nonprofit trade association for talent agencies.
www.agentassociation.com
9255 Sunset Blvd.
Los Angeles, CA 90069
(310) 274-0628

CASTING SOCIETY OF AMERICA
An honorary society of casting directors. To be admitted, one must first apply and then be voted on.
www.castingsociety.com
606 N. Larchmont Blvd., Suite 4B
Los Angeles, CA 90004
(323) 463-1925

COSTUME DESIGNERS GUILD
Union representing motion picture, television and commercial costume designers. Promotes research, artistry, and technical expertise in the field of film and television costume design.
www.costumedesignerguild.com
4730 Woodman Ave., Suite 430
Sherman Oaks, CA 91423
(818) 905-1557

DIRECTORS GUILD OF AMERICA/DGA
Labor organization representing directors, unit production managers, first assistant directors, second assistant directors, technical coordinators, associate directors, stage managers, and production associates in feature films, television, short films, and digital projects.
www.dga.org

LOS ANGELES
7920 Sunset Blvd.
Los Angeles, CA 90046
(310) 289-2000

NEW YORK
110 W. 57th St.
NY, NY 10019
(212) 581-0370

CHICAGO
400 N. Michigan Ave., Suite 307
Chicago, IL 60611
(312) 644-5050

INTERNATIONAL ALLIANCE OF THEATRICAL STAGE EMPLOYEES/IATSE
Union representing technicians, artisans, and craftpersons in the entertainment industry including film and television production as well as live theater and trade shows.
www.iatse-intl.org

LOS ANGELES
10045 Riverside Dr.
Toluca Lake, CA 91602
(818) 980-3499

NEW YORK
1430 Broadway, 20th Fl.
NY, NY 10018
(212) 730-1770

MOTION PICTURE ASSOCIATION OF AMERICA/ MPAA
Trade association for the U.S. motion picture, home video, and television industries.
www.mpaa.org
15503 Ventura Blvd.
Encino, CA 91436
(818) 995-6600

MOTION PICTURE EDITORS GUILD
Union representing motion picture, television, and commercial editors, sound technicians, projectionists, and story analysts.
www.editorsguild.com

LOS ANGELES
7715 Sunset Blvd., Suite 200
Hollywood, CA 90046
(323) 876-4770

NEW YORK
1655 W. 46th St., Suite 900
NY, NY 10036
(212) 302-0700

NATIONAL ASSOCIATION OF BROADCAST EMPLOYEES AND TECHNICIANS-COMMUNICATIONS WORKERS OF AMERICA/ NABET-CWA
Union representing technicians, artisans, and craftspersons in the entertainment industry, including film and television production. Various locals.
www.nabet53.org
1918 W. Burbank Blvd.
Burbank, CA 91506
(818) 846-0490

NATIONAL ASSOCIATION OF TELEVISION PROGRAM EXECUTIVES/NATPE
Nonprofit association of business professionals who create, develop, and distribute content.
www.natpe.org
2425 Olympic Blvd., Suite 600E
Santa Monica, CA 90404
(310) 453-4440
(800) NATPE-GO

PRODUCERS GUILD OF AMERICA/PGA
Organization representing the interests of all the members of the producing team.
www.producersguild.org
8530 Wilshire Blvd., Suite 450
Beverly Hills, CA 90211
(310) 358-9020

SCREEN ACTORS GUILD (SAG)

Labor organization representing actors in feature films, television, short films, and digital projects.
www.sag.org

LOS ANGELES
5757 Wilshire Blvd.
Los Angeles, CA 90036
(323) 954-1600

NEW YORK
1515 Broadway, 44th fl
NY, NY 10036
(212) 944-1030

SOCIETY OF OPERATING CAMERAMEN/SOC

Organization promoting excellence in the fields of camera operation and the allied camera crafts. Open to all experienced operators and offers access to equipment vendors and training sessions with newly introduced equipment.
www.soc.org
P.O. Box 2006
Toluca Lake, CA 91601
(818) 382-7070

TALENT MANAGERS ASSOCIATION/TMA

Nonprofit organization promoting and encouraging the highest standards of professionalism in the practice of talent management.
www.talentmanagers.org
4804 Laurel Canyon Blvd., #611
Valley Village, CA 91607
(310) 205-8495

WOMEN IN FILM/WIF

Professional women's organization founded to empower, promote, nurture and mentor women in the entertainment, communications, and media industries.
www.wif.org
8857 W. Olympic Blvd., #201
Beverly Hills, CA 90211
(310) 657-5144

WRITERS GUILD OF AMERICA/
WGAW (LA) WGAE (NY)

Labor organization representing writers in motion pictures, broadcast cable, and new technology industries.
www.wga.org

LOS ANGELES
7000 W Third St.
Los Angeles, CA 90048-4329
(323) 951-4000

NEW YORK
www.wgaeast.org
5555 W 57th St., Suite 1230
NY, NY 10019
(212) 767-7800

Services/Resources

ABC TALENT DEVELOPMENT PROGRAMS

ABC and Touchstone are equally opportunity employers with a long history of identifying and offering opportunities to diverse talent through the Walt Disney Studio/ABC Entertainment Writing Fellowship, The Talent Development department's Casting Project, DGA Directing Fellowship, Touchstone Partnership and the Scholarship Grant Program for filmmakers, writers, and directors.
http://www.abctalentdevelopment.com
500 S Buena Vista St.
Burbank CA 91521-4395
(818) 460-6055

ACADEMY OF MOTION PICTURE ARTS AND SCIENCES—MARGARET HERRICK LIBRARY

Research and reference collection.
www.oscars.org
333 S. La Cienega Blvd.
Beverly Hills CA 90211
(310) 247-3035

ACTING WORLD BOOKS

Resource for acting publications.
www.actingworldbooks.org
P.O. Box 3899
Hollywood, CA 90078
(818) 905-1345

ACTORS' WORK PROGRAM

Career counseling for members of the Actors' Fund of America.
www.actorsfund.org

LOS ANGELES
5757 Wilshire Blvd., Suite 400
Los Angeles, CA 90036-3635
(323) 933-9244

NEW YORK
729 Seventh Ave., 11th Fl.
NY, NY 10019
(212) 354-5480

AMERICAN FILM INSTITUTE

Organization dedicated to preserving and advancing the art of the moving image through special events, exhibitions, and education. Library open to public for in-house use.
www.afi.com

LOS ANGELES
2021 N. Western Ave.
Los Angeles, CA 90027
(323) 856-7600

WASHINGTON, D.C.
The John F. Kennedy Center for the Performing Arts
(202) 833-2348

AUDIENCES UNLIMITED
A service that contracts with shows to provide an audience.
www.tvtickets.com
100 Universal City Plaza
Bldg 4250MZ
Universal City, CA 91608
(818) 753-3470

BREAKDOWN SERVICES, LTD.
Communications network and casting system that provides integrated tools for casting directors and talent agents and managers, as well as essential information for actors.
www.breakdownservices.com
Los Angeles (310) 276-9166
New York (212) 869-2003
Vancouver (604) 943-7100
London (20) 7437-7631

DRAMA BOOK SHOP
Excellent bookstore for industry trade books. (NY)
www.dramabookshop.com
250 W. 40th St.
NY, NY 10018
(212) 730-8739

DRAMATISTS PLAY SERVICE, INC.
Play publisher.
www.dramatists.com
440 Park Ave. South
NY, NY 10016
(212) 683-8960

LARRY EDMUNDS CINEMA BOOKSHOP, INC.
Resource for industry publications.
www.larryedmunds.com
6644 Hollywood Blvd.
Hollywood, CA 90028
(323) 463-3273

SAMUEL FRENCH, INC.
Publishers of plays. Excellent bookstore.
www.samuelfrench.com

LOS ANGELES
7623 Sunset Blvd.
Hollywood, CA 90046
(323) 876-0570
11963 Ventura Blvd.
Studio City, CA 91604
(818) 762-0535

NEW YORK
45 W. 25th St.
NY, NY 10036

LOS ANGELES PUBLIC LIBRARY—FRANCES HOWARD GOLDWYN/HOLLYWOOD
Regional branch library.
www.LAPL.org
Entertainment Industry Collection
1623 N. Ivar Ave.
Los Angeles, CA 90028
(323) 856-8260

MUSEUM OF TELEVISION AND RADIO
Extensive collection of television and radio programming.
www.mtr.org
465 N. Beverly Dr.
Beverly Hills, CA 90210
(310) 786-1000

NEW YORK PUBLIC LIBRARY FOR PERFORMING ARTS
Extensive combination of circulating, reference, and rare archival collections in the performing arts.
www.nypl.org
40 Lincoln Center Plaza
NY, NY 10019
(212) 621-6600

OFF THE PAGE READING SERIES/SCRIPT CONSULTANT/CAREER COACH—ELLEN SANDLER
ellen@kohncommunications.com
Ellen Sandler is an Emmy-nominated writer, who has written and produced many prime time sitcoms and created original pilots for all the major networks. She is also a personal career coach who teaches producers, writers, and performers the skills of effective pitching as well as a top writing consultant and the director of "Off the Page!" a developmental reading series for spec scripts. You can engage her services to help you write a career-changing spec script by contacting her.

PHASE-L PRODUCTIONS
Offers digital video editing, in-studio taping, air checks, tape duplication, DVD mastering, digital photography headshots, box cover set-up, and photo prints.
7220 Woodman Ave., Suite 201
Van Nuys, CA 91405
(818) 782-4700

SCREEN ACTORS GUILD (SAG)
Labor organization representing actors in feature films, television, short history of promoting sitcom writers. Admission fee for submission. 25 finalists per year. Small tuition.
300 Television Plaza
Burbank, CA 91505
(818) 954-6000

UCLA ARTS LIBRARY
Excellent resource material including special script collections.
www.library.ucla.edu
UCLA
1400 Public Policy Bldg.
Los Angeles, CA 90095
(310) 206-5425

WARM-UP AND DJ
Blas Lorenzo
Klassic ProDukShuns
DJ Interactive Entertainment
klassic@usa.com
(213) 506-1155

WRITERS GUILD FOUNDATION—JAMES R. WEBB MEMORIAL LIBRARY
Collection dedicated to the art, craft, and history of writing for motion pictures, radio, television, and new media. Open to the public and Guild members.
7000 W. Third St.
Los Angeles, CA 90048-4329
(323) 782-4544

Recommended Classes

LOUDER! FASTER! FUNNIER! SITCOM TECHNIQUES CLASS
Taught by co-author Phil Ramuno
phil@sitcomcareer.com
(818) 991-6911

HARVEY LEMBECK COMEDY WORKSHOP HELAINE LEMBECK, MICHAEL LEMBECK
Now in its 40th year, the workshop has three levels but is aimed for the trained/working actor who wants to specialize in comedy. The workshop is designed to teach the actor how to play comedy legitimately in a scene. Uses improv as a tool to enhance the comedic skills for sitcoms, TV, and film. The student participates on stage three to four times each night. An interview is required for these ongoing classes and audition is by arrangement. Critiques are by the teacher only. Classes are often attended by professionals in all areas of the industry. Former students include Robin Williams, Penny Marshall, John Ritter, Jenna Elfman, Bryan Cranston, Kim Cattrall, John Laroquette, Alan Rachins, and Sharon Stone. (310) 271-2831.

ACTING FOR REAL
Suanne Spoke
www.suannespoke.com
A multi-award-winning actor/producer/coach, Spoke produced and starred in the critically acclaimed *Napoli Milionaria* at the Road Theatre; she won an Ovation award for Best Actress and a Los Angeles Drama Critics' Award for Best Production. She has been coaching privately for over seven years while cultivating her own TV and film career, and guest starring in more than 100 TV shows. Her class is geared toward the specific needs of the individual, focusing on character development, expanding one's instrument, and script analysis. Classes run in ten-week sessions (in the NOHO arts district) which include working seminars with casting directors, producers, and directors. Preliminary interviews are required and auditing is available
Call Donne McRae (818) 243-5182 (office) or (818) 618-5857 (cell).

CATLIN ADAMS ACTING LAB
An award-winning director and actress, Adams teaches an all-levels class on Monday nights at the Hudson Avenue Theatre in Hollywood. Classes cover improvisation, sensory work, camera technique exercises, monologue, and scene study. All classes are taught by Adams herself. Learn to prepare for a part, create a character, break down a script, and become your own director. Students work in every class. Class size is strictly limited. For information and interview call (323) 851-8811.

SHARON MADDEN'S CLASS
Madden was founding member of Circle Repertory Company. Teaches children's theatre workshop at Interact Theater in L.A. Her private adult class includes scenes from TV/film, cold reading, camera technique—making choices. She helps actors face their struggle to keep creativity and concentration alive in the face of the unnatural act that is the audition. (323) 655-3795

THE LAURA HENRY ACTING STUDIO
Henry has been the director of her two-year conservatory program in Santa Monica for 12 years. She taught in New York City at The Gately/Poole Acting Studio for eight years. Teaches Meisner technique, audition technique, and other classes. Graduates include: Keiko Agena, *Gilmore Girls*, and Mike O'Malley, *Yes Dear*.
1307 Pico Blvd.
Santa Monica, CA 90405
(310) 399-5744

IMPROV FOR ACTORS
Taught by actor Jeff Doucette at the Third Stage.
2811 W. Magnolia Blvd.
Burbank, CA 91505
(818) 769-3767

HOWARD FINE ACTING STUDIO

Instructors include Fine, Marilyn McIntyre, and other highly qualified acting teachers.
7801 Melrose Ave.
Los Angeles, CA 90046
(323) 951-1174
www.howardfine.com

THE BARN...SCENE STUDY AND WORKSHOPS WITH JOHN SHORT

Scene study at the barn is not about having all the answers. It is about knowing what questions to ask regarding your character and the requirements of the scene. Who am I? What do I want? How am I going to get it? How you answer these fundamental questions determines your unique vision of the character. That vision, combined with the ability to make your scene partner more important than you, is the key to creating work on stage or screen that has nothing to do with "good" acting, and everything to do with being present and alive in your work. Scene study classes and special workshops are taught by veteran actor and teacher John Short, whose credits run the gamut from the Broadway stage to feature films. Auditing is free and highly encouraged.
(323) 610 6560

SECOND CITY

The Writers' Conservatory Program
Uses Second City techniques and exercises to create material through improvisation. Syllabus developed by writer Jim Fisher.
8156 Melrose Ave.
Los Angeles, CA 90046
(323) 658-8190

FULL CIRCLE PRODUCTIONS

The Bay Area's premier school for film and television actors. Teachers have extensive acting and/or directing credits and use no-nonsense, cut-to-the-chase techniques to ensure you'll get the best training possible. FCP's students enjoy an unparalleled booking ratio and their success speaks to the quality of the staff and the curriculum.
1725 Clay St., Suite 100
San Francisco, CA 94109
(415) 982-2024
www.fullcircleproductions.com

Recommended Acting Coaches

PHIL RAMUNO (CO-AUTHOR) (818) 991-6911

sitcomcareer.com

DINAH LENNEY MILLS (323) 664-8186

Private coach for adults and children for theater, television, and film auditions. Worked as a coach on *The Hughleys* for ABC and UPN. Teaches group classes for the Silverlake Children's Theatre and acts as vocal director of bi-annual productions. Also teaches cold reading workshops and on-camera audition technique in UCLA's summer program for young adults and conducts acting seminars. Admission fee for submission. 25 finalists per year. Small tuition.
300 Television Plaza
Burbank, CA 91505
(818) 954-6000

DEBORAH PERLMAN

deborahperlman@warnerbros.com at the Neighborhood Playhouse School. She continues to work as an actor, herself, in all three arenas.

SUANNE SPOKE PRIVATE COACHING

(*See* Acting for REAL under Recommended Acting Classes.)

KITTY SWINK

On-set and private coaching. (818) 508-9169.

GREGG T. DANIEL.

On-set and private coaching. Daniel coaches on UPN's *One on One* (323) 737-2735.

CATLIN ADAMS

Private Coaching (323) 851-8811 (*See* Catlin Adams Acting Lab under Recommended Acting Classes.)

SHARON MADDEN

On-set and private coaching. Wonderful with young talent. (323) 665-3795. (See Sharon Madden above.)

JUDY KERR

On-set and private acting coach, one-time sessions for career coaching. (*See* Recommended books: *Acting Is Everything: An Actor's Guide Book for a Sucessful Career in Los Angeles.*)

MARK TAYLOR

On-set and private coaching. Comedy and drama. (818) 786-5712.

STEVE MUSCARELLA

On-set and off-set coaching. Helps actors with scenes and monologues as well as showcase preparation. Member: DGA, WGA, AFTRA, Academy of Magical Arts. (818) 789-6898. muscarella@earthlink.net.

DENISE DOWSE

Denise is a working actress who offers private coaching sessions for auditions, works on the sitcom *Girlfriends* as their Dialogue/Acting coach, teaches an ongoing Adult Acting Class and is the Resident Director at Amazing Grace Conservatory (AGC), a Performing Arts School for youth ages 6 to 21. Her client list is vast and varied. (Call or email for rates.) Contact number: (323) 369-9582. Email: poohzly@aol.com.

FRED TUCKER

Acting credits include film, TV, and stage. Award-winning stage actor. Private coaching list includes many stand-up comedians. First coaching job was for Gill Hill, Inspector Todd in *Beverly Hills Cop 1, 2,* and *3*. Many years scene study and improv teacher. Presently dialogue and acting coach for UPN sitcom *One On One*. Call or e-mail for rates (310) 413-4605 or freddvision@msn.com.

ART MANKE

Private coach. Manke has over 20 years of experience as an actor, director, and coach. In addition to directing numerous award-winning productions across the country, he was a founding artistic director of LA's acclaimed classical theatre company, A Noise Within, and was trained at the prestigious American Conservatory Theatre. For further information, call (323) 667-1231.

Network Information

ABC ENTERTAINMENT TELEVISION GROUP
500 S. Buena Vista St.
Burbank, CA 91521
(818) 460-7777
www.abc.com

CBS ENTERTAINMENT
7800 Beverly Blvd.
Los Angeles, CA 90036-2188
(323) 575-2345
www.cbs.com

NBC ENTERTAINMENT
3000 W. Alameda Ave.
Burbank, CA 91523-0001
(818) 840-4444

TWENTIETH CENTURY FOX TELEVISION
10201 W. Pico Blvd.
Los Angeles, CA 90035
(310) 369-1000
www.fox.com

UNITED PARAMOUNT NETWORK
11800 Wilshire Blvd.
Los Angeles, CA 90025
(310) 575-7000
www.upn.com

WB NETWORK
4000 Warner Blvd.
Bldg. 34R
Burbank, CA 91522
818-977-5000
www.thewb.com

Selected Studios and Entertainment Groups

BET-BLACK ENTERTAINMENT TELEVISION
One BET Plaza, 1235 W. St. NE
Washington DC 20018-1211
(202) 608-2000
www.bet.com

BIG TICKET TELEVISION
Sunset Gower Studio
1438 N. Gower St.
Box 45, Bldg. 35
Hollywood, CA 90028-8362
(323) 860-7400
www.paramount.com

GREENBLATT JANOLLARI STUDIO
1438 N. Gower St.
Box 20
Bldg. 16, Suite 200
Hollywood, CA 90028
(323) 468-3399

SONY PICTURES ENTERTAINMENT
10202 W. Washington Blvd.
Culver City, CA 90232
(310) 244-4000
www.spe.sony.com

VIACOM ENTERTAINMENT GROUP
5555 Melrose Ave.
Los Angeles, CA 90038
(323) 956-5000

WALT DISNEY PICTURES/TOUCHSTONE PICTURES
500 S. Buena Vista St.
Burbank, CA 91521
(818) 560-1000
www.disney.com

WARNER BROS. TELEVISION
4000 Warner Blvd.
Burbank, CA 91522-0001
www.warnerbros.com

Recommended Publications

ACADEMY PLAYERS DIRECTORY
Print and online casting directories.
1313 N. Vine St.
Hollywood, CA 90028
(310) 247-3058
www.playersdirectory.com

BACKSTAGE
Industry trade publication (NY). Has best theatre information for actors.
www.backstage.com
770 Broadway
NY, NY 10003
(646) 654-5700

BACKSTAGE WEST
Industry trade publication (LA). Has best theatre information for actors.
www.backstage.com
5055 Wilshire Blvd.
Los Angeles, CA 90036-6100
(323) 525-2358

DAILY VARIETY
www.variety.com

Los Angeles
5700 Wilshire Blvd., Suite 120
Los Angeles, CA 90036
(323) 857-6600

New York
360 Park Ave. South
NY, NY 10010
(646) 746-7002

HOLLYWOOD CREATIVE DIRECTORY/HCD
Comprehensive list of contact information for TV and film industry. We highly recommend having this resource in your personal library.
www.hcdonline.com
1024 N. Orange Dr.
Hollywood, CA 90038
(323) 308-3400
(800) 815-0530

HOLLYWOOD REPORTER
5055 Wilshire Blvd., 6th Fl.
Los Angeles, CA 90036
(323) 525-2000
www.hollywoodreporter.com

ROSS REPORTS TELEVISION AND FILM
Listing of agents and casting director contact information.
770 Broadway
NY, NY 10003
(646) 654-5730 (editorials)
(800) 745-8922 (subscription)

Books

ACTING IS BELIEVING
Charles McGaw and Larry D. Clark. Publisher: Harcourt Brace College Publishers.

ACTING IS EVERYTHING: AN ACTOR'S GUIDE BOOK FOR A SUCESSFUL CAREER IN LOS ANGELES
Judy Kerr's personal reference guide now in its eighth edition from her 30 years as an L.A. acting coach. Guide helps actors negotiate their way. Publisher: September Publishing.

ACTING: THE FIRST SIX LESSONS
Richard Boleslavsky. Publisher: Theatre Art Books, Routledge.

THE ACTORS ENCYCLOPEDIA OF CASTING DIRECTORS
Karen Kondazian has compiled insider information and intimate profiles from talking to premier casting directors in film, television, theatre, and commercials from Los Angeles to New York. Publisher: Lone Eagle Publishing Co.

FROM AGENT TO ACTOR
Edgar Small. Published by Samuel French Trade.

THE ART OF ACTING
Stella Adler. Publisher: Applause Books.

THE ARTISTS WAY
Julia Cameron. Publisher: Penguin Putnam, Inc.

AUDITION
Michael Shurtlleff. Publisher: Bantam Books.

AUDITIONING
Joanna Merlin. Publisher: Vintage, Random House.

CLASSIC SITCOMS
Vince Waldron. Publisher: Silman-James Press.

THE COMEDY BIBLE
Judy Carter. Publisher: Simon and Schuster.

THE DIRECTOR'S JOURNEY
Mark W. Travis. Publisher: Michael Wiese Productions.

THE ELEMENTS OF EDITING
Arthur Plotnik. Publisher: Collier Books/Macmillan Publishing Co.

FILM & TELEVISION ACTING
Ian Bernard. Publisher: Focal Press

THE FRASIER SCRIPTS
Created by David Angell/Peter Casey/David Lee. Publisher: Newmarket Press.

GET IN THE CAR, JANE
Billy Van Zandt. Publisher: Falcon Books.

HOW TO AGENT YOUR AGENT
Nancy Rainford. Publisher: Lone Eagle
Publishing Co.

HOW TO AUDITION
Gordon Hunt. Publisher: Quill, Harper Collins.

ICG MAGAZINE
"Father Knows Best? Bruce Finn shoots 24P on
UPN's new comedy *One on One*." March 2002, Vol.
73, No. 3.

IMPROV COMEDY
Andy Goldberg. Publisher: Samuel French Trade.

IMPROVISATION TECHNIQUE
Stephen Book. Publisher: Silmar-James Press

THE LUCY BOOK
Geoffrey Mark Fidelman. Publisher: Renaissance
Books.

A MARTIAN WOULDN'T SAY THAT
Compiled by Leonard B. Stern and Diane L.
Robinson. Publisher: Price Stern Sloan, Inc. The
Putnam Berkley Group, Inc.

NEXT: AN ACTOR'S GUIDE TO AUDITIONING
Ellie Kanner, C.S.A., and Paul G. Bens, Jr. Publisher:
Lone Eagle Publishing Co.

NONLINEAR
Michael Rubin. Publisher: Triad Publishing Co.

RESPECT FOR ACTING
Uta Hagen. Publisher: Wiley Publishing, Inc.

SANFORD MEISNER ON ACTING
Sanford Meisner and Dennis Longwell. Publisher:
Vintage, Random House.

THE SEINFELD SCRIPTS
Publisher: Harper Perennial.

A SENSE OF DIRECTION
William Ball. Publisher: Drama Book Publishers.

STAND UP COMEDIANS ON TELEVISION
Museum of Television & Radio. Publisher: Harry N.
Abrams, Inc.

TIPS
Jon Jory. Publisher: Smith Krause Book.

**THE TUMULTUOUS LIFE AND COMIC ART OF
LUCILLE BALL**
Stefan Kanfer. Publisher: Alfred Knopf.

THE WAY OF THE ACTOR
Brian Bates. Publisher: Shambhala Publications, Inc.

WRITING FOR TELEVISION COMEDY
Jerry Rannow. Publisher: Allworth Press.

On-Line Resources

Alan Rafkin script archive at Syracuse University.
   http://libwww.syr.edu/information/media/
   archive/rafkinscripts.htm.
Drew's Script-O-Rama
   (transcribed scripts)
http://www.script-o-rama.com/.
The Internet Movie Data Base—includes TV credits
   www.imdb.com
www.TVGuide.com
   Great data about the TV business
www.TVtome.com
   More great data.

Comedy Clubs — Los Angeles

ACME COMEDY THEATER
La Brea STREET No.
Hollywood, CA 90036
(323) 525-0202

GROUNDLINGS
7307 Melrose Ave.
Los Angeles, CA 90046
Exec Dir. Krista Gano
FAX (323) 934-8143
(323) 934-9700

ICE HOUSE
Pasadena, CA
(626) 577-1894

THE IMPROV
8162 Melrose Ave.
Los Angeles, CA 90046
(323) 651-2583
FAX (323) 651-0710

Comedy Clubs — New York

THE BOSTON COMEDY CLUB
82 West 3rd St.
NY, NY
(212) 477-1000

CAROLINE'S ON BROADWAY
1626 Broadway
NY, NY 10019-7408
(212) 757-4100

COMEDY CELLAR
115 MacDougal St.
NY, NY
(212) 254-3480

COMIC STRIP LIVE
1568 Second Ave.
NY, NY
(212) 861-9386

DANGERFIELD'S
1118 First Ave.
NY, NY
(212) 593-1650

GLADYS' COMEDY ROOM
145 W. 45th St.
NY, NY
(212) 832-1762

GOTHAM COMEDY CLUB
34 W. 22nd St.
(212) 367-9000

NEW YORK COMEDY CLUB
241 E. 24th St.
NY, NY
(212) 696-5233

STAND-UP NY
236 West 78th St.
NY, NY
(212) 595-0850

THE UPRIGHT CITIZENS BRIGADE THEATER
161 W. 22nd St.
NY, NY
(212) 366-9176

Sitcom Jobs

PRODUCTION

These positions are actual jobs available on one network sitcom. The amount of people in each category and sometimes the titles vary by show. Not all of these people are credited on the air.

EXECUTIVE PRODUCER (Nonwriting): May be production company executives, star, star's manager, star's lawyer, director or miscellaneous others.

EXECUTIVE PRODUCER (Writing): The show runner and sometimes the show's star.

CO-EXECUTIVE PRODUCER: Three of the "senior" writers.

SUPERVISING PRODUCER: Two of the "next echelon" writers.

PRODUCER: Five people including writers and the actual producer who hires the crew and more writers.

STORY EDITOR: Writer.

STAFF WRITER: The three lowest links of the writer chain.

DIRECTOR: Some shows have only one and others have several that rotate.

CASTING DIRECTOR: Individual or two-person team.

CASTING ASSOCIATE: Assists the casting director.

DIRECTOR, ADMINISTRATIVE AFFAIRS: Production company official.

ASSISTANTS: Two assistants to the production company executives, two more to the show's star, and one each to the show runner and actual producer.

ASSOCIATE PRODUCER: Handles many of the show producer's functions.

PRODUCTION SECRETARY: Also works for the show's producer.

PRODUCTION ASSISTANTS: Three office "runners."

NIGHT P.A.: Delivers scripts.

STAGE P.A.: Takes phone messages during rehearsals.

WRITER'S ASSISTANTS: Three script typists and would-be writers.

ASSOCIATE DIRECTOR: The Director's first assistant on a taped show. First AD on a film show runs the stage.

STAGE MANAGER: The Director's assistant who runs the stage. Second AD on a film show assists the first AD.

2nd STAGE MANAGER: 2nd stage assistant to the Director on a tape show.

3rd STAGE MANAGER: Only used on shows with many background actors. 2nd Second AD on film shows.

PRODUCTION ASSOCIATE: The Script Supervisor under another name.

TEACHER: Also responsible for child welfare considerations. Not a necessary position on shows without child actors. Sometimes there are multiple teachers.

BABY COACH: Works with infants.

DIALOGUE COACH: Works with the children who were in school during a rehearsal, stands in for them, and is available to the adults for running lines.

DIALOGUE/STAND-IN: Stand-in for the show's star and available to run lines with any actor.

SECURITY: Star's bodyguard and watches the stage.

POSTPRODUCTION AND MUSIC

EDITOR: Assembles and edits show.

POST PRODUCTION COORDINATOR: Schedules all postproduction needs.

AVID LOADER/ON-LINE EDITOR: Transfers footage to the computerized edit system and conforms the final edit decision list from the system to the master tapes.

MUSIC DIRECTOR: Composes theme music, music cues, and chooses any commercial music cues.

POST MIXER: Sweetens all the audio elements.

AUDIENCE REACTION: The "laugh" man.

RECORDIST: Assists the Mixer.

WARDROBE

COSTUME DESIGNER: Heads the wardrobe department.

WARDROBE SUPERVISOR: Second in command.

COSTUMERS: Four assistants also referred to as "dressers."

LIGHTING AND GRIP

LIGHTING DIRECTOR: Would be the Director of Photography on a film show.

GAFFER: In charge of hanging and focusing the lighting instruments.

BOARDMAN: Switches on the lighting instruments and controls levels.

ELECTRIC: Three lighting assistants.

KEY GRIP: Sets up the walls of the set.

LADDER: Works on ladders for set needs.

MAKEUP AND HAIR

MAKEUP: Three people. One is sometimes dedicated to the star.

HAIR: Two people. One is sometimes dedicated to the star.

TECHNICAL CREW

TECHNICAL DIRECTOR: Switches cameras on line feed. Heads camera department on tape shows.

TECHNICAL COORDINATOR: Assists director in coordinating camera blocking. Heads department on film shows.

AUDIENCE SWITCHER: Switches cameras' video assist on film shows.

AUDIO MIXER: Mixes sound.

A2: Assists the Mixer and plays back sound effects.

P.A. MIXER: Balances the audience mikes and the speakers in the audience.

CAMERAS: Four operators.

FIRST ASSISTANT CAMERA: Focus puller. Takes responsibility for camera being loaded correctly (Film).

SECOND ASSISTANT CAMERA: Helps load film (Film).

DOLLY GRIP: Operates dolly that camera is on (Film).

VIDEO: Balances the video feeds from all the cameras.

VTR: Records the line feed and the four isos.

BOOMS: Two operators.

Camera Utility: Two cable pullers/assistants.

BOOM UTILITY: Two boom pushers/cable pullers.

ART DEPARTMENT

PRODUCTION DESIGNER: Created the set design.

SET DESIGNER: Assistant to Designer. Responsible for this show.

SET DECORATOR: Responsible for all set items that are not working props.

LEAD PERSON: Second in command to Decorator. Stands by all rehearsals.

SWING DECORATOR: Helps position the dressings.

DIRECTOR, ART DEPARTMENT: Sometimes designs sets.

PROPMASTER: Buys, rents, and places working props.

ASSISTANT PROPMASTER: Stands by all rehearsals.

PROPS/SWING: Helps position props.

COORDINATOR, CONSTRUCTION: Self-explanatory.

COORDINATOR, STAGING SERVICES: Self-explanatory.

ART DEPARTMENT SECRETARY: Episodic Expense Coordinator.

SET DESIGNERS: Three other designers for other shows from this company.

ART DEPARTMENT PAS: Three "runners."

WAREHOUSE/PROPS AND WAREHOUSE/SCENERY

TRANSPORTATION: Two people to truck walls and large set pieces.

MISCELLANEOUS

CRAFT SERVICE: Keeps snacks and nourishment for everyone on stage.

OUTSIDE CONTRACTORS

AFTRA: Actor's Union representative. SAG on a film show.

AUDIENCE TICKETS: Provides tickets to public.

AUDIENCE PAGES: Check tickets, manage guest list, and seat the audience.

BOOM: Microphone rentals.

CAPTIONING: Has to do with credits.

EXTRAS CASTING: Supplies background artists and sometimes stand-ins.

FAN MAIL: Sorts, delivers, and sometimes answers fan mail.

INTERNATIONAL DISTRIBUTION: Self-explanatory.

MUSIC CLEARANCE: Gets permissions for all music used in show.

OFF-LINE: Editing facility.

ON-LINE: Possibly a different facility.

POST SOUND: Postproduction sound facility.

RESEARCH: Including script commercial conflicts and clearances.

VIDEO TRUCK: Includes cameras, videotape machines, and control rooms.

Above-the-line:
> Actors, director, and producers above-and below-the-line are either under contract to the studio, sign a production company deal-memo, or get paid by the day.

Act break:
> The dividing point in the story usually punctuated by a twist in the plot that makes the audience want to come back after the second commercial break.

AD:
> The director's assistants. Evolved differently in film and live television (which became videotaped television). Film shows have an Assistant Director, Second Assistant, and sometimes a Second 2nd AD. Taped shows have an Associate Director, Stage Manager, and Second Stage Manager. The new DGA contract will change the title of Technical Coordinators to Associate Directors.

Air check:
> Recording a show off the air for purposes of archiving it or checking its content.

Air show:
> The live performance of a show in front of cameras and audience while film or tape is recording.

Background artists:
> Extras. Members of the Screen Actors Guild.

Below-the-line:
> The crew and production staff. Some are paid only for the weeks they work. Others are "carried" and receive payment for the weeks that a show is not in production and on hiatus. Above-the-line staff includes the writers, producers, and the director. Above-and below-the-line are either under contract to the studio, sign a production company deal-memo, or get paid by the day.

Blow:
> A final joke at the end of a scene, usually a big joke. See *Button*.

Boom:
> The stand for the microphone.

Booth:
> The video control room or hub.

Breakdown:
> The tool by which agents submit their clients for a possible audition. A breakdown, at its best, is a description of the character and what makes that character tick. At its least, it is a summation of how a character serves the plot. It gives the actor insight into what the writers had in mind.

Business:
> Any physical action; any movement or gesture. It may support dialogue or exist on its own.

Button:
> Joke at the end of a scene, usually a small joke. Emphasis given to the end of any joke. See *Blow*.

Callback:
> A reference to previously mentioned material or piece of business. Repeating a big joke. A second audition for an actor.

Call time:
> The time an actor or crew member is expected to be on stage ready to work.

Carrying:
> Having scripts in hands.

Cold open:
> Short scene which precedes the first act. It appears before the opening credits to entice or tease the audience into not changing the channel and instead watching the entire episode. The networks try to get the viewing audience to watch their channel without switching after each program ends. They sometimes make the teaser so "cold" or unanticipated that it may start immediately as the other show ends, without even a station break to separate them.

Collate:
> Putting the script in order with the new pages.

Counter:
> To adjust your position after another actor moves.

Coverage:
> All the camera shots. If a show has many characters, the producers may want you to "cover" all the actors with close-ups.

Craft service:
> One or two people who provide snacks (and sometimes meals) for the crew working on stage.

Cueing:
> Saying the words aloud for one character with a partner saying the lines for all the other characters. Also, to signal an action, such as an entrance.

Cue bite:
> To take out the pauses between the lines.

Dissolve:
> An edit that simultaneously eliminates one image while creating the next.

Deadpan:
> A face that shows no emotion, e.g., a poker face. The human face has been referred to as a "pan" since the 19th century, possibly because the face is broad and shallow like a dishpan.

Dichotomy:
> Literary tool employed to evoke humor. It divides an idea into separate contradictory classes, thereby bringing out the funny aspect.

Director's cut:
> The first completed assembly of the show. The DGA contract stipulates that directors get to edit their show first, or at least give notes on the first assembly.

Dissolve:
> The fade on image out as the next image fades in.

Dollies:
> A sophisticated wagon for the camera. It is usually pushed but can also be pulled. It can operate on the floor or on tracks. The film camera operator rides on the wagon.

Double take:
> A sight gag involving rapidly turning the head twice.

Doubling:
> Having multiples of props, wardrobe, or actors.

Dovetailing:
> See *Cue bite.*

Downstage:
> The part of the stage closer to the audience. It is so named because in the past when stages (not audiences) were raked (tilted), as the actors walked away from the audience, they literally were traveling up the lower part of the stage.

Down to time:
> The time that network is allowing for this program, including opening titles and end credits.

Dramedy:
> Show that has both comedy and drama.

Dress show:
> First audience show. This name came from live television's final dress rehearsal. This show is taped and/or filmed and serves as the first of at least two performance choices for the editor.

Dressed:
> Decorated.

Dry blocking:
> A part of rehearsal in which the crew watches the actors perform the scene just to see where the actors go and listens to what they say.

Echo:
> An exact callback. Repetition of same word or business.

End credits:
> The end of the show where the names of the crew are listed.

ESU:
> Engineering setup.

Feed:
> To cue actors on a specific line. Usually preceded by an actor calling for a line by saying, "Line!" See *Setup.*

First assembly:
> The director's cut.

50/50:
> The mirrorlike physical relationship between two actors. It facilitates each actor's being equally visible to the audience or cameras.

First team:
> The actors who are in the scene. They are replaced by stand-ins called the second team.

Fourth wall:
> A theatre term referring to the imaginary wall through which the audience is watching. Breaking the fourth wall in theatre is when a character speaks directly to the audience. Breaking the fourth wall in television is when the actor looks directly into the camera lens and appears to be talking directly to the viewers.

Gaffer:
> A person on the electrical crew in charge of hanging and focusing the lighting instruments.

Getting read:
> The show runner reading spec script.

Give it away:
> To prematurely reveal something to the audience. To telegraph what or where the joke will be.

Green bed:
> Floor or walkway hanging above the lighting grid.

Handle:
> One or more incidental words that lead in a sentence. It gives dialogue a conversational tone.

Hanging:
> Attaching lamps to the grid for use in lighting a show.

Hold:
Waiting for the audience to finish laughing.

Hiccup:
A reset of 30 seconds or less. A short pause in the scene usually taken so cameras, sets, or props can change, move, or reset. The cameras continue to roll and the delay is edited out later. The film or tape continues to roll during a hiccup.

Hi-def:
High-definition TV.

Irony:
A literary device in which the meaning of the words used is the opposite of their usual sense.

Iso coverage:
Cameras that are not on-line as the active camera of the switched feed are also being recorded or "isolated" for use during postproduction.

J.T.C.:
Joke to come.

Jumped laughs:
Continuing with dialogue when the audience wants to laugh. Causes a problem by shortening the laugh and causes the audience not to hear dialogue that follows.

Land:
The ability of a joke to get a laugh or score.

Laying pipe:
Providing the exposition.

Line feed:
The edit made live during a taping.

L.T.C.:
Abbreviation for "line to come."

Live cutting:
An edit that is simultaneously broadcast or taped.

Load in:
Moving scenery on to the sound stage at the beginning of the week.

Match action:
To repeat exact physical action of what has been done before in order to maintain continuity from one take to another. Used during overlap or reset, or repeated takes or coverage.

Mislead:
To intentionally take the audience in one direction with information or an idea so that you can surprise them by going in the other direction. The information given before a turn.

Monitors:
TV screens that show either the live feed or the isos.

Off book:
When an actor no longer needs to carry a script in his hands because he has memorized the words. This makes it easier for him to act, handle props, and move about the stage more freely.

Opening titles:
The opening of the show, sometimes accompanied by the theme song. Opening titles always give the name of the show, the names of the actors, and often the name of the show creators.

Operative word:
The word to be stressed. The important word to understand the plot or the joke.

Overlap:
To repeat action or dialogue on a subsequent take.

Over the top:
A description for a performance that is too large or exaggerated.

Page 1 rewrite:
A complete reworking of the script beginning with the first page.

Patter:
Amusing lines delivered rapidly by a performer(s).

Pay it off:
Deliver the punchline.

Pedestal dolly:
A heavy-duty microphone stand on wheels— only, in this case, the mike is a camera with extended arms to control the panning, tilting, focus, and the zoom lens. This "ped" also has a pneumatic assist to raise or lower the camera's height.

Picking up the cues:
See *Cue bite.*

Pickups:
Retakes after the audience has gone home. Partial sections of a scene reshot after whole scene has been completed.

Pilot:
The first script of a series; the actual first show of a series.

Pipe:
The exposition in a script.

Pitch:
Telling your original idea to a network, in hopes that they will like the idea enough to order a script. Suggesting individual jokes as part of an ongoing rewriting process.

Playback:
An already recorded portion of the show. Because of the time code imprinted on tape, and the script supervisor's records, it is easy to locate an exact part of the already recorded scene.

Practical:
A light or appliance that functions and is used by an actor in a scene.

Producer's cut:
Second version of a show (after Director's Cut) on which the producers have given notes.

Punch:
To review the joke and make it better. Also, to emphasize a line in a performance.

Punchline:
The funny part of the joke. It will not be funny without the setup.

Quad split:
Simple four-way output of each of the cameras.

Replace:
To come up with an entirely new joke.

Resets:
Changing camera positions or scenery. It may be a long enough pause to require the film or tape to stop.

Residuals:
Payments negotiated by a union for reuse of a TV show.

Retake:
Doing a scene over.

Room:
The writer's room or the audition office.

Room tone:
The sounds that go on in an empty room with no one moving. It may appear silent to the naked ear, but actually there is ambient sound. During pickups it is common to record 45 seconds of room tone in a swing set used only on that episode. It is prelaid for scenes with no background actors.

Second:
DGA position of Second AD or Second Stage Manager.

Second banana:
The second character of importance. A term from burlesque.

Second team:
The stand-ins.

Setup:
The statement or premise that has to be understood for a joke to get a laugh. The front half of the joke.

Set-line:
The edge of the set. This line is called the proscenium line in the theatre.

Shooting off:
Composing a camera shot beyond where there is a set.

Show runner:
The head writer. His official title is Executive Producer.

Shtick:
An extreme piece of physical business such as a pratfall. The old Yiddish term for piece or routine. It described the physical comedy or little dances of vaudeville.

Sides:
A few pages of the script. Used at an audition, these pages are an actor's guide to the story and character.

Sight gag:
A joke whose laugh is predicated upon a visual.

Slate:
To identify yourself at the beginning of an audition tape.

Slow burn:
Sight gag involving slow turn of the head.

Speed-thru:
An exercise in which actors recite their lines or dialogue at a quicker pace than normal (sometimes devoid of meaning).

Spit take:
A sight gag involving spitting.

Staffing:
Getting a season as a writer on a series.

Standing sets:
Sets that are used every week.

Subtext:
What an actor is thinking while he says the line; *Sub* meaning "under" and *text* meaning "wording." It is the silent or hidden message. Subtext is an important tool for an actor not only when understating something but also whenever a character is thinking something different from, or more complex than, what his actual words (or lack of words) allow him to say aloud.

Suits:
Network or studio executives named because of the odd uniform they wear.

Sweetening:
Adding laughs or the entire process of audio postproduction.

Swing sets:
Sets that are new to a particular episode. On some very busy shows, the crew actually swings them into a space between two regular sets.

Table draft:
The version of the script that actually gets read the first time the cast is assembled. This reading takes place around a table rather than on a set.

Tag:
Short, final scene before or during the end credits.

Take:
Each redo of a scene or portion of a scene. It is assigned a take number for keeping things straight during editing.

Tally light:
> A light (usually red) on the camera that comes on when that camera is on-line.

Teaser:
> A short scene that precedes the first act. This scene introduces the theme of the episode.

Telegraph:
> To give away what is about to come. Tipping the joke.

Throw it away:
> To not emphasize information. A direction given to make information more casual so as not to telegraph the joke that is coming.

Tipping the joke:
> To telegraph information that is coming.

Topper:
> A punchline on top of another punchline.

Turn:
> The point between the setup and punchline or mislead and punchline where the information or emotion switches unexpectedly to another direction. Often accompanied by a physical turn.

Tweaking:
> Adjusting lighting instruments.

24P:
> A video recording method progressively scanning 24 frames each second. Because of electricity's 60 cycles, standard video uses two scans of each frame that is then interpolated together to make each video frame. This creates 30 frames of video for each second of action.

Twist:
> An unexpected plot point. A surprise.

Understatement:
> A joke employing irony. It deliberately states the truth inaccurately or too weakly in order to make the audience laugh.

UPM:
> Unit Production Manager. Directors Guild members since 1964.

Video village:
> The bank of monitors and podiums set up on the stage floor as the technical hub.

Walla:
> Nondescript conversations mixed into the sound track.

Warm-up:
> A stand-up comic hired to be the official host for the audience.

Wrapped:
> The finish of the day, episode, or series for an individual or the entire company.

Wrinkle:
> The complication during Act Two.

Year is of first airing. Listed networks aired first run episodes.

1947   *Mary Kay and Johnny* (DUMONT/NBC/CBS)
     15-min., then 30, then 15 daily

1948   *The Growing Paynes* (DUMONT)
     The Laytons (DUMONT)

1949   *The Goldbergs* (CBS/NBC/DUMONT/SYND)
     a.k.a. *Molly*
     The Aldrich Family (NBC)
     Mama (CBS) a.k.a. *I Remember Mama*
     The Life of Riley (NBC)
     Mixed Doubles (NBC)
     The Family Genius (DUMONT)
     The Hartmans (NBC) a.k.a. *The Hartmans at Home*
     The Ruggles (ABC)
     That Wonderful Guy (ABC)
     Wesley (CBS)

1950   *The Stu Erwin Show* (ABC) a.k.a. *Life With Stu Erwin, The New Stu Erwin Show, The Trouble With Father*
     Young and Gay (CBS) later *The Girls*
     The George Burns and Gracie Allen Show (CBS) sitcom with variety
     The Jack Benny Program (CBS) sitcom with variety
     Menasha the Magnificent (NBC)
     Mama Rosa (ABC)
     The Hank McClune Show (NBC)
     Beulah (ABC)

1951   *Young Mr. Bobbin* (NBC)
     I Love Lucy (CBS)
     The Amos & Andy Show (CBS) a.k.a. *Amos 'n' Andy*
     Actors Hotel (ABC) summer series
     The Egg and I (CBS) 15-min. daily
     Those Endearing Young Charms (NBC)
     Meet Corliss Archer (SYND)

1952   *My Hero* (NBC) a.k.a. *The Bob Cummings Show*
     My Little Margie (CBS/NBC)
     The Abbott and Costello Show (SYND)

Meet Millie (CBS)
Our Miss Brooks (CBS)
Leave it to Larry (CBS)
My Friend Irma (CBS)
Doc Corkle (NBC)
Heaven For Betsy (CBS) two 15-min. sitcoms a week
It's a Business (DUMONT)
Life With Luigi (CBS)
The Adventures of Ozzie and Harriet (ABC)
I Married Joan (NBC) a.k.a. *The Joan Davis Show*
A Date With Judy (ABC)
Boss Lady (NBC)

1953   *Make Room for Daddy* (ABC/CBS) later *The Danny Thomas Show*
     Where's Raymond? (ABC) a.k.a. *The Ray Bolger Show*
     Ethel and Albert (NBC/CBS/ABC) last regular live sitcom ending in 1956
     Bonino (NBC)
     Mr. Peepers (NBC)
     The Red Buttons Show (NBC) started earlier as a variety show
     Life with Father (CBS)
     My Favorite Husband (CBS)
     Private Secretary (CBS) a.k.a. *Susie*
     Meet Mr. McNutley (CBS) a.k.a. *The Ray Milland Show, Meet Mr. McNulty*
     Life With Elizabeth (SYND)
     The Alan Young Show (CBS) started earlier as a variety show
     Topper (CBS)
     Pride of the Family (ABC)
     Marge and Jeff (DUMONT) 15 min. daily
     My Son Jeep (NBC)
     The Adventures of Colonel Humphrey J. Flack (ABC/DUMONT/SYND)
     Jamie (ABC)
     Take It From Me (ABC) a.k.a. *The Jean Carroll Show*
     The Pride of the Family (ABC)

1954   *Mickey Rooney Show* (NBC) a.k.a. *Hey
     Mulligan*
  The Duke (NBC) summer series
  Willy (CBS)
  The World of Mr. Sweeney (NBC) 15 min.,
     started as part of a variety show
  It's a Great Life (NBC)
  Dear Phoebe (NBC)
  That's My Boy (CBS)
  Honestly, Celeste! (CBS)
  Father Knows Best (CBS)
  December Bride (CBS)
  The Donald O'Connor Texaco Show (NBC)
  The Halls of Ivy (CBS)
  The Marriage (NBC)

1955   *The Honeymooners* (CBS) started earlier as
     part of a variety show
  Professional Father (CBS)
  Norby (NBC)
  The Eddie Cantor Comedy Theater (SYND)
     anthology, sitcom some weeks
  It's Always Jan (CBS)
  You'll Never Get Rich (CBS) later *The Phil
     Silvers Show* a.k.a. *Sgt. Bilko*
  The Bob Cummings Show (NBC/CBS) a.k.a.
     Love That Bob
  The People's Choice (NBC)
  Homer Bell (SYND) sitcom-western
  The Great Gildersleeve (SYND)
  So this is Hollywood (NBC)
  The Soldiers (NBC) summer series
  The Whiting Girls (CBS) summer series

1956   *Stanley* (NBC)
  The Brothers (CBS)
  The Adventures of Hiram Holiday (NBC)
  Oh! Susanna (CBS/ABC) a.k.a. *The Gayle
     Storm Show*
  Hey, Jeannie (CBS)
  The Charles Farrell Show (CBS)
  Joe & Mabel (CBS) summer series

1957   *Bachelor Father* (CBS/NBC/ABC)
  Sally (NBC)
  Blondie (NBC)
  The Eve Arden Show (CBS)
  The Real McCoys (ABC/CBS)
  A Date with the Angels (ABC)
  Mr. Adams and Eve (CBS)
  Leave it to Beaver (CBS/ABC)
  How to Marry a Millionaire (SYND)
  Dick and the Dutchess (CBS)
  The Marge and Gower Champion Show (NBC)
  The Thin Man (NBC)
  The Lucille Ball-Desi Arnaz Show (CBS) 60
     min., first episode 75 min.

1958   *The Donna Reed Show* (ABC)
  The Ann Southern Show (CBS)

  The George Burns Show (CBS)
  How to Marry a Millionaire (SYND)
  The Ed Wynn Show (NBC)
  Love That Jill (ABC)
  The Adventures of Tugboat Annie (SYND)
     a.k.a. *Tugboat Annie*
  This is Alice (SYND)

1959   *Dennis the Menace* (CBS)
  The Many Loves of Doby Gillis (CBS) a.k.a.
     Doby Gillis
  Fibber McGee and Molly (NBC)
  The Betty Hutton Show (NBC)
  Hennesey (CBS)
  The Dennis O'Keefe Show (CBS)
  Too Young to Go Steady (NBC) 8 episodes, all
     live
  Love and Marriage (NBC)

1960   *The Tab Hunter Show* (NBC)
  Pete and Gladys (CBS)
  Bringing up Buddy (CBS)
  The Andy Griffith Show (CBS) a.k.a. *Mayberry
     RFD*
  Happy (NBC)
  The Tom Ewell Show (CBS)
  My Sister Eileen (CBS)
  The Jim Backus Show (SYND) a.k.a. *Hot Off
     the Wire*
  My Three Sons (ABC/CBS)
  Peter Loves Mary (NBC)
  Angel (CBS)
  Harrigan and Son (ABC)
  The Flintstones (ABC/NBC) animated
  Guestward Ho! (ABC)

1961   *Car 54, Where Are You?* (NBC)
  Calvin and the Colonel (ABC) animated
  The Dick Van Dyke Show (CBS)
  The Bob Cummings Show (CBS)
  Margie (ABC)
  Ichabod and Me (CBS)
  Top Cat (ABC) animated
  The Alvin Show (CBS) animated
  Mrs. G Goes to College (CBS) a.k.a. *The
     Gertrude Berg Show*
  The Joey Bishop Show (NBC/CBS) later *The
     New Joey Bishop Show*
  Hazel (NBC/CBS)
  The Hathaways (ABC)
  Holiday Lodge (CBS) summer series
  Mister Ed (Synd)
  One Happy Family (NBC)
  Westinghouse Playhouse (NBC) a.k.a. *The
     Nanette Fabray Show*, then *Yes, Yes
     Nanette*
  Father of the Bride (CBS)

1962   *The Jetsons* (ABC/CBS/NBC/SYND) animated
  The Lucy Show (CBS)

Ensign O'Toole (NBC)
Fair Exchange (CBS)
Going My Way (ABC)
McKeever and the Colonel (NBC)
Oh, Those Bells! (CBS)
Room For One More (ABC)
It's A Man's World (ABC)
Our Man Higgins (ABC)
The Beverly Hillbillies (CBS)
McHale's Navy (ABC)
I'm Dickens, He's Fenster (ABC)
Don't Call Me Charlie (NBC)
Mr. Smith Goes to Washington (ABC)

1963   *Grindl* (NBC)
Petticoat Junction (CBS)
The Patty Duke Show (ABC)
Glynis (CBS)
Harry's Girls (NBC)
My Favoirte Martian (CBS)
The New Phil Silvers Show (CBS)
Broadside (ABC)
The Farmer's Daughter (ABC)
The Bill Dana Show (NBC)

1964   *No Time for Sergeants* (ABC)
My Living Doll (CBS)
Wendy and Me (ABC)
The Bing Crosby Show (ABC)
Many Happy Returns (CBS)
The Tycoon (ABC)
Mickey (ABC)
The Cara Williams Show (CBS)
Bewitched (ABC)
The Bailey's of Balboa (CBS)
Karen (NBC) part of 90 Bristol Court trilogy
Tom, Dick and Mary (NBC) part of 90 Bristol Court trilogy
Harris against the World (NBC) part of 90 Bristol Court trilogy
The Munsters (CBS)
The Addams Family (ABC)
Vallentine's Day (ABC)
Gomer Pyle, U.S.M.C. (CBS)
Gilligan's Island (CBS)
Many Happy Returns (CBS)
Broadside (ABC)

1965   *The John Forsythe Show* (NBC)
F Troop (ABC)
My Mother the Car (NBC)
Mr. Roberts (NBC)
Please Don't Eat the Daisies (NBC)
Hogan's Heroes (CBS)
Gidget (ABC)
Green Acres (CBS)
O.K. Crackerby! (ABC)
Mona McCluskey (NBC)
Tammy (ABC)
Camp Runamuck (NBC)

I Dream of Jeannie (NBC)
Get Smart (NBC/CBS)
The Smothers Brothers Show (CBS) sitcom, not a variety show
The Wackiest Ship in the Army (NBC) 1-hour sitcom
Hank (NBC)

1966   *It's about Time* (CBS)
Hey Landlord (NBC)
The Abbott and Costello Show (SYND) animated
Run, Buddy, Run (CBS)
Family Affair (CBS)
The Jean Arthur Show (CBS)
The Double Life of Henry Phyfe (ABC)
The Hero (NBC)
The Rounders (ABC)
The Pruitts of Southhampton (ABC) a.k.a. *The Phyllis Diller Show*
Love on a Rooftop (ABC)
Occasional Wife (NBC)
The Tammy Grimes Show (ABC)
That Girl (ABC)
Pistols 'n' Peticoats (CBS)
The Monkees (NBC)

1967   *The Mothers-in-Law* (NBC)
Mr. Terrific (CBS)
Good Morning World (CBS)
The Second Hundred Years (ABC)
He and She (CBS)
The Flying Nun (ABC)
Accidental Family (NBC)
Captain Nice (NBC)
Rango (ABC)

1968   *Here's Lucy* (CBS)
Mayberry R.F.D. (CBS)
The Doris Day Show (CBS)
Julia (NBC)
The Good Guys (CBS)
Blondie (CBS)
The Ugliest Girl in Town (ABC)
Here Come the Brides (ABC)
The Ghost and Mrs. Muir (NBC/ABC)

1969   *To Rome with Love* (CBS)
My World and Welcome to It (NBC)
The Bill Cosby Show (NBC)
The Queen and I (CBS)
The Governor and J.J. (CBS)
The Courtship of Eddie's Father (CBS)
The Debbie Reynolds Show (NBC)
The Brady Bunch (ABC)
Mr. Deeds Goes to Town (ABC)
Love, American Style (ABC) 60-min. anthology
Room 222 (ABC)

1970   Make Room for Granddaddy (ABC)
        The Nanny and the Professor (ABC)
        Barefoot in the Park (ABC)
        The Odd Couple (ABC)
        Nancy (NBC)
        The Tim Conway Show (CBS)
        The Partridge Family (ABC)
        The Mary Tyler Moore Show (CBS) a.k.a. Mary
            Tyler Moore
        Arnie (CBS)

1971   The Jimmy Stewart Show (NBC)
        The Chicago Teddy Bears (CBS)
        Getting Together (ABC)
        Doctor in the House (SYND) British
        From a Bird's Eye View (NBC)
        The New Andy Griffith Show (CBS) a.k.a.
            Headmaster
        Shirley's World (ABC) filmed all on location
        Funny Face (CBS)
        All in the Family (CBS) later Archie Bunker's
            Place
        The New Dick Van Dyke Show (CBS)
        The Partners (NBC)
        The Good Life (NBC)

1972   M*A*S*H (CBS)
        The Sandy Duncan Show (CBS)
        Maude (CBS)
        Sanford and Son (NBC)
        Me and the Chimp (CBS)
        The Don Rickles Show (CBS)
        The Super (ABC) summer series
        Wait 'til Your Father Gets Home (SYND) ani-
            mated
        Temperatures Rising (ABC) later The New
            Temperatures Rising
        The Paul Lynde Show (ABC)
        Bridget Loves Bernie (CBS)
        The Little People (NBC) later The Brian Keith
            Show
        The Bob Newhart Show (CBS)
        The Corner Bar (ABC)

1973   Diana (NBC)
        The Addams Family (NBC/ABC) animated
        Here We Go Again (ABC)
        My Favorite Martians (CBS) animated
        Ozzie's Girls (SYND)
        Thicker Than Water (ABC)
        A Touch of Grace (ABC)
        Lotsa Luck (NBC)
        Bob & Carol & Ted & Alice (ABC)
        Callucci's Deptartment (CBS)
        Roll Out! (CBS)
        Adam's Rib (ABC)
        Needles and Pins (NBC)
        The Girl with Something Extra (NBC)
        Love Thy Neighbor (ABC) summer series

        Thicker Than Water (ABC)
        Dusty's Trail (SYND)

1974   Happy Days (ABC)
        Partridge Family: 2200 A.D. (CBS) animated
        That's My Mama (ABC)
        Good Times (CBS) first spinoff of a spinoff
        Rhoda (CBS)
        Paper Moon (ABC)
        Barney Miller (ABC)
        Chico and The Man (NBC)
        Friends and Lovers (CBS) a.k.a. Paul Sand in
            Friends and Lovers
        The Texas Wheelers (ABC)

1975   Phyllis (CBS)
        Welcome Back, Kotter (ABC)
        The Jeffersons (CBS)
        Joe and Sons (CBS)
        Barney Miller (ABC)
        One Day at a Time (CBS)
        When Things Were Rotten (ABC)
        On the Rocks (ABC)
        The Cop and the Kid (NBC)
        Grady (NBC)
        Hot L Baltimore (ABC)
        We'll Get By (CBS)
        Sunshine (NBC)
        Karen (ABC)
        Far Out Space Nuts (CBS)
        The Bob Crane Show (NBC)
        The Montefuscos (NBC)
        Fay (NBC)
        Big Eddie (CBS)
        Doc (CBS)
        King of Kensington (SYND) Canadian
        The Ghost Busters (CBS)

1976   All's Fair (CBS)
        What's Happening! (ABC/SYND)
        Ball Four (CBS)
        Laverne and Shirley (ABC)
        Alice (CBS)
        The Practice (NBC)
        The Tony Randall Show (ABC)
        The Nancy Walker Show (ABC)
        Popi (CBS)
        Big John, Little John (NBC)
        C.P.O. Sharkey (NBC)
        The Dumplings (NBC)
        Good Heavens (ABC)
        Sirota's Court (NBC)
        Viva Valdez (ABC)
        Ivan the Terrible (CBS) summer series
        The McLean Stevenson Show (NBC)
        Holmes and Yoyo (ABC)
        Mr. T and Tina (ABC)
        The Practice (ABC)

1977   On Our Own (CBS)

The Betty White Show (CBS)
Soap (ABC)
Three's Company (ABC)
Busting Loose (CBS)
Fish (ABC)
Carter Country (ABC)
Loves Me, Loves Me Not (CBS)
A Year at the Top (CBS)
Tabitha (ABC)
Sanford Arms (NBC)
Blansky's Beauties (ABC)
Operation Petticoat (ABC)
We've Got Each Other (CBS)
All That Glitters (SYND)
Sugar Time! (ABC)
The Kalliaks (NBC)
Fernwood 2night (SYND) later *America 2night*
Szysznik (NBC)
The Love Boat (ABC) 60-min. anthology
The San Pedro Beach Bums (ABC)

1978   WKRP in Cincinnati (CBS)
Taxi (ABC/NBC)
The Ted Knight Show (CBS)
In the Beginning (CBS)
Mork and Mindy (ABC)
The Waverly Wonders (NBC)
Who's Watching the Kids (NBC)
Diff'rent Strokes (NBC/ABC)
A.E.S. Hudson Street (ABC)
Another Day (CBS)
Baby, I'm Back (CBS)
Free Country (ABC)
Please Stand By (SYND)
Joe and Valerie (NBC)
The Hee Haw Honeys (SYND)
Apple Pie (ABC)
The Harvey Korman Show (CBS)
Husbands, Wives & Lovers (CBS)
Quark (NBC)
Que Pasa, U.S.A.? (PBS)
The Roller Girls (NBC)

1979   Out of the Blue (ABC)
A New Kind of Family (ABC)
Stockard Channing in Just Friends (CBS) later *Just Friends*
Angie (ABC)
Miss Winslow & Son (CBS)
Joe's World (NBC)
13 Queens Boulevard (ABC)
Turnabout (NBC)
Billy (CBS)
Brothers and Sisters (NBC)
Co-Ed Fever (CBS)
Delta House (ABC)
Dorothy (CBS)
Flatbush (CBS)
Hanging In (CBS)
The Associates (ABC)

The Last Resort (CBS)
Struck by Lightning (CBS)
Hello Larry (NBC)
Benson (ABC)
The Ropers (ABC)
Detective School (ABC)
Working Stiffs (CBS)
The Bad News Bears (CBS)
The Facts of Life (NBC)
The Baxters (SYND)
Highcliffe Manor (NBC)
House Calls (CBS)
Makin' It (ABC)
The Mary Tyler Moore Hour (CBS) sitcom within variety show

1980   Flo (CBS)
Ladies' Man (CBS)
House Calls (CBS)
Sanford (NBC)
Too Close for Comfort (ABC/SYND) later *The Ted Knight Show*
Bosom Buddies (ABC)
It's a Living (ABC/SYND) a.k.a. *Making a Living*
I'm a Big Girl Now (ABC)
Fawlty Towers (SYND) British
Good Time Harry (NBC)
Good Time Girls (ABC)
Me and Maxx (NBC)
Nobody's Perfect (ABC)
One in a Million (ABC)
Phyl and Mikhy (CBS)
The Stockard Channing Show (CBS)
The Six O'Clock Follies (NBC)
Semi-Tough (ABC)
Breaking Away (ABC)
When the Whistle Blows (ABC)
United States (NBC/ABC)
Mr. And Mrs. Dracula (ABC)

1981   Private Benjamin (CBS)
Harper Valley PTA (NBC) a.k.a. *Harper Valley*
The Two of Us (CBS)
Mr. Merlin (CBS)
Love, Sidney (NBC)
Best of the West (ABC) sitcom-western
Lewis & Clark (NBC)
Gimme a Break! (NBC)
Park Place (CBS)
Checking In (CBS)
Laverne & Shirley (ABC) animated
Open All Night (ABC)
Maggie (ABC)
The Brady Brides (NBC)
Mr. Merlin (CBS)

1982   9 to 5 (ABC/SYND)
Gloria (CBS)
Newhart (CBS)

Square Pegs (CBS)
Filthy Rich (CBS)
Family Ties (NBC)
Report to Murphy (CBS)
Teachers Only (NBC)
One of the Boys (NBC)
No Soap, Radio (ABC)
Making the Grade (CBS)
Joanie Loves Chachi (ABC)
Star of the Family (ABC)
It Takes Two (ABC)
Cheers (NBC)
Police Squad! (ABC)
The New Odd Couple (ABC)
Silver Spoons (NBC/SYND)
Herbie the Love Bug (CBS)
Baker's Dozen (CBS) sitcom-drama
Madame's Place (SYND)

1983   *Mama's Family* (NBC)
Goodnight, Beantown (CBS)
AfterMASH (CBS)
Just Our Luck (ABC)
It's Not Easy (ABC)
Buffalo Bill (NBC)
Foot in the Door (CBS)
Reggie (ABC)
Small & Frye (CBS)
We Got It Made (NBC/SYND)
Webster (ABC)
Mr. Smith (NBC)
Ace Crawford, Private Eye (CBS)
Amanda's (ABC)
At Ease (ABC)
Baby Makes Five (ABC)
Condo (ABC)
Oh Madeline (ABC)
Jennifer Slept Here (NBC)
Zorro and Son (CBS)
Gun Shy (CBS)

1984   *Punky Brewster* (NBC)
Kate & Allie (CBS)
Three's a Crowd (ABC)
Night Court (NBC)
Charles in Charge (CBS/SYND)
Shaping Up (ABC) a.k.a. *Pablo* (ABC)
The Four Seasons (CBS)
Mama Malone (CBS)
Spencer (NBC) later *Under One Roof*
Brothers (SHOWTIME)
Empire (CBS)
Domestic Life (CBS)
Double Trouble (NBC)
The Duck Factory (NBC)
E/R (CBS)
Maggie Briggs (CBS) a.k.a. *Suzanne Pleshette
   is Maggie Briggs*
Dreams (CBS)
It's Your Move (NBC)

Who's the Boss (ABC)
The Cosby Show (NBC)
1st & Ten (HBO)
Down to Earth (TBS)

1985   *Mr. Belvedere* (ABC)
Growing Pains (ABC)
Charlie & Co. (CBS)
Golden Girls (NBC)
227 (NBC)
Small Wonder (SYND)
Foley Square (CBS)
Hail to the Chief (ABC)
It's Punky Brewster (NBC) animated
The Lucy Arnaz Show (CBS)
Mary (CBS)
Off the Rack (ABC)
You Again? (NBC)
Still the Beaver (DISNEY/TBS) a.k.a. *The New
   Leave it to Beaver*
What's Happening Now! (SYND)
Washingtoon (SHOWTIME)
Check It Out (SYND) Canadian
Rocky Road (TBS)
Sara (NBC)

1986   *Valerie* (NBC/CBS) later *Valerie's Family, The
   Hogan Family*
Easy Street (NBC)
My Sister Sam (CBS)
Throb (SYND)
Perfect Strangers (ABC)
ALF (NBC)
What a Country! (SYND)
He's the Mayor (ABC)
Head of the Class (ABC)
Gung Ho (ABC)
Joe Bash (ABC)
Me & Mrs. C (NBC)
Mr. Sunshine (ABC)
Dads (ABC)
The Cavenaughs (CBS)
Bridges to Cross (CBS)
All is Forgiven (NBC)
Fast Times (CBS)
Fathers and Sons (NBC)
Hangin' In (SYND) Canadian
Leo & Liz in Beverly Hills (CBS)
The New Gidget (SYND)
One Big Family (SYND)
The Redd Foxx Show (ABC)
Tough Cookies (CBS)
Together We Stand (CBS) later *Nothing is Easy*
Better Days (CBS)
Sledge Hammer! (ABC)
Life with Lucy (ABC)
The Ellen Burstyn Show (ABC)
Amen (NBC)
Designing Women (CBS)
Sanchez of Bel Air (USA)

You Again? (NBC)
The Last Precinct (NBC)
Melba (CBS)
Safe At Home (TBS)

1987 *Married...with Children* (FOX)
The Charmings (ABC)
Mr. President (FOX)
Duet (FOX)
My Two Dads (NBC)
Bustin' Loose (SYND)
Dennis the Menace (SYND) animated
Down and Out in Beverly Hills (FOX)
Karen's Song (FOX)
Mama's Boy (NBC)
Marblehead Manor (SYND)
Out of This World (SYND)
The Popcorn Kid (CBS)
Pursuit of Happiness (ABC)
Roomies (NBC)
She's the Sheriff (SYND)
Sweet Surrender (NBC)
The Tortellis (NBC)
You Can't Take it with You (SYND)
Frank's Place (CBS)
The 'Slap Maxwell' Story (ABC)
A Different World (NBC)
Full House (ABC)
I Married Dora (ABC)
Everything's Relative (CBS)
Women in Prison (FOX)
Beans Baxter (FOX)
Second Chance (FOX) later *Boys Will Be Boys*
Roxie (CBS)
Nothing in Common (NBC)
Harry (ABC)
Beverly Hills Buntz (NBC)
Hooperman (ABC)
D.C. Follies (SYND)
The Days and Nights of Molly Dodd (NBC/LIFETIME)
The Dom DeLuise Show (SYND)
Good Morning, Miss Bliss (NBC) later *Saved by the Bell*
The New Monkees (SYND)
Rags to Riches (NBC)
Take Five (CBS)
Trying Times (PBS)

1988 *Day By Day* (NBC)
Coming of Age (CBS)
Roseanne (ABC)
It's Garry Shandling's Show (SHOWTIME/FOX)
Murphy Brown (CBS)
The Van Dyke Show (CBS)
Annie McGuire (CBS)
Just the Ten of Us (ABC)
The Wonder Years (ABC) sitcom-drama
The Thorns (ABC)

Eisenhower & Lutz (CBS)
Family Man (ABC)
First Impressions (CBS)
My Secret Identity (SYND) Canadian
The Munsters Today (SYND)
Just in Time (ABC)
Trial and Error (CBS)
Baby Boom (NBC)
Dear John... (NBC)
Dirty Dancing (NBC)
Raising Miranda (CBS)
Empty Nest (NBC)
Starting from Scratch (SYND)
Learning the Ropes (SYND)
Tattinger's (NBC) later *Nick & Hillary*

1989 *Anything but Love* (ABC)
Free Spirit (ABC)
Homeroom (ABC)
Sister Kate (NBC)
Coach (ABC)
Open House (FOX)
Major Dad (CBS)
The People Next Door (CBS)
The Famous Teddy Z (CBS)
Chicken Soup (ABC)
The Nutt House (NBC)
Family Matters (ABC/CBS)
Ann Jillian (NBC)
FM (NBC)
Have Faith (ABC)
Heartland (CBS)
Knight & Daye (NBC) summer series
Live-In (CBS)
Nearly Departed (NBC)
The Robert Guillaume Show (ABC)
13 East (NBC)
Saved by the Bell (NBC)
Living Dolls (ABC)
Doctor, Doctor (CBS)
Doogie Howser, M.D. (ABC)
Hey Dude (NICK)
One of the Boys (NBC)
The Simpsons (FOX) animated

1990 *Wings* (NBC)
Get a Life (FOX)
Good Grief (FOX)
True Colors (FOX)
Parker Lewis Can't Lose (FOX)
Uncle Buck (CBS)
City (CBS)
The Fresh Prince of Bel-Air (NBC)
The Marshall Chronicles (ABC)
Harry and the Hendersons (SYND)
His & Hers (CBS)
Molloy (FOX)
New Attitude (NBC)
Normal Life (CBS)
Wish You Were Here (CBS)

Singer & Sons (NBC)
Bobby's World (FOX) animated
Down Home (NBC)
Dream On (HBO/FOX)
Little Rosie (ABC) animated
The Fanelli Boys (NBC)
A Family for Joe (NBC)
Working Girl (NBC)
Sydney (CBS)
Sugar and Spice (CBS)
You Take the Kids (CBS)
Ferris Bueller (NBC)
Married People (ABC)
Lenny (CBS)
Babes (FOX)
Grand (NBC)
Going Places (ABC)
Evening Shade (CBS)
Bagdad Café (CBS)
The Family Man (CBS)
Seinfeld (NBC)
Evening Shade (CBS)
Parenthood (NBC)
Working It Out (NBC)
American Dreamer (NBC)
My Talk Show (SYND) sitcom-talk show
Maniac Mansion (FAM)
Big Brother Jake (ABC FAMILY)
What a Dummy (SYND)

1991   Blossom (NBC)
Eerie, Indiana (NBC)
Roc (FOX)
Herman's Head (FOX)
Man of the People (NBC)
Pacific Station (NBC)
Home Improvement (ABC)
Sibs (ABC)
Good & Evil (ABC)
Charlie Hoover (FOX)
Davis Rules (ABC/CBS)
Dinosaurs (ABC)
Good Sports (CBS)
The Man in the Family (ABC)
The New WKRP in Cincinnati (SYND)
Sunday Dinner (CBS)
Walter & Emily (NBC)
Hi Honey, I'm Home (ABC/NICK)
Baby Talk (ABC)
The Royal Family (CBS)
Teech (CBS)
Drexell's Class (FOX)
Step by Step (ABC/CBS)
Princesses (CBS)
Brooklyn Bridge (CBS)
Flesh 'n' Blood (NBC)
The Torkelsons (NBC) a.k.a. Almost Home
Nurses (NBC)
Top of the Heap (FOX)
Salute Your Shorts (NICK)

Morton & Hayes (CBS)
Harry and the Hendersons (SYND)
Welcome Freshmen (NICK)
Clarissa Explains It All (NICK)
Stat (ABC)

1992   Great Scott! (FOX)
Flying Blind (FOX)
Woops! (FOX)
Hearts Afire (CBS)
Love & War (CBS)
Hanging with Mr. Cooper (ABC)
Laurie Hill (ABC)
Arresting Behavior (ABC)
Billy (ABC)
Down the Shore (FOX)
Grapevine (CBS)
Top of the Heap (FOX)
Stand by Your Man (FOX)
Rachel Gunn, R.N. (FOX)
Scorch (CBS)
Vinnie & Bobby (FOX)
The Powers That Be (ABC)
Julie (ABC)
Home Fires (NBC)
Fish Police (CBS) animated
The Larry Sanders Show (HBO)
Mad about You (NBC)
Delta (ABC)
Room for Two (ABC)
Martin (FOX)
Rhythm & Blues (NBC)
Camp Wilder (ABC)
The Golden Palace (CBS)
Bob (CBS)
California Dreams (NBC)
The Jackie Thomas Show (ABC)
Frannie's Turn (CBS)
Here and Now (NBC)
Out All Night (NBC)

1993   Good Advice (CBS)
Living Single (FOX)
Daddy Dearest (FOX)
Dave's World (CBS)
Phenom (ABC)
Saved by the Bell: The New Class (NBC)
Saved by the Bell: The College Years (NBC)
Almost Home (NBC)
Bakersfield, P.D. (FOX)
Big Wave Dave's (CBS)
Black Tie Affair (NBC)
The Boys (CBS)
The Building (CBS)
Cutters (CBS)
Dudley (CBS)
Home Free (ABC)
The Second Half (NBC)
Tall Hopes (CBS)
Getting By (ABC/NBC)

Thea (ABC)
Joe's Life (ABC)
Grace under Fire (ABC)
The Trouble with Larry (CBS)
The Nanny (CBS)
The Sinbad Show (FOX)
Frasier (NBC)
Boy Meets World (ABC)
It Had to Be You (CBS)
Family Album (CBS)
George (ABC)
Where I Live (ABC)
The Mommies (NBC)
Café Americain (NBC)
The John Larroquette Show (NBC)
The Adventures of Pete & Pete (NICK)
Running the Halls (NBC)
Danger Theater (FOX)
A League of Their Own (CBS)

1994 These Friends of Mine (ABC) later *Ellen*
 Sister, Sister (ABC/WB)
 Absolutely Fabulous (COMEDY CENTRAL)
  British
 On Our Own (ABC)
 Hardball (FOX)
 Wild Oats (FOX)
 Blue Skies (ABC)
 Me and the Boys (ABC)
 Muddling Through (CBS)
 704 Hauser (CBS)
 Monty (FOX)
 The Good Life (NBC)
 The George Carlin Show (FOX)
 The Critic (ABC/FOX) animated
 Someone Like Me (NBC)
 Tom (CBS)
 The Martin Short Show (NBC)
 Thunder Alley (ABC)
 All-American Girl (ABC)
 The Boys Are Back (CBS)
 Daddy's Girls (CBS)
 Friends (NBC)
 Madman of the People (NBC)
 The Five Mrs. Buchanans (CBS)
 Something Wilder (NBC)
 My Brother and Me (NICK)
 Weird Science (USA)
 The Mighty Jungle (ABC FAMILY)

1995 Hope & Gloria (NBC)
 Brotherly Love (NBC)
 Minor Adjustment (NBC)
 Kirk (WB)
 Simon (WB)
 Cleghorne! (WB)
 Too Something (FOX) later *New York Daze*
 Women of the House (CBS)
 Pig Sty (UPN)
 Pride & Joy (NBC)

The Pursuit of Happiness (NBC)
First Time Out (WB)
Can't Hurry Love (CBS)
If Not for You (CBS)
Partners (FOX)
Ned and Stacy (FOX)
In the House (NBC)
Hudson Street (ABC)
News Radio (NBC)
The Parent 'Hood (WB)
The Drew Carey Show (ABC)
The Naked Truth (ABC)
Hang Time (NBC)
Bless This House (CBS)
The Wayans Bros. (WB)
Unhappily Ever After (WB)
The Crew (FOX)
The Single Guy (NBC)
Caroline in the City (NBC)
Dweebs (CBS)
The Bonnie Hunt Show (CBS) a.k.a. *Bonnie*
The Jeff Foxworthy Show (ABC)
Maybe This Time (ABC)
The Preston Episodes (FOX)
Home Court (NBC)
Cybill (CBS)
High Society (CBS)
Almost Perfect (CBS)
Misery Loves Company (FOX)
My Wildest Dreams (FOX)
Night Stand with Dick Dietrick (SYND)
 sitcom-talk show
The Office (CBS)
Platypus Man (UPN)
A Whole New Ballgame (ABC)
Bringing Up Jack (ABC)
Double Rush (CBS)
Fudge (ABC)
The George Wendt Show (CBS)
Muscle (WB)
Stark Raving Mad (NBC)
Love & Money (CBS)
If Not for You (CBS)
The New Get Smart (FOX) a.k.a. *Get Smart*

1996 3rd Rock from the Sun (NBC)
 Boston Common (NBC)
 The Steve Harvey Show (WB)
 Life with Roger (WB)
 Mr. Rhodes (NBC)
 Malcolm and Eddie (UPN)
 Good Behavior (UPN)
 Sparks (UPN)
 Life's Work (ABC)
 Spin City (ABC)
 Moesha (UPN)
 Townies (ABC)
 Men Behaving Badly (NBC)
 Nick Freno, Licensed Teacher (WB)
 The Jamie Foxx Show (WB)

Suddenly Susan (NBC)
Sabrina, the Teenage Witch (ABC)
Clueless (ABC/UPN)
Everybody Loves Raymond (CBS)
Love and Marriage (FOX)
Aliens in the Family (ABC)
Arli$$ (HBO)
Party Girl (FOX)
My Guys (CBS)
The Last Frontier (FOX)
Kenan & Kel (NICK)
Homeboys in Outer Space (UPN)
Good Company (CBS)
Cosby (CBS)
Buddies (ABC)
Campus Cops (USA)
Champs (ABC)
Common Law (ABC)
The Faculty (ABC)
Ink (CBS)
Local Heroes (FOX)
The Louie Show (CBS)
Lush Life (FOX)
Pearl (CBS)
Public Morals (CBS)
The Show (USA)
Something So Right (NBC)

1997   *King of the Hill* (FOX) animated
Jenny (NBC)
The Tom Show (WB)
Alright, Already (WB)
George & Leo (CBS)
Soul Man (ABC)
Over the Top (ABC)
Hiller and Diller (ABC)
Lost on Earth (USA)
Just Shoot Me (NBC)
Hitz (UPN)
USA High (USA)
Union Square (NBC)
Head over Heels (UPN)
Dharma & Greg (ABC)
Working (NBC)
The Smart Guy (WB)
Veronica's Closet (NBC)
You Wish (ABC)
City Guys (NBC)
Teen Angel (ABC)
Meego (CBS)
The Gregory Hines Show (CBS)
Apt. 2-F (MTV)
Arsenio (ABC)
Austin Stories (MTV)
Between Brothers (FOX/UPN)
Breaker High (UPN)
Built to Last (NBC)
Chicago Sons (NBC)
Claude's Crib (USA)
Life...and Stuff (CBS)

Student Bodies (SYND)
Good News (UPN)
Fired Up (NBC)
Pauly (FOX) a.k.a. *The Pauly Shore Show*
Police Academy: The Series (SYND)
Social Studies (UPN)
Temporarily Yours (CBS)
The Tony Danza Show (NBC)

1998   *Holding the Baby* (FOX)
That 70s Show (FOX)
The Army Show (WB)
The King of Queens (CBS)
The Brian Benben Show (SHOWTIME)
Conrad Bloom (NBC)
Will & Grace (NBC)
Ask Harriet (FOX)
Guys Like Us (UPN)
DiResta (UPN)
The Secret Life of Desmond Pfeiffer (UPN)
The Hughleys (ABC/UPN)
Sports Night (ABC)
Costello (FOX)
Encore! Encore! (NBC)
Maggie Winters (CBS)
For Your Love (WB)
Becker (CBS)
Jesse (NBC)
Malibu, CA (SYND)
One World (NBC)
Living in Captivity (FOX)
Getting Personal (FOX)
Brother's Keeper (ABC)
The New Addams Family (FAM/FOX KIDS)
That's Life (ABC)
Two of a Kind (ABC)
The Secret Lives of Men (ABC)
Reunited (UPN)
The Love Boat: The Next Wave (UPN) 60-min.
  anthology
Style and Substance (CBS)
Kelly Kelly (WB)
House Rules (NBC)
You're the One (WB)
The Simple Life (CBS)
The Closer (CBS)
Oh Baby (LIFETIME)
Cousin Skeeter (NICK)
Power Play (UPN) Canadian
Damon (FOX)
Just You and Me (CBS) a.k.a. *First Impressions*
Lateline (NBC)
Maggie (LIFETIME)

1999   *Futurama* (FOX) animated
Dilbert (UPN)
The Parkers (UPN)
Grown Ups (UPN)
It's Like, You Know... (ABC)
The Family Guy (FOX) animated

The Mike O'Malley Show (NBC)
Shasta McNasty (UPN)
Two Guys, A Girl and a Pizza Place (ABC)
  later *Two Guys and a Girl*
Norm (ABC)
Oh Grow Up (ABC)
Work with Me (CBS)
Then Came You (ABC)
Action (FOX)
Stark Raving Mad (NBC)
Love or Money (CBS)
Katie Joplin (WB)
Ladies Man (CBS)
Odd Man Out (ABC)
Oh Grow Up (ABC)
The PJs (FOX/WB) animated
Payne (CBS)
Strangers with Candy (COMEDY CENTRAL)
Thanks (CBS)
Everything's Relative (NBC)
Family Rules (UPN)
Home Movies (UPN) animated
I was a Sixth Grade Alien! (FOX FAMILY)
Zoe, Duncan, Jack & Jane (WB) later *Zoe...*
Movie Stars (WB)

2000 *Tucker* (NBC)
The Geena Davis Show (ABC)
Madigan Men (ABC)
Hype! (WB)
Nikki (WB)
Yes, Dear (CBS)
Daddio (NBC)
Girlfriends (UPN)
The Michael Richards Show (NBC)
DAG (NBC)
Bette (CBS)
Welcome to New York (CBS)
Cursed (NBC) later *The Weber Show*
People Who Fear People (ABC)
Titus (FOX)
Clerks (ABC) animated
Even Stevens (DISNEY)
Talk to Me (ABC)
Then Came You (ABC)
The Trouble with Normal (ABC)
Normal, Ohio (FOX)
Noah Knows Best (NICK)
Manhattan, AZ (USA)
M.Y.O.B. (NBC) summer series
The War Next Door (USA)
Baby Blues (WB) animated
Battery Park (NBC)
The Brothers Garcia (NICK)
Curb Your Enthusiasm (HBO)
Grapevine (CBS)
Malcolm in the Middle (FOX)
Sammy (NBC) animated
Strip Mall (COMEDY CENTRAL)

2001 *All About Us* (NBC)
Men, Women & Dogs (WB)
Off Center (WB)
What about Joan (ABC)
Bob Patterson (ABC)
Emeril (NBC)
Three Sisters (NBC)
Scrubs (NBC)
Undeclared (FOX)
My Wife and Kids (ABC)
According to Jim (ABC)
Go Fish (NBC)
The Bernie Mac Show (FOX)
Inside Schwartz (NBC)
The Tick (FOX)
The Ellen Show (CBS)
Danny (CBS)
That's Life (CBS)
Maybe It's Me (WB)
Reba (WB)
Raising Dad (WB)
The Oblongs (WB) animated
Kristen (NBC)
Lizzie McGuire (DISNEY)
One on One (UPN)
So Little Time (FAM)
Some of My Best Friends (CBS)
Taina (NICK)
The Fighting Fitzgeralds (NBC)
Grosse Pointe (WB)
That's My Bush! (COMEDY CENTRAL)
Grounded for Life (FOX, then WB)
The Job (ABC)

2002 *8 Simple Rules for Dating My Teenage Daughter* (ABC)
Andy Richter Controls the Universe (FOX)
Baby Bob (CBS)
Bram and Alice (CBS)
The George Lopez Show (ABC)
Greetings from Tucson (WB)
What I Like about You (WB)
That 80s Show (FOX)
Life with Bonnie (ABC)
Still Standing (CBS)
Less Than Perfect (ABC)
Good Morning, Miami (NBC)
Greg the Bunny (FOX)
Imagine That (NBC)
In-Laws (NBC)
Leap of Faith (NBC)
Watching Ellie (NBC)
The Rerun Show (NBC)
Hidden Hills (NBC)
Half and Half (UPN)
Wednesday 9:30 (8:30 Central) (ABC) later *My Life in Television*

Beware of Dog (ANIMAL PLANET)
Do Over (WB)
Family Affair (WB)
Less than Perfect (ABC)
The Michael Richards Show (NBC)

2003   *Abby* (UPN)
Arrested Development (FOX)
Eve (UPN)
Half and Half (UPN)
Happy Family (NBC)
I'm with Her (ABC)
It's All Relative (ABC)
Like Family (WB)
Lost at Home (ABC)
Luis (FOX)
Married to the Kellys (ABC)
The Mullets (UPN)
My Big Fat Greek Life (CBS)
The O'Keefes (WB)
Oliver Beene (FOX)
The Ortegas (FOX)
The Pitts (FOX)
Regular Joe (ABC)
Rock Me Baby (UPN)
Two and a Half Men (CBS)
Wanda at Large (FOX)
Whoopi (NBC)
On the Spot (WB) improv-sitcom
Back to Kansas (ABC)
The Stones (CBS)
Coupling (NBC)
The Tracy Morgan Show (NBC)
The Ortegas (FOX)
A Minute with Stan Hooper (FOX)
Cracking Up (FOX)
All of Us (UPN)
The Opposite Sex (UPN)
All about the Andersons (WB)
Run of the House (WB)
The Help (WB)
The Mayor (WB)
A.U.S.A. (NBC)
Charlie Lawrence (CBS)
Happy Family (NBC)
Hope & Faith (ABC)
Romeo! (NICK)
That's So Raven (DISNEY)
Reno 911 (COMEDY CENTRAL)

Appendix 4 SITCOM EXERCISES

APPENDIX TO CHAPTER 2 SITCOM EXERCISE

<u>STYLE AND SUBSTANCE - PILOT</u>
(B)
<u>INT. CHELSEAS'S OFFICE - LATER THAT MORNING (D-1)</u>

(Chelsea, Jane, Terry)

CHELSEA IS LISTENING TO TERRY, HER YOUNG MALE SECRETARY, RUN DOWN
A LIST OF PHONE MESSAGES. CHELSEA MAKES HIM NERVOUS.

> TERRY
>
> Francine Messinger called and said thanks for the
> padlocks.

> CHELSEA
>
> That's Nancy Kissinger, and she's thanking me for
> the gravlax. ✓✓✓

> TERRY
>
> Right. Franklin Carter called...

> CHELSEA
>
> Frank Langella. ✓✓✓

> TERRY
>
> Okay. Needs advice on planting an urban garden.

> CHELSEA
>
> An herb garden.✓✓✓ Breathe, Terry.

> TERRY
>
> Okay. Ken Klein called...

> CHELSEA
> Kevin Kline? ✓✓✓

> TERRY
> No.

> CHELSEA
> Calvin Klein? ✓✓✓

TERRY SHAKES HIS HEAD NO.

> CHELSEA (cont'd)
> Kelly Klein. Carol Kane. Carole King. ✓✓✓ (A BEAT)
> Beverly Sills?

> TERRY
> Yes. You're good at this. ✓✓✓

> CHELSEA
> Thank you, Terry. Much better today. ✓✓✓

> TERRY
> I thought so too. ✓✓✓

TERRY EXITS AS JANE ENTERS.

> JANE
> Hi, Chelsea. Listen I don't want to be a bugaboo,
> but have you had a chance to sign that budget
> agreement yet?

CHELSEA STARES AT HER FOR A SECOND.

> JANE (cont'd)
> Jane Sokol. From Ferber Communications?

> CHELSEA
> Jane, please. I know who you are. What a darling
> suit.

> JANE
> Thanks. I really need you to sign that agreement.
> Being put in charge of your office is the first major
> assignment the company's given me, so I want to keep
> Mr. Ferber happy happy. So sign sign. ✓✓✓

                        CHELSEA
        I'll look at it right away.

JANE NOTICES A PURSE ON THE DESK.

                        JANE
        We have the same purse.

                        CHELSEA
        Really?

                        JANE
        Yes. It's exactly the same purse.

                        CHELSEA
        How about that?

                        JANE
        I mean...it's the same purse. (A BEAT) That's my
        purse, isn't it? ✓✓✓

                        CHELSEA
        Why don't we talk about something else? (PICKING
        SOMETHING UP FROM THE DESK) Oh, look. A recipe for
        flan. ✓✓✓

                        JANE
        Chelsea. You have my purse.

                        CHELSEA
        Don't get upset, Jane. You're new here, I want to
        get to know you. You know the old saying. The
        fastest way to get to know another woman is to look
        in her purse.

                        JANE
        Here's another old saying. I want my purse back.
        ✓✓✓

                        CHELSEA
        You have something to hide?

                        JANE
        No.

>   CHELSEA
>   I'd let you look in my purse.

>   JANE
>   I doubt that.

>   CHELSEA
>   I would.

>   JANE
>   Right.

>   CHELSEA
>   Go ahead.

>   JANE
>   Where is it?

>   CHELSEA
>   At home. ✓✓✓ But if it were here, I'd let you look
>   at it.

>   JANE
>   Chelsea, this is a major invasion of my privacy.

CHELSEA HOLDS OUT A SMALL JAR OF JAM TO JANE.

>   CHELSEA
>   Jane, I'd like you to have this. It's a jar of my
>   lovely homemade preserves. I hope you like rhubarb.
>   ✓✓✓

>   JANE
>   Do you honestly believe that giving me a little jar
>   of jam will make this okay?

>   CHELSEA
>   I have a bigger jar. ✓✓✓

>   JANE
>   That is so not my point.

>   CHELSEA
>   Oh, I get it. There's a jam hater in our midst, is
>   there? ✓✓✓

                    JANE
Oh, please. I love jam.

                    CHELSEA
I wish I could believe that.

                    JANE
I am crazy about jam.

                    CHELSEA
You do not seem jam friendly to me. ✓✓✓

                    JANE
(AFTER A BEAT) Okay. Okay. You want to look in my
purse? You go right ahead. This is unbelievable.

                    CHELSEA
Oh, pooh. You really know how to take the fun out of
things.

CHELSEA STARTS DIGGING AROUND IN THE PURSE.

                    CHELSEA (cont'd)
Somebody clips coupons. ✓✓✓

CHELSEA TAKES A COUPON OUT AND GRIMACES.

                    CHELSEA (cont'd)
Macaroni and cheese? From a box? ✓✓✓

                    JANE
It's filling and inexpensive.

                    CHELSEA
I can't argue, Jane, but if those were the only
criteria for nourishment, there'd be a lot more
recipes for dirt. ✓✓✓ (DIGGING) Lip gloss,
rouge...I see tweezers. Eyebrows on the march, Jane?
✓✓✓

                    JANE
Are we done yet?

                    CHELSEA
Oh, Jane. Jane, Jane, Jane...

CHELSEA REMOVES A PACKAGE OF HOSTESS SNOBALLS FROM THE PURSE.

> CHELSEA (cont'd)
> Hostess Snoballs? Why, Jane? ✓✓✓

> JANE
> I like them. They're fun.

> CHELSEA
> Have you heard the expression, "You are what you
> eat?" Add bangs and a business suit, this is you,
> Jane. ✓✓✓

> JANE
> I'll be going now...

JANE GATHERS UP HER PURSE AND STARTS TO EXIT. CHELSEA HOLDS UP A
SMALL PHOTOGRAPH.

> CHELSEA
> Who's this?

> JANE
> Give me that, please.

> CHELSEA
> Brother?

> JANE
> None of your business.

> CHELSEA
> Friend?

> JANE
> I'm not telling you.

> CHELSEA
> Fiancé?

> JANE
> (A BEAT) No.

> CHELSEA
> You paused. ✓✓✓

                    JANE
Darn!

                    CHELSEA
What's his name?

                    JANE
Why would I tell you?

                    CHELSEA
Because I really think you want to talk about it.
Mint? ✓✓✓

CHELSEA HOLDS OUT A SMALL CONTAINER OF MINTS.

                    JANE
(GRABBING THEM) Those are mine. ✓✓✓ Chelsea, I
appreciate your trying to be friendly, but I'm not
going to discuss my personal life with you.

                    CHELSEA
He looks like a Paul.

                    JANE
I'm here to do a job. It's a job I take seriously.

                    CHELSEA
Doug? Dennis?

                    JANE
There's a line between business and personal...

                    CHELSEA
Tony? Mike?

                    JANE
I'm a professional, and I'm going to maintain a
professional...

                    CHELSEA
Chuck?

                    JANE
(END OF ROPE) Steve! Steve! The man's name is Steve!
✓✓✓ Are you happy now?

CHELSEA

I knew you wanted to talk about it. ✓✓✓

JANE

I don't! This is the office. The office is where we talk about office things. My ex-fiancé is not an office thing.

CHELSEA

Your ex-fiancé?

JANE

Darn! ✓✓✓

CHELSEA

What happened? He hit you, didn't he? (TO THE PHOTO) You bastard. ✓✓✓

JANE

This is really inappropriate, How would you like it if I just waltzed in here and started asking you about your divorce? Which by the way, I would never do. I know it must've been difficult and I hope you're okay.

CHELSEA

(THROWN) I'm sorry?

JANE

I said I hope you're okay.

CHELSEA

(COVERING) Well, yes...of course I am. My husband wasn't giving me what I needed, he was a lox, I kicked him out. Let's get back to you. ✓✓✓

JANE

Look, I need that agreement signed and on my desk by the end of the day.

CHELSEA

I'll look it over right now. Jane, if I upset you, I'm sorry. It was wrong to take your purse.

                              JANE
          Okay. I'll be in my office if you need me.

JANE EXITS AND CLOSES THE DOOR BEHIND HER. CHELSEA TAKES OUT THE
SNOBALLS AND TAKES A BITE OF ONE. JANE ENTERS.

                         JANE (cont'd)
          Where are they?

A BEAT, THEN CHELSEA MAKES A MUFFLED RESPONSE.

                            CHELSEA
          Where's what? ✓✓✓

CHELSEA HANDS THE REMAINING SNOBALL BACK TO JANE.

                                        FADE OUT.[1]

APPENDIX TO CHAPTER 3 SITCOM EXERCISE

                             LUIS
                           "PILOT"

INT. DONUT SHOP - DAY

(LUIS, GREG, MARLY)

GREG KISSES MARLY. HE NOTICES LUIS WATCHING AND BREAKS IT OFF.

                             GREG
          Oh, I guess I shouldn't kiss your daughter in front
          of you, huh?

                             LUIS
          You can kiss my daughter in front of me. You just
          can't kiss my daughter in front of me without a job.

                             GREG
          What else can I do in front of you if I get a job?
          Grab her ass?

>   LUIS
> A good job, yes.

>   GREG
> What can I do for eighty-five grand and a dental
> plan?

>   LUIS
> You make eighty-five grand a year, you can grab my
> ass.

>   GREG
> (RE: GREG'S SMALL HANDS AND LUIS'S LARGE ASS)
> I don't think that's possible.

LUIS TAKES A BEAT THEN LUNGES AT HIM.

>   GREG (cont'd)
> You know, Luis, most artists don't achieve success
> until after they're dead.

>   LUIS
> How 'bout I make you successful right now? (THEN,
> RE: GREG'S DONUT) Did you pay for that?

>   GREG
> Of, course.

>   LUIS
> (MENACING) Did you?

>   GREG
> Yes!

>   LUIS
> (MENACING) Did you?

>   GREG
> Marly, can I borrow a dollar? (THEN) I'm kidding. Of
> course I paid for it. I mean, come on. (LOUD
> WHISPERS) Marly. Dollar bill. Quickly!

                    LUIS
I don't get it. She's a smart girl. <u>What does she</u>
<u>see in you?</u>

                    GREG
<u>Maybe a guy who loves her, who's sensitive,</u>
<u>talented, and from time to time</u> (OFF LUIS) <u>not</u>
<u>afraid to show fear.</u> (LOUD WHISPER, TO MARLY)
Dollar...bill. Now. If you love me!

MARLY BRINGS HIM A DOLLAR.

                    GREG (cont'd)
Here you go.

                    LUIS
I don't understand you. I mean, <u>how can you let a</u>
<u>woman pay your bills?</u>

                    GREG
It'd be a hell of a lot easier if you didn't bring
it up all the time. (THEN, RE: DOLLAR) <u>Do I got some</u>
<u>change skating my way, how does that work?</u>

APPENDIX TO CHAPTER 4 SITCOM EXERCISES

                <u>HOME IMPROVEMENT</u>
                    "PILOT"
                    <u>ACT TWO</u>
                    <u>SCENE 2</u>
<u>EXT. BACKYARD - DUSK (DAY 2)</u>

<u>SPFX: BARBEQUE SMOKE FROM WILSON'S YARD</u>

(WE SEE WILSON BARBEQUING. TIM SEARCHES FOR THE DISHWASHER PARTS)

                    TIM
What a mess.

                    WILSON
Hi, ya, Tim.

PHYSICAL COMEDY - CAN'T SEE HIS FACE

> TIM
>
> Hi Wilson. Mmm. Smells good. What are you cooking?
> Baby back ribs?

> WILSON
>
> Squirrel.

TWIST-K SOUND

> TIM
>
> Squirrel. What's that taste like?

> WILSON
>
> Sort of like chipmunk.

K SOUND

> By the way, a couple of those bolts landed in the
> birdbath.

K SOUND

> TIM
>
> I was a little surprised by the torque on that
> compressor.

CHARACTER TRAIT - INEPT WITH TOOLS

> WILSON
>
> I tell you, Tim, this is what it's all about. Catch
> of the day cooking, sun setting, men standing around
> the campfire telling stories.

PLAY ON WORDS - RUN OF 3 WITH ALLITERATION OF K SOUNDS AND S SOUNDS

> TIM
>
> Can I tell you one?

> WILSON
>
> Campfire's lit, good neighbor.

CALL BACK

> TIM
>
> Jill didn't get the job she wanted. I tell her not
> to feel bad and she gets angry at me.

> WILSON
>
> Hmm.

**NOT APPARENT FROM THE WRITING, BUT ACTOR MADE THIS INTO AN INTER-
ESTING CHARACTER TRAIT**

> TIM
>
> And then I tell her what to do, she gets all bent
> out of shape and storms out of the room.

> WILSON
>
> Sounds like you were having an asymmetrical
> conversation.

> TIM
>
> Asymmetrical. How do you spell that?

> WILSON
>
> Let's just say one-sided.

PLAY ON WORDS

(TIM DOES A KNOWING GRUNT)

> WILSON (CONT'D)
>
> You see, Tim,

CHARACTER TRAIT - PHILOSOPHER

> by nature, men are problem solvers. But Jill didn't
> want you to solve her problem.

> TIM
>
> She didn't?

> WILSON
>
> No. She just wanted you to listen while she shared
> her feelings.

                              TIM
          Just stand there and listen? That's like doing
          nothing.

CHARACTER TRAIT - *NAÏVE ABOUT WOMEN*

                              WILSON
          Sometimes the best thing you can do is nothing.

(TIM DOES AN UNDESTANDING GRUNT)

                              TIM
          I get it. Jill got mad at me because I didn't listen
          to her.

MISLEAD

                              WILSON
          No, she got mad at you because you blew up the damn
          dishwasher.

TURN - *ALLITERATION* [2]

                         STYLE AND SUBSTANCE
                              "PILOT"
                             ACT ONE
                               (A)

FADE IN:

INT. OUTER LOBBY - MORNING (D-1)

(Jane)

CAMERA STARTS IN CLOSE ON A BEAUTIFUL FLORAL ARRANGEMENT ON A
TABLE IN THE OUTER LOBBY (THE SHOW TITLE WILL BE SEEN HERE).
CAMERA PANS UP AND WE SEE THE SIGN ON THE WALL: "CHELSEA STEVENS,
A DIVISION OF FERBER COMMUNICATIONS." WE FIND JANE TALKING ON HER
CELLULAR PHONE.

---

[2] From the pilot episode of *Home Improvement*, created by Matt Williams, David McFadzean, and
Carmen Finestra. Used by permission of Touchstone Television. All Rights Reserved.

JANE

Everything's under control, Mr. Ferber. You sent me
to run things here, that's what I'm doing. No,
Chelsea hasn't signed the budget agreement yet. Yes,
I did promise I'd have that signed by the end of my
first week. Yes, that would be tomorrow. Yes, I'm
aware I'm saying yes a lot. Yes.

RUN OF THREE

Mr. Ferber, I've just had a little trouble pinning
Chelsea down, but I will pin her. Consider her
pinned. Yes.

CALLBACK

Thank you sir.

JANE CLICKS OFF, GROWLS AND <u>EXITS</u> INTO THE OFFICES.

<u>INT. PRODUCTION OFFICES - CONTINUOUS (D-1)</u>

(Chelsea, Jane, Trudy, Mr. John, Terry, Office Extras)

JANE ENTERS AND CROSSES OVER TO WHERE TRUDY IS MAKING HERSELF A
CUP OF COFFEE.

JANE

Hi, Trudy. Have you seen Chelsea?

TRUDY

Not yet. She hasn't signed your budget thing, huh?

JANE

I'm getting desperate.

TRUDY

Jane, let me give you some advice. When you deal
with Chelsea, you always, always have to remember
one important thing.

MISLEAD

                    JANE
What's that?

                    TRUDY
She's a freak.

TURN - K SOUND

                    JANE
She's not a freak.

                    TRUDY
Oh, yes, she is. Last Christmas, she made a
gingerbread house? It was built to code.

ABSURD-K SOUND

There was a guest gingerbread house in the back.

ABSURD - K SOUND

                    JANE
Okay, she's a little obsessive, but she's built a
very successful business. The magazine, the
television show...

                    TRUDY
It's a great big freakdom.

PLAY ON WORDS - CALLBACK

                    JANE
Then why are you here?

                    TRUDY
Because I'm the best food stylist in the world and
Chelsea knows it.

TRUDY OPENS HER PORTFOLIO AND FLIPS THROUGH IT.

                    TRUDY (cont'd)
My award-winning chocolate sundae.

                    JANE
That ice cream looks delicious.

MISLEAD

> TRUDY
> Thank you. It's lard.

TURN

> I can recreate any dish for photographic purposes. I use whatever it takes. That chocolate sauce?

> JANE
> It looks good.

MISLEAD

> TRUDY
> Quaker State motor oil.

TURN

> That's thirty weight, if memory serves.

TOPPER

> (TURNING THE PAGE) This is my fettuccine alfredo.

> JANE
> The noodles look real.

> TRUDY
> Oh, they are.

MISLEAD

> JANE
> How about the sauce?

> TRUDY
> Sears Weatherbeater house paint.

TURN

> And that's one coat, Jane.

TOPPER - K SOUND

MR. JOHN CROSSES OVER. HE'S A DAPPER MAN IN HIS FIFTIES.

>   TRUDY (cont'd)
> Perhaps we should ask Mr. John.

>   MR. JOHN
> Ask me what?

>   TRUDY
> Do you think Chelsea's a freak?

>   MR. JOHN
> No, I don't. I've been designing for Chelsea Stevens
> for ten wonderful years, and I believe her to be the
> apotheosis of taste and style.

MISLEAD

>   TRUDY
> She's not in yet.

>   MR. JOHN
> She's a freak.

TURN - CALLBACK

> (TO TRUDY) Let's tell her about the gingerbread
> house.

>   TRUDY
> I already did.

>   MR. JOHN
> (TO JANE) It had plumbing.

TOPPER

> Guy and I still talk about it.

>   JANE
> Guy?

>   MR. JOHN
> My life partner. I'm sorry if my frankness shocks
> you, Jane, but I'm proud of my relationship and I

> MR. JOHN (cont'd)
>
> don't hide the fact.

> JANE
>
> I'm fine.

> MR. JOHN
>
> Well. I know you've come from the Midwest...so if I do say anything that makes you uncomfortable, I hope you'll speak up.

MISLEAD

> JANE
>
> It's not a problem. I am an adult.

> MR. JOHN
>
> Thank you, Jane. It's like I was saying to Guy in the shower this morning as we were lathering up...

TURN

> JANE
>
> Oh, dear.

> MR. JOHN
>
> Too much?

UNDERSTATEMENT

CHELSEA STEVENS, THE JUGGERNAUT OF STYLE AND TASTE, ENTERS FROM THE OUTER LOBBY. SHE CARRIES A SMALL WICKER BASKET COVERED WITH A RED-CHECKERED NAPKIN.

> CHELSEA
>
> Good morning, everyone!

STAFFERS ADLIB GREETINGS.

> CHELSEA (cont'd)
>
> This morning before breakfast while I was restocking my trout pond and shearing my lamb,

ABSURD

                         CHELSEA (cont'd)
I realized I wanted to tell you all how much I
appreciate the hard work you do. But then later,
while I was airing out my quilts and making
prosciutto jerky,

ABSURD - K SOUND

I reminded myself that we can always work harder. I
guess what I'm trying to say is...

MISLEAD

be more like me.

TURN

And one more thing. In the magazine, on the
show...no more kiwi. Kiwi is over. If I could talk
to a kiwi,

K SOUNDS

do you know what I'd say? I'd say "Get out, get a
shave, you're through."

RUN OF 3 - PERSONIFICATION

No kiwi. Let's all say it.

                         ALL
No kiwi.

ABSURD - K SOUND

                         CHELSEA
Thank you. And the big news. My divorce becomes final
today, so I think we all know what that means.

MISLEAD

A BEAT, THEN SHE PUTS THE BASKET ON THE TABLE.

                         CHELSEA (cont'd)
That's right. I made scones!

TURN - K SOUND

CHELSEA DISAPPEARS INTO HER OFFICE.

                    MR. JOHN
        She seems down today.

UNDERSTATEMENT [3]

---

[3] Used by permission of Touchstone Television. All Rights Reserved.

Appendix 5 **ADDITIONAL EXERCISES**

ADDITIONAL EXERCISE SCENE 1
Home Improvement
Used by permission of Touchstone Television. All Rights Reserved.

"Pilot"
(PARTIAL SCENE)
<u>ACT TWO</u>
<u>SCENE 1</u>

<u>INT. KITCHEN/FAMILY ROOM-LATER THAT DAY SATURDAY MORNING (DAY 2)</u>

(TIM, JILL)

(TIM ENTERS FROM THE BACKYARD AS JILL CROSSES TO THE KITCHEN)

JILL

What did you do? Show me right now.

TIM

Honey, honey. You're so cute when you're panicked.
That little vein in your forehead pops out.

JILL

What the hell is that?

TIM

That is a new and improved dishwasher.

JILL

Take it out.

TIM

You can't stand the fact that I improved this
dishwasher.

(TIM PICKS UP A DIRTY DISH)

TIM

Remember that plate with the dried egg yolk this morning.

(TIM PLACES THE DISH IN THE DISHWASHER, CLOSES THE DOOR, AND TURNS IT ON)

SPFX: COMPRESSOR HUMS

TIM (CONT'D)

Hear that purr? That's a five horsepower, Blastmaster Compressor. Air delivery systems, eighteen standard cubic feet per minute. That, my dear wife, is a man's dishwasher!

SPFX: EXPLOSION

THE BACK END OF THE DISHWASHER BLOWS OFF AND SHOOTS ACROSS THE FAMILY ROOM SCATTERING DEBRIS EVERYWHERE.

SPFX: SPARKS

(JILL DOESN'T MOVE, SHE SIMPLY STARES AT TIM FOR SEVERAL BEATS, THEN:)

TIM

Mark, you didn't tighten that hex bolt like I asked you.

(MARK AND RANDY ENTER FROM THE STAIRS)

RANDY

Whoa. Neat.

JILL RUNS TO THEM.

TIM

Get back. Get back.

JILL

Stay away from there. There's broken glass. You'll hurt yourself.

                    RANDY
    I'm going to call Tommy. He's got to see this.

(RANDY EXITS)

                    JILL
    No. Stay off the phone! I'm expecting a call about
    my job.

                    MARK
    Daddy already got that call.

                    TIM
    Mark, haven't you caused enough trouble with that
    hex bolt.

                    MARK
    Sorry. You didn't get the job, Mom.

                    TIM
    Get out.

(MARK EXITS UP THE STAIRS. JILL TURNS AND STARES AT TIM FOR A
BEAT)

                    JILL
    I didn't get the job?

                    TIM
    No, I was waiting for the right time to tell you.
    Then the dishwasher exploded, and that wasn't it.

SPFX: SPARKS.

                    TIM (CONT'D)
    Sweetheart, I'm really, really sorry. You okay?

                    JILL
    I'll get the broom.

(JILL CROSSES TO THE CLOSET. SHE REENTERS CARRYING A BROOM AND
DUST PAN, CROSSES TO THE FAMILY ROOM)

TIM

Don't worry about all this. I'll clean it up. Let's look on the bright side. It wasn't a full load.

JILL

I asked you not to touch the dishwasher but you didn't listen, did you? Fine. I'm not going to get angry. It's alright. Only makes more work for me. But I don't mind. I like to work. Too bad no one will hire me.

TIM

Everything will be all right.

JILL

Don't tell me how to feel.

TIM

I'm just saying if it was me.

JILL

It's not you, Tim. It's me.

TIM

All I'm saying is, you don't have to work.

JILL

I see. You don't want me to work, do you?

TIM

No. I mean that make enough money for both of us.

JILL

This is not about money. This is about my creative expression as a woman. My autonomy.

TIM

Autonomy. How do you spell that?

JILL

I don't want to talk about it.

TIM

You know what you should do?

                    JILL

Oh great. Now I'm getting advice from a man who
prances around on TV, grunting like a baboon.

                    TIM

What does that have to do with?

                    JILL

...while that Binford Tool Girl flashes her big
headlights.

                    TIM

Lisa?

                    JILL

Yes Lisa.

                    TIM

She's there for the female point of view.

                    JILL

Oh, I know what point of view she's there for. The
side view.

                    TIM

What does Lisa have to do with this? She didn't take
your job. She's got a job.

(JILL EXITS. TIM STARTS TO <u>CROSS</u> TO THE BACKYARD)

SPFX: SPARKS

ADDITIONAL EXERCISE SCENE 2
"Home Improvement"
Used by permission of Touchstone Television. All Rights Reserved.

                    "PILOT"
                (PARTIAL SCENE)
                   <u>ACT ONE</u>
                   <u>SCENE 2</u>
<u>INT. KITCHEN/FAMILY ROOM - LATE SATURDAY MORNING (DAY 2)</u>

(TIM, JILL, BRAD, RANDY, MARK)

BRAD <u>ENTERS</u> FROM THE BACK DOOR, <u>RACES</u> THROUGH THE FAMILY ROOM

WITH A FOOTBALL UNDER HIS ARM.

                    JILL
     No running in the house.

                    TIM
     Brad, cover the ball with both hands. You don't want
     to fumble.

(BRAD <u>EXITS</u>)

                    JILL
     Tim.

                    TIM
     You heard your mother. No running in the house. See
     you later.

                    JILL
     Where are you going?

                    TIM
     Sears. They're having their Saturday Sales
     Spectacular.

                    JILL
     You can't go. I've got this job interview.

                    TIM
     What job interview?

                    JILL
     I've been telling you every day this week. Personnel
     manager at Kingman-Hartwell.

                    TIM
     You never told me you had a job interview.

                    JILL
     Don't you ever listen to me? It was the last thing
     that I said to you in bed last night.

                    TIM
     If you recall, the last thing you said to me in bed
     last night was 'no.'

                    JILL
You're thinking of tonight!

                    TIM
You split my sides, sometimes you do!

                    JILL
Look, sweetie, I have to leave in an hour. You've
got to stay here and watch these kids.

                    TIM
Fine. I'll be back in twenty minutes.

                    JILL
Twenty minutes! Who are you kidding? You'll be down
there drooling, fondling tools, your eyes bugging
out. You don't even look at me that way.

                    TIM
I would if you had two speeds and were reversible!

                    JILL
Tim.

                    TIM
You won't even know I'm gone.

(TIM <u>HEADS</u> FOR THE GARAGE DOOR. JILL DANGLES THE TAPE MEASURE
OVER THE TRASH COMPACTOR)

                    JILL
Tim, walk out that door, this goes in the trash
compactor.

                    TIM
No! Not my Binford Power Tape with positive toggle
lock.

                    JILL
Kiss it goodbye!

                    TIM
No. No. Don't turn that on.

                              JILL
          Are you staying?

                              TIM
          Yes. Boy you're mean to me. Ew, food boogers.

(JILL KISSES HIM)

                              JILL
          Since you're staying, could you load the dishwasher?

                              TIM
          Why not, you've broken my spirit.

                              JILL
          Tim, this job is important to me. Aren't you excited
          about me going back to work?

                              TIM
          Yeah, sure.

                              JILL
          'Yeah, sure?' Could you maybe work up a little more
          enthusiasm?

                              TIM
          I'm sorry, honey. I'm really excited, you won't be
          laying around the house, mooching off me and the
          boys.

(JILL SLAPS TIM IN THE BUTT)

                              TIM (CONT'D)
          Oooh! Get the other cheek. I'm your love slave.

(RANDY COMES IN THE DOOR)

                              RANDY
          Is it okay if I go over to Tommy's?

                              TIM
          What?

                              RANDY
          Is it okay if I go over to Tommy's?

                          TIM
        Sure.

(RANDY <u>STARTS</u> TO LEAVE)

                          JILL
        Wait, where's Mark?

                          RANDY
        He's out back playing.

                          JILL
        Hold it, where's that rope?

                          RANDY
        Rope?

                          MARK (OS)
        Help!

(RANDY <u>RUNS AROUND</u> TO THE OTHER DOOR)

                          JILL
        I'm going out in the backyard. If I find your brother
        tied to the barbeque again, you're grounded for a
        week.

                          RANDY
        Don't come out yet. Just give me a second.

(RANDY <u>RUNS OFF</u>)

                          JILL
        One daughter. That's all I wanted. One daughter.

                          TIM
        Well, there's a simple operation we can perform on
        the boys right here at home.

                          JILL
        You're sick.

                          JILL
        Honey, don't put that in there. You have to rinse it
        off first.

                    TIM
I have to wash the dish before I put it in the
dishwasher?

                    JILL
The spray isn't strong enough to take off that egg
yolk.

                    TIM
Well it would be if we had a man's dishwasher. But
you insisted on buying the Lady Soft Touch Décor
series.

                    JILL
I'm so sorry. The grunting, hairy ape model was sold
out.

(JILL GRUNTS. TIM GRUNTS)

                    JILL
Just rinse the dishes.

                    TIM
Honey, I can fix the spray in this dishwasher.

                    JILL
No, Tim! It's not broken!

                    TIM
All it needs is more power.

                    JILL
Every time you fix something, the fire department
shows up.

                    TIM
This would be easy. All I have to do is get a
compressor, rewire it, and—

(JILL COVERS TIM'S MOUTH WITH HER HAND. TIM TRIES TO TALK)

                    JILL
I am not going to let you ruin a perfectly good
dishwasher just so you can get out your tools and
play. No.

                    TIM

Play? I happen to be the host of my own home
improvement show.

                    JILL

Don't touch the dishwasher!

(JILL <u>EXITS</u>)

                    TIM

Don't touch the dishwasher! I'll show her. I'll
strap a four twenty-seven v-eight engine on this
sucker. Have enough power to blow everything off
that dish in there, including that sissy little
flower pattern.

(JILL <u>REENTERS</u>)

                    JILL

I heard that.

                    TIM

Aaahh! Jill, this is my house, my dishwasher, and
I'll rewire it if I want.

                    JILL

No! You're not going to rewire it and screw it up
like you did the blender. End of discussion.

(JILL <u>EXITS</u>)

                    TIM

I don't know what her problem is. It's the only
blender in town that can puree a brick!

ADDITIONAL EXERCISE SCENE 3
8 Simple Rules
From the pilot episode *8 Simple Rules...for Dating my Teenage Daughter* written by
Tracy Gamble.
Used by permission of Touchstone Television. All Rights Reserved.
The character of Paul was played by John Ritter
The character of Bridget is played by Kaley Cuoco
The character of Kerry is played by Amy Davidson

<u>ACT TWO</u>
<u>SCENE K</u>
<u>INT. LIVING ROOM - LATER THAT NIGHT (NIGHT 2)</u>

<u>KERRY</u> SITS IN A CHAIR READING "THE BELL JAR." <u>PAUL ENTERS</u> THE
FRONT DOOR <u>WITH BRIDGET</u>, HOME FROM THE MALL. THEY CROSS TO THE
COUCH.

                    PAUL
     So you never really planned on going to the library,
     did you?

                    KERRY
     Sure she did. Right after her Mensa meeting.

BRIDGET JUST FOLDS HER ARMS AND SHOOTS KERRY A LOOK OF DISGUST.

                    KERRY
               (TO BRIDGET; AS IF TO A CHILD)
     "Mensa" is a club for geniuses.

                    BRIDGET
     I know what Mensa is.

                    PAUL
     Kerry, this is private.

                    KERRY
     Okay. (THEN) "Geniuses" are really smart people.

                    PAUL
     Kerry, beat it.

KERRY STARTS TOWARD THE KITCHEN.

                    PAUL
     Bridgie, the truth?

                    BRIDGET
     (NODS: SADLY) All right. I was trying to run into
     Kyle. I was hoping he'd ask me to the Homecoming
     Dance, but that's not going to happen.

PAUL'S MOVED A BEAT AND TAKES HER HAND.

                    PAUL
Ooh, honey. I'm sorry.

                    KERRY
She's already going to Homecoming with Dustin.

                    PAUL
Bridget. You already have a date?

                    BRIDGET
Yeah, but I could do a lot better...

SHE STRIKES A "LOOK AT ME" POSE.

                    PAUL
I'm past deadline and I'm sitting here feeling sorry
for you when you went to the mall scamming for
someone "better"?

                    BRIDGET
(TO KERRY) Did he just say "scamming"?

                    KERRY
He also says "chill."

                    BRIDGET
Eew. And look at his pants.

                    KERRY
I know.

PAUL LOOKS AT HIS PANTS.

                    PAUL
All right. Kerry, out! Bridget, you are grounded for
a month.

                    BRIDGET
What? (BLASÉ) Oh, no. How 'bout one week and I clean
my room?

                    PAUL
We're not negotiating. Three weeks!

                    BRIDGET
Be serious. One week, I clean my room annnnnd...no
allowance.

                    PAUL
Forget it! Two weeks.

                    KERRY
Well, let that be a lesson to <u>her</u>.

                    PAUL
(LOSING IT) You know, Kerry, I'm sick of your smart
ass attitude. Guess what? You're not going to
Homecoming either!

                    KERRY
I wasn't going to Homecoming anyway!

                    PAUL
How come?

                    KERRY
'Cause it's stupid! 'Cause it's for idiots!
'Cause...

THESE WORDS HANG IN THE AIR. <u>KERRY BOLTS UPSTAIRS</u>.

                    PAUL
'Cause no one asked her.

                    BRIDGET
("DUH") Uh, yeah.

Appendix 6 **SET PLAN**

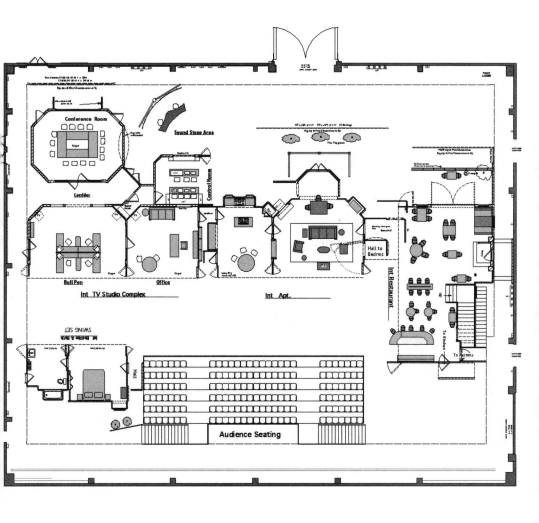

ABOUT THE AUTHORS

Emmy Award–winning **Mary Lou Belli** currently directs UPN's new hit sitcom *Eve* starring the MTV Award–winning hip-hop artist. She began her directing career with multiple episodes of *Charles in Charge* and *Major Dad*, and continues with such current shows as *Girlfriends*, *The Hughleys*, *Sister, Sister*, and *One on One*. Known for her work in children's programming, Mary Lou coached on NBC's Saturday morning hit *Saved by the Bell—The New Class*. She went on to direct *USA High*, *One World*, Nickelodeon's *Amber, Amber*, and Fox's teenage soap opera, *Tribes*.

After receiving a BA in theatre from Penn State, Mary Lou acted in musical theatre and soaps in New York, followed by a Los Angeles career producing and directing theatre. She has over 75 play productions to her credit, mostly world or West Coast premieres, including Cecile Callan's controversial *Angels Twice Descending* (optioned as a television movie by Fox), Wil Calhoun's *The Balcony Scene* (coproduced Off-Broadway with her partner Ian Praiser at NY's Circle Rep (starring Cynthia Nixon), and then placed in development as a feature at TRISTAR).

Among the awards she holds the dearest is her citation from the Los Angles Mayor Tom Bradley for her work with abused children.

She lives with her actor husband, Charles Dougherty. They have two children.

Single-camera and multi-camera directing credits for **Phil Ramuno** include almost one hundred episodes of many sitcoms, as well as *Into The Night Starring Rick Dees* (ABC late night), *America's Funniest People*, and six years of documentary, news, and public affairs for Group W in Boston.

Phil's introduction to sitcoms was as an assistant director on the legendary *Soap*. He later directed multiple episodes of such sitcoms as *Gimme a Break*, *Charles in Charge*, *The Ted Knight Show*, *9 to 5*, and *Grace under Fire*. Phil has helmed eight pilots for ABC, CBS, FOX, Nickelodeon, TLC, Universal Studios, Columbia, Orion, and Disney.

For the stage, Phil directed several award-winning plays in Los Angeles. He has co-run workshops for handicapped actors in Southern California, and won an award from the State of California for the best direction of a handicapped actor (on the sitcom episode on *Throb*). He has taught various subtleties of television production and acting for sitcoms at his alma mater Emerson College, Emerson College Los Angeles Campus, Endicott College, the Lake Arrowhead Workshops, and the Directors Guild Workshop. Phil is currently teaching at USC Film Graduate School.

He and his wife, Jackie Zebal Ramuno, live in Los Angeles with their children Jeff and Jessica.